Jesus Is the Only
Hope We Have

Jesus Is the Only
Hope We Need

Jesus Is the Only
Hope We Have

Jesus Is the Only
Hope We Need

Speaking Jesus from the Heartland

LARRY SCANTLAND

XULON PRESS

Xulon Press
2301 Lucien Way #415
Maitland, FL 32751
407.339.4217
www.xulonpress.com

Unless otherwise indicated, Scripture quotations taken from *The Holy Bible, New International Version*,® NIV.® Copyright © 1973, 1978, 1984, 2011 by Biblica, Inc. ™ Used by permission of Zondervan. All rights reserved worldwide. www.zondervan.com

Scripture taken from the *HOLY BIBLE, NEW INTERNATIONAL VERSION*. Copyright © 1973, 1978, 1984 International Bible Society. Used by permission of Zondervan Bible Publishers. (denoted with*)

Scripture taken from the *New King James Version* ®. Copyright © 1982 by Thomas Nelson, Inc. Used by permission. All rights reserved. (denoted with**)

Printed in the United States of America.

PAPERBACK ISBN-13: 978-1-6312-9235-4

HARDCOVER ISBN-13: 978-1-6312-9236-1

EBOOK ISBN-13: 978-1-6312-9237-8

This book is dedicated to my loving wife, Rhonda, for the life we share in this earthly walk.
This book is dedicated to my Savior Jesus for the full and meaningful life, now and forevermore.

Dear Reader,

*I*t is my prayer that you will be drawn to the Savior Jesus through reading any part of this book and that you will take our Lord God at His Word and believe all that He says.

Jesus truly is the *only hope* we have.
Jesus truly is the *only hope* we need.

Thank you, Jesus, for reaching down to a sinner, such as I.
Thank you, Lady, for reaching out to this ordinary guy.
I'll be grateful, oh so grateful, throughout eternity.
For my Jesus and my Lady for the love you've given me.

Table of Contents

And Three Fell

What persons fall at the feet of Jesus?
What happens when persons fall at the feet of Jesus?
Mark 4:35–41 and 5:1–43

*I*t was evening, and Jesus and his disciples had left the crowd behind, and sailed in a boat together, along with other boats across the Sea of Galilee. A violent storm had suddenly broken out, and the waves came up over their boat until it was nearly swamped. While the disciples fretted—Jesus slept. They woke Him up and threw an unwarranted question at him. "Teacher, don't you care if we drown?"

Had Jesus *ever* given them *any* reason to believe that He would not care if they drowned? After all, this is the same Jesus who had demonstrated kindness, selflessness, mercy, tenderness, gentleness, and love— every minute of every hour of every day that He had spent with them. Did they have any reason to question His caring? But you know how it is when you are desperate, when trouble is overwhelming you, when you are overcome with fear.

Jesus got up, rebuked the wind, and said to the waves authoritatively, "Quiet! Be still!"

Immediately the wind died down, and it became completely calm. What was their reaction? We're told that they were terrified, and asked each other in wonderment, "Who *is* this? Even the wind and the waves obey him!" Well, they went across the Sea of Galilee, and came to a region of Gerasenes. Do you know what awaited them there? Do you think Jesus knew what was waiting there? Thank for a moment—is Jesus

1

ever caught off guard...ever surprised? Think, also, and keep in mind, this is Jesus who came to seek and save that which is lost.

This is Jesus who came to give hope to the hopeless. What awaited Him there was the epitome of lostness and hopelessness. Keep in mind, this is Jesus who gave His life as a ransom for those held captive. This is Jesus who is afraid of *nothing*. So, what awaited Him?

A *crazy* man with an evil spirit lived in the tombs. Matthew actually refers to two men. Mark and Luke mention one, perhaps because he was the prominent one and the only one to confront Jesus. Why did he live in the tombs? In that day, the very poor would often live in the tombs along with the dead, who were buried there. It is likely that this man was very poor. But it was much more than that.

We know that he had often been chained hand and foot, and we are told that no one could bind him anymore. He was a wild man, a man to stay away from. The townspeople believed that. Was he a man to be feared? The townspeople believed that. We are told that no one was strong enough to subdue him. Was he a pathetic figure? Was there any hope for this wretched creature? What would the townspeople say?

Stay away from there.
No one can do anything for him.
It is hopeless.

Yet, was his life *really* hopeless? Was he *really* doomed? Do you suppose that anyone in that community saw him as one created in God's image, just as they were?

How about you? Do you ever look at folks differently? Perhaps you have no trouble at all seeing some of them as God's creations, but maybe, for others, it is easy to overlook the fact that God created *them* in His image, just as He did you.

Well, this man saw Jesus from a distance, and he ran, and *he fell on his knees in front of Jesus*. He shouted at the top of his voice, "What do you want with me, Jesus, Son of the Most High God? Swear to God that you won't torture me!"

For Jesus had said to him, "Come out of this man, you evil spirit!"

Then Jesus asked him, "What is your name?"

"My name is Legion," he replied, "for we are many."

Do you see who had control of this man? The demons are the ones who spoke. We are told that the demons pleaded with Jesus because they were fearful of eternal punishment and being sent into the Abyss (Luke 8). Even the demons recognize the omnipotence of Jesus.

Jesus cast them out of this poor man and into a herd of pigs numbering about 2,000, who then rushed down a steep bank into the lake and drowned. Now, I can't even begin to imagine what that must have been like. It isn't in the experience banks of most of us, is it?

But, herein lies a tragedy—many in that community were more troubled about the financial loss of the pigs, rather than being joyful over the deliverance of a poor, wretched soul—one created in God's image.

Now, think of it. If this Jesus had power even over demons, what other marvelous things were in store for those in this community who would seek to follow Him? Just think of what a difference Jesus could make in their community.

Think of the difference Jesus could make in *your* life.

So picture this—just a few moments earlier—a naked, demon-possessed, wild creature—now a completely changed man, dressed, at the feet of Jesus, and in his right mind. Hallelujah! Do you rejoice at this conversion? Do you rejoice at this one—once bound for hell but now having a home waiting in heaven?

Those missing the whole point pleaded with Jesus to leave. This is the giver of Life, the Savior of the world, the only Hope, the Lord of all—yet they pleaded with Jesus to leave.

Have you ever done that—asked Jesus to leave? Have you ever not been comfortable with Jesus in your presence? I dare say that we all have. Yet, it is only in His presence that we find peace. I wonder if any of these folks were ever in His presence again.

Now the delivered one pleaded with Jesus also… he pleaded to go with Him, but Jesus told him to go home and tell them. Tell them how much the Lord has done for you, and how much He has had mercy on you. Did he do that? Oh yes. He went and began to tell all around the ten city region how much Jesus had done for him, and all the people were amazed.

What kind of person falls at the feet of Jesus? This one was in bondage—in need of deliverance. What happened to this one who fell at the feet of Jesus? He was delivered and freed to bear witness to the power of the Lord Jesus over Satan and his demons, and to spend eternity in heaven.

Now after this, Jesus crossed over by boat to the other side of the lake. (Do you think the disciples kept a wary eye out for storms?) Wait a minute—had Jesus gone all the way across the great sea, through a threatening storm, and back, for that one soul? It would seem so, but that shouldn't surprise us, should it?

Jesus once said, "Suppose one of you has a hundred sheep and loses one of them. Does he not leave the ninety-nine in the open country and go after the lost sheep until he finds it?" (Luke 15:4).

To what lengths will Jesus go in order to save you? To what lengths indeed! How far is it from His throne in heaven to Calvary's cross?

Well, now they were back on the shore, and the crowd gathered around Him. Jairus came and *fell at the feet of Jesus*. Jairus was a synagogue ruler, one who supervised the worship, perhaps a worship leader, as we would say. Jairus fell at Jesus's feet, pleading with Him. Why? Because his beloved daughter, twelve years old, lay dying. Jairus pleaded with Jesus to come and put His hands on her so that she would be healed and live. So Jesus went with him.

But wait! Just then something else happened.

Would Jesus be delayed from such an important round? What could be more important than saving a young girl from dying, we might ask. But, understand this—Jesus is not the same as you and me.

Jesus does not have our limitations.

Jesus does not operate in the same way we do.

Jesus is not on the same time schedule as we are.

Jesus hurries not.

Jesus worries not.

Jesus has no reason to.

Jesus is Almighty God in the flesh.

Jesus is Lord.

Now, as Jesus and the crowd were surging forward, He turned around and asked caringly, "Who touched my clothes?" His disciples were taken aback, perhaps even in sarcastic tones, saying, "You see the people crowding against you, and yet you ask, 'Who touched me?'"

But Jesus kept looking around to see who had done it. He knew power had gone out from Him. Realizing that she couldn't go unnoticed, the woman then came forward, and *fell at His feet,* trembling with fear. Did she have *anything* to fear from the Loving One? The Healer? The Lifter of men's souls? The unknown frightens us, though, doesn't it? Do you have anything to fear from the Loving One, Jesus, who would be your Savior?

Then, she told Him the whole truth—about how she had been bleeding for twelve years. She had suffered continually. She had seen and been cared for by many doctors. She had spent all the money she had, yet she grew worse. Then, she heard about Jesus. Her last hope? Yes, but the only hope she needed. Her faith led her to push through the crowd just so she could touch His clothes because she believed that if she could only do that, she would be healed.

Remember what Jesus said about faith even as small as the mustard seed (Matt. 17:20)? That tiny seed, commonly planted then, yielded the largest of all plants in the garden. What happened when this woman touched Jesus's clothes? Her bleeding stopped, and she was freed from her suffering. Hallelujah! Do you rejoice at her physical healing?

Jesus said to her, "Daughter, your faith has healed you. Go in peace, and be freed from your suffering." She was not only delivered physically, but more importantly, she was delivered spiritually because of her faith

5

in the Lord Jesus. "For it is by grace you have been saved, through faith—and this is not from yourselves; it is the gift of God—not by works, so that no one can boast" (Eph. 2:8). Like the demoniac, she was saved. Do you rejoice at her spiritual healing?

What kind of person falls at the feet of Jesus? This one was desperate, in need of deliverance and without hope.

What happens to one who falls at the feet of Jesus? She was delivered, given hope, and was saved to spend eternity in heaven.

Now what about Jairus? While this was going on; what was he doing? Was he marking time? Did he continually glance toward home, thinking of every precious moment that was slipping by? It would have been only natural, wouldn't it?

Then, while Jesus was still speaking, the dreaded news came to him—it's too late. "Your daughter is dead. Why bother the teacher anymore?" We don't know what Jairus thought, or what he said. We can only imagine what we would have thought. In all likelihood, Jairus was distraught that Jesus would delay, knowing how serious this was. This woman could have waited; Jesus could have come back to her. His daughter was at death's door. Now, it is too late.

Have you ever thought that? It's too late. Is it ever too late? Mark this: it is *never* too late for Jesus. It is never *too late* for Jesus. It is never too late for *Jesus*.

Jesus told Jairus, "Don't be afraid; just believe." His message is the same to you and me: Don't be afraid; just believe (John 16:33). I have overcome the world, He tells us.

When arriving at Jairus's home, He only allowed his closest disciples to follow him—Peter, James, and John, and as they entered, there was the usual commotion—mourners, wailers, criers (perhaps even some of them professionals). Imagine their reaction when Jesus went in and said to them, "Why all this commotion and wailing? The child is not dead, but asleep."

Their reaction? They laughed at him. After He put them all out (I love that), He took the child's father and mother, and the disciples who were with Him, and went into the room where the child lay. I ask you again... are there any surprises awaiting the Creator of the universe? Does He ever just say, "I didn't see that coming?"

He took her by the hand and said to her—what translates into English as, "Little girl, I say to you, get up." Wow, was He in control? I'll say. She immediately got up and walked around. Hallelujah! Do you rejoice that she was raised to life? They were all astonished. You know what Jesus said—Get her something to eat.

What kind of person falls at the feet of Jesus? This one was needy, desperate, afraid, and needed hope. What happens to one who falls at the feet of Jesus?

The demoniac fell in front of Jesus, needing deliverance and freedom from the worst type of bondage we could imagine—demon possession that brought banishment and isolation from fellow man. He not only received that, but deliverance and freedom to dwell in the Lord's house for all eternity.

The diseased woman fell at the feet of Jesus, trembling in fear. She needed deliverance from years of pain and suffering physically and emotionally. She not only received that, but deliverance for all eternity to dwell in the Lord's house forever.

The synagogue ruler fell at the feet of Jesus, pleading for his daughter's life. He needed Jesus to save her and to save his wife and him from the horror of losing their child. His daughter was delivered from death, and they were delivered from sorrow.

What do you think this man's story would be in the coming days? Do you think that a man who was bold enough to fall at the feet of Jesus in front of so many others would be backward about sharing this miracle of God through the years to family, friends, and acquaintances? I imagine that this day's events were recounted at family dinners and events many, many times throughout the years.

Now—

What do you need? What deliverance do you need? What hope do you need?

Whatever it is that you need in this moment, Jesus is waiting to *be* what you need.

You see—

Everything is made right at the feet of Jesus.

Everything is *made right* at the feet of Jesus.

Everything is made right at the *feet of Jesus.*

God calls you to the feet of Jesus so that He can make everything right in your life.

Everything that is of greatest importance.

Jesus is the *only hope* you have.

Jesus is the *only hope* you need.

O Father God, our Hope in Christ Jesus, I pray for the one reading this to fall at Your feet spiritually, if not physically, and to submit to Your power to save and to deliver in whatever ways this one needs. Hallelujah! In the name of Jesus, your Son and our Savior. Amen.

Are You Being Filled?

*D*o you ever think about what you lack? Does it keep you from being content? We are inundated with messages coming at us, reminding us of things we "need." If we just had this new device, our lives would be more efficient. If we just used this new product, our day would go smoother. If we just adhered to this new way, our being would be more complete. Messages continually bombard us, always about something new that we don't have, and how much better our lives would be if we did have "it"... ever the focus on that which we don't have instead of on that which we do.

Can we just get off the not-so-merry-go-round for a moment, take a deep breath, be still, and reflect on God's truth? After all, it is our Creator who has showed us what true contentment, true peace, and true meaning in life really is—whether we stand in a green field of plenty, or in a brown desert of barrenness. Maybe it's really not about having more. Maybe it's really not even about having less. Pride can be the motivation for either.

Maybe it really is not about what we have at all, but about *what* has us, or better yet, *who* has us. Truth is, either the Lord has us, or Satan has us. And our contentment depends wholly on this. Our security depends wholly on this. Our assurance depends wholly on this.

What about a widow living below the poverty level? Could she be content? Could she have a full and meaningful life? It is hard to imagine otherwise when you read this: "As Jesus looked up, he saw the rich putting their gifts into the temple treasury. He also saw a poor widow put in two very small copper coins. 'Truly I tell you' he said, 'this poor widow has put in more than all the others. All these people gave their gifts out of their wealth; but she out of her poverty put in all she had to live on'" (Luke 21:1-4).

Why would she do that? What would be her motivation? Surely if she needed that to live on, she should have kept it for herself, right?

Now we don't know what might have gone through her mind, what battles she may have fought internally before this scene, or how she may have tried to justify keeping what little she had, but, apparently her trust was not in how many coins she possessed. Instead, her trust was in the one who made the coins in the first place. Jesus held her up as an example—not because of what she had but because of what she gave. It was not because of what she possessed, but because of who possessed her. So, was she giving out of the green field of plenty or the brown field of barrenness? Maybe one was within and one was without.

What about another widow living below the poverty level—this one with a son and in a land parched and suffering with famine? She didn't have enough food for even the two of them, and her son was about to die, yet read on in 1 Kings 17:7-12...

"Some time later the brook dried up because there had been no rain in the land. Then the word of the Lord came to him: 'Go at once to Zarephath in the region of Sidon and stay there. I have directed a widow there to supply you with food.' So he went to Zarephath. When he came to the town gate, a widow was there gathering sticks. He called to her and asked, 'Would you bring me a little water in a jar so I may have a drink?' As she was going to get it, he called, 'And bring me, please, a piece of bread.' 'As surely as the Lord your God lives,' she replied, 'I don't have any bread—only a handful of flour in a jar and a little olive oil in a jug. I am gathering a few sticks to take home and make a meal for myself and my son, that we may eat it—and die.'"

Do you think that this widow—even though she had heard from the Lord Himself—wondered why Elijah didn't go to someone else who had more to give than she? Surely, there were others in that community who had more than enough. Surely her circumstances looked more like the brown desert of barrenness than the green field of plenty, didn't it?

We don't know what doubts or conflicts she may have felt, but we do know that she obeyed the Lord through His servant.

"Elijah said to her, 'Don't be afraid. Go home and do as you have said. But first make a small loaf of bread for me from what you have and bring it to me, and then make something for yourself and your son. For this is what the Lord, the God of Israel, says': 'The jar of flour will not be used up and the jug of oil will not run dry until the day the Lord sends rain on the land'" (1 Kin. 17:13-14).

We are seeing now that what matters is not what she has, but what she does with what she has—and ultimately what God does with what she has, right?

"She went away and did as Elijah had told her. So there was food every day for Elijah and for the woman and her family. For the jar of flour was not used up and the jug of oil did not run dry, in keeping with the word of the Lord spoken by Elijah" (1 Kin. 17:15-16).

How many times does the word of the Lord not come true? How often is the word of the Lord mistaken? You know as well as I that the answer is never. Here again, the Lord did exactly what He said He would do. He always does. The widow and her son were fed along with Elijah from what started out as not even enough for two. Out of little, God provided much. Out of not enough, God provided more than enough. But another test was coming.

"Some time later the son of the woman who owned the house became ill. He grew worse and worse, and finally stopped breathing. She said to Elijah, 'What do you have against me, man of God? Did you come to remind me of my sin and kill my son?' 'Give me your son,' Elijah replied. He took him from her arms, carried him to the upper room where he was staying, and laid him on his bed. Then he cried out to the Lord, 'Lord my God, have you brought tragedy even on this widow I am staying with, by causing her son to die?' Then he stretched himself out on the boy three times and cried out to the Lord, 'Lord my God, let this boy's life return to him!'" (1 Kin. 17:17-21).

You see, we all face crises of faith. Will we pass the test?

To pass we must trust in the one who has His eyes ever upon us, the one who knows our every thought, the one who knows our every sin, and yet He loves us still. And when we do pass the test, we move up closer to this one who loves us so much, the one who gave the very best He had.

We are weak, but He is strong. It is in our weakness that His strength is made known—just as this widow and even Elijah experienced.

"The Lord heard Elijah's cry, and the boy's life returned to him, and he lived. Elijah picked up the child and carried him down from the room into the house. He gave him to his mother and said, 'Look, your son is alive!' Then the woman said to Elijah, 'Now I know that you are a man of God and that the word of the Lord from your mouth is the truth'" (1 Kin. 17:22-24).

What does it take for you and me to give testimony that the word of the Lord is truth? What about when He says that He has come so that we may have life to the full, and a life full of meaning?

You may say that your life is full already. You may say that your life has meaning already. But full of what? Is it full of things? Activities? Survival? Pleasures? Profession? All of those may have their place, but are they the most important? Are they what will lead you closer to your God? Are they what will bring you peace and contentment? Would they lead you to give out of barrenness, not out of plenty? Will you pass the test of trust?

You may say that your life is empty and your cupboard is bare. Life is a struggle of just getting one foot in front of the other. It isn't even day to day but more like hour to hour. You cannot even fathom a life that is full and meaningful. Will you pass the test of trust?

Jesus understands each of us. In fact, He understands exactly what each and every one of us face. You see, He knows what it is to have it all—more than Solomon, more than the richest person on earth today, and more than you. He owns it all. Everything that is belongs to Him, and it is He who sustains all creation. If He didn't want you to be in this life, He wouldn't have created you. But He *did* create you so He could love you and be loved by you.

Imagine Him looking down from His throne over all His creation. in perfect peace and in perfect relationship with His Heavenly Father with no reason to leave the security and glory of His place in heaven.

Except—we needed a Savior and we could never conjure one up— try though we do.

Except—the Savior we needed could only be one, the perfect one, the Son of God, the King Himself, the Messiah, the Christ, Immanuel—*Jesus*.

But no king is going to give up His throne for a stable, His royal robes for peasant clothes, His presence with the perfect Father for life among sinners, His divine nature for human nature. Surely not.

Hallelujah, this one did.

Hallelujah, this King became a servant.

Hallelujah, Jesus set it all aside for you and me.

What were Jesus's earthly possessions? By the time a man reaches thirty or so, he should have quite a few possessions, right? A house, a donkey, tools of his trade. Jesus didn't have a house. He didn't have a donkey. He didn't have tools of his trade. He had no regular place to lay his head, and no earthly possessions (other than the fact that ultimately he owns it all).

But what he did possess—grace and truth, forgiveness and mercy, hope and love—He offered to all he met, no matter their status, no matter their situation, no matter their skin color, no matter whether they lived in the brown desert of barrenness or the green field of plenty.

In this earthly life, He had a stone for a pillow, sandals on His feet, and only the clothes on His back when arrested. He was subjected to all the human emotions and frailties—the same as you and me. Yet He epitomized contentment. He epitomized trust in his Father even when facing the cruelest fate known to man. And He would pass the test of trust—in His Heavenly Father.

When He set his face to Jerusalem, He knew what was ahead:

adoration would turn to ridicule,

praise would turn to scorn,

blessings would turn to curses,

smiles would turn to sneers,

open hands would turn to clenched fists.

It was not because of anything He had ever done wrong. It was all because of what I have done wrong—and you, too. Jesus would stand in the most barren place imaginable. No, He would hang on the most barren place imaginable, on a hill of death bound by nails to a wooden cross. No longer spotless—because He bore all our sin. No longer under the watchful eye of His Father who turned away in anguish and sorrow. No longer full of life, but bleeding out from the cross. Yet, through it all, Jesus would love all those who hated him. He would pray for forgiveness for those who rejected him. He would save all those who trusted in Him.

Out of the barrenness of that crucifixion, Jesus poured out Himself: His blood to cover our sins, His life to fill us with Himself. When He breathed His last, He said it was finished. He had accomplished what He came here to do—all of it. That which His heavenly Father called Him to do, He did without fail.

Will I be able to say that when my time is done? Likely not, but it is just that that I want to do. What about you? What does it take to live out the full and meaningful life?

Piles of money at the end? You will leave it here.

Houses and lands accumulated? You will leave them here.

Degrees, awards, trophies amassed? You will leave them here.

Cars, planes, boats collected? You will leave them here.

Children, grandchildren, great-grandchildren? They can't go with you when your time is up.

Is the full and meaningful life realized through earthly treasures? Hardly.

Jesus said, "Do not store up for yourselves treasures on earth, where moth and rust destroy, and where thieves break in and steal. But store up for yourselves treasures in heaven, where moth and rust do not destroy, and where thieves do not break in and steal. For where your treasure is, there will your heart be also" (Matt. 6:19–21*).

That is where Jesus laid His treasures up, and He still is laying up more treasures—for those who will follow Him.

To be filled with Christ Jesus, we have to be emptied out of selfishness and pride. We would want it to be as simple as turning off one spigot and turning on another. But it isn't. Whatever you have learned, whatever you have become proficient at, likely has taken some time and practice, probably with some setbacks along the way, as well.

My walk with the Lord is just so, probably like most.

I have emptied out a small space and asked the Lord to fill it.

He has, but I needed more of Him, and He wanted more of me.

I emptied out a little larger space and asked the Lord to fill it.

He has, but I needed more of Him, and He wanted more of me.

And so it goes.

I have never been completely emptied out of self and completely filled with the Spirit of Jesus, but I aspire to exactly that. We should pray as Paul did "that you, being rooted and established in love, may have power, together with all the saints, to grasp how wide and long and high and deep is the love of Christ, and to know this love that surpasses knowledge—that you may be filled to the measure of all the fullness of God" (Eph. 3:17–19*).

Filled to the measure of all the fullness of God! That should be my goal—and yours, becoming mature, "attaining to the whole measure of the fullness of Christ" (Eph. 4:13). You see, we "have been given fullness in Christ" (Col. 2:10*). I want that. Don't you?

"His divine power has given us everything we need for a godly life through our knowledge of him who called us by his own glory and goodness. Through these he has given us his very great and precious promises, so that through them you may participate in the divine nature, having escaped the corruption in the world caused by evil desires" (2 Pet. 1:3–4).

Emptying out of the world, and all that passes away, to be being filled with God's own nature—the very Spirit of Jesus Himself—now that is worth living for.

Paul, in this same Spirit, was able to declare that he had learned (didn't come easily or naturally) to be content, no matter what the circumstances, whether the green field of plenty, or the brown desert of barrenness (Phil. 4:12–13). That is the contentment that only comes from the indwelling, the infilling of Jesus's Spirit.

I have experienced some of these life tests to be passed in order to go deeper in my relationship with the Lord Jesus. I learned that I don't have enough within me to pass those tests, not enough within me to stand strong in the face of adversity. Yet, as I become weak, He becomes stronger. Whether I am in the green field of plenty or in the brown desert of barrenness, Jesus calls me to give. It is the same with you. However, what He calls you to give is you. What He calls me to give is me.

Think of the poster of Uncle Sam pointing his finger at you, stating "I Want You." This portrays an image of authority, for sure, and a call to duty, for sure. Well, Jesus is calling you also—and me. He is stating "I Want You," but He isn't pointing a long, bony finger at you or me. His look isn't stern or foreboding. He isn't dressed in patriotic colors. His look is love for you and me. His arms are open wide, revealing the scars from the nails driven through Him instead of you and me. He is dressed in white for purity and righteousness, which He offers to you and me. What He offers can be found nowhere else. It can't be manmade. It isn't contingent on what we possess or don't possess. It hinges only on our need for forgiveness, security, hope, and salvation. That is what Jesus offers to all who will repent and call on His name.

You see, what is important is that we each give, and it doesn't matter whether out of plenty or out of want when it is we ourselves that are being given and given to the only one who can make us more than we are. He made the two widows more than they were on their own. He made what they had more than they could have on their own. He made the apostle Paul more than he could have been on his own.

Jesus showed us that He can be made nothing, be made in human likeness, be made a servant, be made to dwell among us sinners, and yet, through it all, pour out himself completely so you and I can be poured into Him and even be filled with Him.

Will you call on His name to repent and be saved?

Will you call on His name to be filled with His Spirit from now on?

When the tests come in this life, and they will, may I be found faithfully giving of myself, emptying of myself in order to continually be being filled with Jesus.

How about you?

O Lord God, I pray for the one reading this, whether in the brown desert of barrenness or the green field of plenty, to trust You that the source of contentment in this life is You in Christ Jesus. In the name of Jesus our Fulfillment. Amen.

Know That I Am God

These days are heavy and are weighing me down;
I can't bear the load. I'm coming unwound.
It's time to close my eyes and hear Your voice,
So calm, so kind.

When I'm neither hot nor cold,
And my days are same old, same old,
I need Your victory, I need to be bold.
It's time to close my eyes, and hear Your voice,
So strong, so clear.

When it's all about me, and pride gets in the way,
My downfall is coming; I know I need to pray.
It's time to close my eyes, and hear Your voice,
So true, so wise.

Be still and know that I am God.
Hide My Word deep in your heart.
Trust Me and follow Me;
I am faithful forever to you.

Be Still and Know that I Am God

Psalm 46:10 says it all

*T*hese days are heavy, and weighing me down; I can't bear the load...I'm coming unwound. Does that hit close to home for you? Are your days heavy? Is the load becoming too much to bear? Or has it been too much to bear for some time now? Are you becoming unwound? What do you do when it is more than you can bear?

There are a lot of ways to deaden our senses and mask our pain, aren't there? And there is a lot of pain around us. Think about how much bad news we hear in a day's time. Compare that to how much good news we hear in a day's time.

Rhonda and I used to watch the first ten minutes or so of the 10 o'clock news, but concluded it was too depressing before we went to sleep. What is usually in that first part of the news? Accounts of killings, shootings, robberies, tragedies, and disasters—in other words, gloom and despair!

We now hear news of terrible things, tragedies, disasters, and so on not just from our neighborhood, city, state, or even country, but from all around the world. And bad news travels fast, doesn't it? Gossip travels fast, too, doesn't it?

Do you remember the *Hee Haw* version of gloom, despair, agony on me. Deep, dark depression, excessive misery. It was sung in a humorous way, wasn't it? But the real gloom and despair displayed around us is no laughing matter, is it?

How many times do we hear of something good that has occurred or something good that someone has done? How often do you hear of souls saved that day? Yet, that is happening around us.

God is always at work around us to do good, to bring good, to save souls, and to help those who will call upon Him. He never slumbers; He never sleeps. What is the Lord God of all creation saying to us through all this? Stick your head in the sand? Ignore all the bad stuff going on around you? Pretend that the world is heaven? No, but I do think that He is saying to you and me to *be still, and know that I am God*. Why? Because it is always important to recognize who is in control. Because it is always important to trust in the one who is in control.

What happens when we put our trust in fellow man? What happens when we put our trust in our leaders? Aren't we let down, disappointed, disillusioned, and even misled? We see evidence of betrayal by fellow man and by our leaders daily, don't we?

Does our heavenly Father betray us? Does He let us down?

Does He ever throw up His hands and say, "Well, I just give up"?

Does He ever, in fact, give up on you and me?

Does He ever mislead us?

No, no, no, no, and *no*!

Compassionately, caringly, He says to you and me through all the trials and tribulations of this world to *be still, and know that I am God*. Hide My Word deep in your heart. Trust Me and follow Me. I am *faithful* forever to you. James 1:17 tells us, "Every good and perfect gift is from above, coming down from the Father of the heavenly lights, who does not change like shifting shadows."

Psalm 9:9–10 says, "The Lord is a refuge for the oppressed, a stronghold in times of trouble. Those who know your name trust in you, for you, Lord, have never forsaken those who seek you." In Hebrews 13:5, the Lord assures us that "Never will I leave you; never will I forsake you" (same promise that He had made throughout time, even back to the Israelites as recorded in Deuteronomy). This follows a warning for us not to trust in money, or in what this world has to offer. It won't satisfy, will it? It won't last, will it?

We need to know, for sure, that there is a higher purpose—a higher calling—in this life than just what we see in this world, in this temporary place. Deep within, we desire more than what this life offers. God has placed eternity in our hearts. And God delivers more—in fact, He delivers more than all we could ever hope or imagine. He says that to you and me in Ephesians 3:20: "Now to him who is able to do immeasurably more than all we ask or imagine, according to his power that is at work within us." And, His power is at work within us when we are trusting in Him, when we are plugged into Him, and when we are following Him. So calmly, so kindly, He says "Be still, and know that I am God." Hide My Word deep in your heart, trust Me, and follow Me. I am faithful forever to you.

Maybe you are not putting your trust in fellow man or in mortal leaders, but you are putting your trust in you. You have gotten this far on your own; you are a "self-made" man or "self-made woman." Really? Is there even such a thing? You mean to say that no one helped you, sacrificed for you, or eased your path along the way? It brings to mind the old adage about whoever represents himself in a court of law has a fool for a client.

If you are trusting in yourself to carry the day, trusting in your own devices and your own wits, then you will find it all the more frustrating and depressing when you come to the realization that you cannot do it alone. You are on a dead-end street my friend.

"Pride goes before destruction, a haughty spirit before a fall" (Prov. 16:18). But, at the end of that dead end, there is one who waits for you with open arms. He says, "Blessed are the meek, for they will inherit the earth" (Matt. 5:5). Why, because the meek are the ones who are like Jesus. Like John the Baptist who said, "He must become greater, I must become less" (John 3:30). Not, it's all about me, but, instead, it is all about Him! Here is what Jesus did, and He did it for you—and me:

"Who, being in very nature God, did not consider equality with God something to be used to his own advantage; rather, he made himself nothing by taking the very nature of a servant, being made in human likeness. And being found in appearance as a man, he humbled himself by becoming obedient to death—even death on a cross!" (Phil. 2:6–8).

Does that sound like your pride? Far from it! Does a king really give up all that he has to become a servant? Does a king really give up heaven for earth? Does a king really sacrifice for his servants?

When it's all about you and pride gets in the way, your downfall is coming. You know you need to pray, so close your eyes, and hear His voice, so wise, so true: Be still and know that I am God; hide My Word deep in your heart; trust Me and follow Me. I am faithful forever to you.

What about when you are neither hot nor cold? You are just kind of pluggin' along, just getting by. You have fallen into familiar patterns, perhaps ruts, and you just don't see anything getting any better. You had visions earlier on of rising higher and accomplishing more, having more of an impact in this life or on others. But here you are, not really enthused about much of anything. Maybe you don't want to be too excited about things because that usually leads to a letdown. Maybe you don't want to invest in anything too much because often that leads to disappointment and pain.

God wants to assure you and me that He is the *God of victory*. "But thanks be to God! He gives us the victory through our Lord Jesus Christ" (1 Cor. 15:57). You need to be set free from the humdrum. Jesus said, "Then you will know the truth, and the truth will set you free" (if you are one of His disciples and hold to His teaching) (John 8:31–32).

You see, if the Son sets you free, you will be free indeed (John 8:36). Do you want to be free? Do you want some purpose? A reason to live? "Be still, and know that I am God." Hide My Word deep in your heart; trust Me and follow Me. I am faithful forever to you.

When God called Moses to go to Pharaoh and bring the Israelites out of Egypt, do you remember what Moses asked God? He said, "What if they ask me what your name is." What did God say? "I AM WHO I AM" This is what you say: "I AM has sent me to you."

In John 8:58, Jesus said, "I tell you the truth...before Abraham was born, I am!" God never was. God never will be. God IS. God always *is*. Yesterday, God *is*. Today, God *is*. Tomorrow, God *is*. For all eternity, God *is*. God never changes. God never sleeps. God never shuts down. People talk about 24/7. They will be there 24/7—yada, yada, yada 24/7. Really?

God *does* 24/7...all day, every day, every week, every month, every year, for all time.

God is never too busy for you.

God is never uncaring about you.

God is never lukewarm about you.

He can't be lukewarm when He gave His one and only Son to die in your place.

God loves you more than you can ever hope or imagine.

God is real.

God waits for you to put your trust in Him.

Psalm 46:10 states, Be still and know that I am God." As you are being still before the Lord at this moment, He is drawing you to Him by the power of His Holy Spirit. He wants to do in your life that which you cannot. Please know that you cannot save yourself. You cannot give meaning to your life on your own. You cannot find peace and salvation on you own. You cannot enter God's heaven on your own. Now is the time to *be still, and know that He is God*, and trust Him.

O Lord God, I pray for the one reading this to be still, trust You, and know that You are God. Truly You are God of all creation, and please make that known to this one now in the name of Your Son and our Savior Jesus. Amen.

Breeding Ground

*W*hat are breeding grounds? They are places to reproduce, to give rise to, to raise, to educate, to train, and to nourish. Are they good or bad? They are not inherently good or bad, are they? It certainly would be bad if there were no breeding grounds to reproduce the things we need, wouldn't it?

Consider pastures, where cows, horses, sheep, and the like are bred;

Or farmyards, where chickens and pigs are grown;

Or fields, where beans, corn, potatoes, grains, and the like are harvested;

Or forests, where oak, maple, pine, walnut, and pecan trees thrive;

Or laboratories, where bacteria and the like are cultivated.

But, also consider these: How about places of desolation where hopelessness, despair, and heartache are bred? These exist all over the world, even in the U.S., don't they? They exist in our presence, don't they?

How about places of worship, where numerous results are bred, depending on whom or what is being worshipped? In many of these places, there is worshipping of the created instead of the Creator—false gods instead of the one true and living God.

How about places of family love, where worth, peace, contentment, and purpose are bred? How about places of family discord and strife, where doubt, fear, disobedience, and even hatred are bred? How about the mind and the heart, where character, purpose, behavior, and paths for life are bred? When I say character, purpose, and behavior, do you think of good or bad? These can be either—can't they—because one's beliefs, attitude, purpose, and practice can go in either direction.

What things are you breeding in your mind and your heart? What are you planting? Are you planting anything purposeful? Or, are you letting the field of your mind grow wild? Have you ever observed a garden spot that started out with so much promise? You uproot or kill all the weeds; you break the ground and till it, making it ready for the seeds or plants; you sow or plant, you fertilize and water, and then you are done. You leave it alone to do its thing. How will that work out for you? After all, you did all the right things at the beginning, didn't you? That's what really matters, isn't it? Oh, how we wish it were that easy, huh?

We start out with such good intentions, we are full of energy, and we have hope; the vision is fresh in our minds. Then we let our guard down, and we begin to lack commitment. We get sidetracked, and we rationalize that it isn't that big a deal anyway.

Take the garden, for example. If we leave it alone after even a great beginning, what will happen? Weeds, vines, and critters will creep in. It's the darndest thing—I don't know where they come from, but if you till it and plant it, the weeds will come. They aren't weak either; if fact, they often are stronger than the crop you desire. They will take over in due time, unless you take action. If you stand by, all your initial hard work will produce little but frustration. I know. I have been there and done that. It aggravated me no end, but that's the way it is. Everything in this life needs tending in order for it to be better. Can you think of one thing that gets better on its own without any care-tending? Everything in this life needs tending in order for it to be better.

Think about a young child. What if you bring that child into this world and then leave him or her on their own to just fend for themselves? What would the result be? There is plenty of evidence around us. If that child is not loved, nurtured, taught, corrected, disciplined, hugged, assured, protected, and provided for, then what is likely to happen in that child? The result will be less than desirable in all likelihood. That may have been your childhood experience.

But what if you do take care of that child, love him or her, provide for him or her, show respect for him or her, encourage, teach, discipline, spend time with, and set the good example in love? Wouldn't you have the expectation of a better result—a productive harvest?

God says, "Start children off on the way they should go, and even when they are old they will not turn from it" (Prov. 22:6).

You, very likely, won't see it all through their teen years, and perhaps even in some of the adult years, but your efforts will be rewarded in God's good time. Please don't give up on the harvest after you have worked so hard in the planting, nurturing, and tending. And, it is never too late to recommit to those. "Let us not become weary in doing good, for at the proper time, we will reap a harvest if we do not give up" (Gal. 6:9).

Now, let's go back to your mind and your heart. What's growing in there? Is it despair? Is it hopelessness? Is it discontentment? Is it a sense of failure? Is it cluttered with all the madness of the world around us? How is the 24/7 news coverage of seemingly every tragedy and disaster on the face of the earth working out for us? Is darkness ruling in your mind and your heart? Is it the burden of the past? Is it fear of the future? What is your albatross?

God tells us in Philippians 4 that we ought to think about whatever is true, whatever is noble, whatever is right, whatever is pure, whatever is lovely, whatever is admirable, whatever is excellent, whatever is praiseworthy. You may think that might put you *out of touch* with the world. Bingo.

Now, is God telling us to not be *in*formed about the world around us? No, but God *is* telling us to not be *con*formed to this world, but, instead, be *trans*formed by the renewing of our minds (Rom. 12:2). What happens then? Then, we will be able to tap into God's will—His good, pleasing, and perfect will. Then, we will be more ready to not be anxious about things, but instead to bring them to the Father in prayer with thanksgiving to receive the peace that He offers—the peace that cannot be explained and that transcends all understanding, guarding our hearts and minds in Christ Jesus (Phil. 4). Could it get any better than that?

Let me ask you something—is God out of touch? Does He not know what is going on in the world? After all, didn't He create everything that is? Doesn't He understand computers, science, behavior, and relationships better than anyone ever? So, how do we begin to think about what is true, noble, right, pure, lovely, admirable, excellent, and praiseworthy? We begin with the one who is all this—Jesus, the Christ, the Son of God.

When you and I see Jesus for who He is, when you and I begin to think on Him and reflect on who He is to us, and when you and I stop, be still, and know that He is God, then we begin to plant the good seed in the field of our minds and hearts, which will, in time, bear forth the good crop, the good fruit, of a life worth living.

You see, He is the one True Vine, and we are His branches if we have surrendered ourselves to Him. In doing so, we are joined together with Him. And, here's the thing—apart from Him, we are nothing. Apart from Him, we can do nothing (John 15:5).

Someone wrote that it is wrong to compare the challenges ahead of us with our own energy level. How true! The issue is not our strength, but His strength, which is limitless—which is sufficient (2 Cor. 12:9). How have you done on your own, by your own wit and your own devices? If you are like me, you haven't done so well on your own. No one has; no one does.

Compared to Jesus, we have all fallen short. We have all sinned. We have all gone our own way. Have we suffered? Have we paid a price? Have we damaged the relationship with our Creator God? Yes, and so much so that we can never make it right. We can never do enough or be enough to make it right. But there is one who can.

Actually, there is one who has. He made it right on Calvary. He took all your sin and my sin on Himself, and all our sin was crucified there that day so that when the Christ—the Lamb of God—gave up His last breath, it was finished. All had been atoned for and paid for—your sin and mine.

Grace and mercy abounded from the cross in Jesus. Mercy that stays the hand of execution for you and me. Because as Scripture teaches us, the wages of sin is death. That is what we deserve—death. But Jesus, in mercy, paid the price with His life.

Grace opens the floodgate of God's blessings to you and me so that we can experience all the fullness of God just like Jesus. Mercy keeps us from getting what we deserve. Grace avails to us that which we don't deserve, all because of Jesus, the Christ. Apart from Him, we have no hope. Apart from Him, we have no lasting purpose. Apart from Him, there is no good crop, no good fruit. It is only in Jesus that the breeding ground of our minds and hearts yields anything of value. He gives us the focus of our higher calling. It is He who lifts us up to soar on wings like the eagles. Catch this vision:

"He gives strength to the weary and increases the power of the weak. Even youths grow tired and weary, and young men stumble and fall; but those who hope in the Lord will renew their strength. They will soar on wings like eagles; they will run and not be weary, they will walk and not be faint" (Is. 40:29–31).

There is a saying in our industry that when you are busy fighting the alligators, it's hard to remember that the reason you were put there in the first place was to clean out the swamp. Let's keep the focus where it needs to be. Focusing on who we are—apart from Jesus—misses the whole point of creation. Focusing on who we are *in Jesus* keeps us on point. It keeps us following the one who knows the Way, because *He is the Way*.

What is in your mind right now? The Holy Spirit can cut through all the weeds, the bad seed in your mind and heart. It is the Holy Spirit who draws you to your heavenly Father, not to punish you, but to love you into right relationship with Him and to love you into His presence here and now and for all eternity. He will show you that Jesus is your Hope, your Peace, your Purpose.

It is up to you to agree with God and His Word. Be in the Word; abide in the Lord Jesus. The field of your mind will be growing God's seed, and harvest—the good harvest—will be reaped in God's time.

O Lord God, I pray for the one reading this to open her or his mind and heart to what You can plant there, to what You can grow there, all of which leads to goodness and mercy. In the name of the Lamb of God, Jesus. Amen.

Communication

*A*re you ever frustrated in trying to communicate with someone? Did you ever stop to think about how many means of communication are available to you and me today?

Land line telephone (we actually still have one),
cell telephone,
text messaging,
Twitter,
Facebook,
pager,
facsimile,
Skype,
Facetime,
email,
snail mail (formerly USPS), and
Face-to-face,

So many ways, but how good are we—really—at communicating? Are you ever frustrated because you can't reach someone, even with all the many options you have? Are you ever frustrated when you leave messages, but then the person doesn't respond? What about the frustration when your device signals its battery is low or even dead? What about when your call is dropped or you have no signal? Remember the commercial "Can you hear me now?" What about when you hear a busy signal, and you really *need* to speak to that person? What about when computers or servers are down? It seems as though nothing can be done when that happens, right?

I was in a training session one time. Our trainers were loading a new software program on our laptops, which should have taken only a few minutes, but it took about two hours because of the differences between our computers, and how they were receiving the data.

What about when the fax doesn't go through because it is out of paper, out of toner, or jammed up on the other end? What about when a communication is lost in the mail? What about when there is no response because you are just being ignored? That caller ID business works both ways, doesn't it?

What about a part of the address being incorrect or incomplete that prevents the communication from arriving, whether it be on a letter or an email (any discrepancy prevents email from going through—one omitted period in my email address has kept many from being delivered). What about unlisted numbers or numbers that have been written down incorrectly?

In spite of the many ways in which we *can* communicate, just how well are we *really* communicating? How's your communication when you reach someone from another country, who doesn't speak your language very clearly? Many calls today are routed to another country for customer service, which often ends up being anything but customer service when the two parties can't understand each other. And even when you are in face-to-face conversation with someone, is that person giving you their undivided attention, or are they distracted or disinterested—perhaps thinking about what they are going to say next?

"People who have nothing to say are never at a loss in talking" (Josh Billings).

"We never listen when we are eager to speak" (Francois de La Rochefoucauld).

How many really good listeners do you know? Are you a good listener? Each of us should practice becoming a *really good listener*, and it may take a lot of practice to get there.

On my visits with customers, I regularly pray that God will help me be a good listener, in order that I hear what my customer's needs are. It is tempting to be thinking what it is that I want to say and completely miss what my customer has to say. I've done that, and when I have, the visit doesn't go as well as it should, and I haven't taken care of our customer as I need to.

How many times have you finished speaking to someone only to find out that they weren't listening to you at all? Communication problems that you and I experience today are the source of deep frustration and often lead to disappointment, loneliness, and isolation.

How well have you been listening to your heavenly Father?

Did you know that the Lord God Almighty, the Creator of all that is, Creator of you and me, has been communicating to each of us all our lives? And, did you know that He is always listening to what you have to say to Him? When you thought there was no one there, that you were all alone, that no one really cared, someone is there and does care. He is not only the Great Communicator—He is the Perfect Communicator! What He says is to the point—no idle chatter, no meaningless words, no surface talk. You and I are pretty good at surface talk, idle chatter, and meaningless words, aren't we? We can chat up sports, weather, and entertainment until we are exhausted—and most of it nothing more than surface conversation. But God gets to the heart of the matter *every time*. What He says is *exactly* what you and I need to hear. What is the message He is communicating to you and me?

That He is busy? Too busy for you; too busy for me?

That He is out of reach?

That He is out of touch?

That He has no cell service where He is?

That His computer is down?

That He is not interested in what happens to you?

That He has abandoned you?

That is absolutely *not* the truth in any way, shape, or form! You see, this is the truth: God, the Father, is communicating to you and me all our lives. And, here is what He is saying:

He does care about us.

He is interested in what happens to us.

He does love us deeply.

He created us to love Him.

He does listen to us, and He hears what we have to say.

He does want to help us.

He does not abandon us.

He does have something to say to us, and it is exactly what we need to hear. You know, a battery can be fully charged, but until it is connected, its power isn't utilized. By itself, it is useless. Until we are connected to God, His power is not made known to us or through us. And, we are connected to God the Father through Jesus alone by the power of His Holy Spirit.

If you want to be heard, speak to the one who always listens. You need no mechanical device—no phone, no fax, no computer, no stationary, no pen. You need only to speak, and the God of all the universe listens.

Do you understand how He hears each one of us, and all of us? I don't either. But we don't have to understand *how* He does it; just to know *that* He does it. It is ours to believe, even when we don't understand. It is ours to trust, even when we don't understand. He is listening right now, hearing every word, every thought in that brain of yours that He created.

Have you ever heard the phrases: Well, he is just so busy, he doesn't have time right now; or he can't be disturbed right now; or he has so many irons in the fire, he can't take time for that right now? Those are human limitations—not so with Almighty God, not so with All-Loving God. He is always accessible. How can this be? Does He have much responsibility? Well, uh, just sustaining the earth, the galaxies, the universe, the heavens, and all creation 24/7. We *talk* a lot about 24/7, but God *does* 24/7. He has no downtime.

How can He hear you and hear me? How does He have time to listen? Why would He want to listen to me? I can only answer the first two questions with He is omnipotent—all powerful. He is greater and more majestic, more powerful, than your or my finite mind can even comprehend. As for why He would want to listen to you and to me, well, He makes that clear—because He loves you, He loves me, and He wants the absolute best for you and me.

So, what do you need in order to communicate with God? The tried and true—all the time working—no downtime—no busy signal—prayer. I can testify that God has heard me all hours of the day and night. You see, scripture tells us that He never slumbers or sleeps (Ps. 121:3–4).

Have you ever wanted to just talk to someone, but they were asleep? Then, when they were finally awake, the time wasn't right anymore, or you even forgot whatever it was. Not so with God the Father. He is always available.

In the first part of that same Psalm—"I lift up my eyes to the hills... where does my help come from? My help comes from the Lord—the Maker of heaven and earth" (Ps. 121:1-2*). Isn't it just like a loving Father to make Himself available to everyone? You see, when you seek God's attention, you have it. "If you seek him, he will be found by you" (1 Chr. 28:9). "But if from there you seek the Lord your God, you will find him if you seek him with all your heart and with all your soul" (Deut. 4:29). When you earnestly desire God's presence, He is there with you.

What is it you need most? I don't mean things—what do you *really need?* "Ask, and it will be given to you; seek and you will find; knock and the door will be opened to you. For everyone who asks receives; the one who seeks finds; and to the one who knocks, the door will be opened" (Matt. 7:7–8). You see, God has been communicating with man from the beginning. "For since the creation of the world God's invisible qualities—his eternal power and divine nature—have been clearly seen, being understood from what has been made, so that people are without excuse" (Rom. 1:20).

God is communicating to you and me through his beautiful creation all around us. He is communicating to you and me through the prophets of old that He would send His Son one day to become one among us, and to *save* us. The Old Testament points to the coming of the Savior. Then He did send His Son to communicate the love of the Father and to become the sacrifice that paid the penalty for your sin and my sin.

God is communicating to you and me through His personal love letter—the Bible—of the depth of His love, forgiveness, mercy, grace, and peace. Oh, how He loves the folks in the Bible—folks who disobeyed Him, ignored Him, rejected Him, and dishonored Him, folks who lied, cheated, stole, murdered, were adulterous, and idolatrous— sinners. If *we* were treated so, what would *we* do? Would we offer our only beloved son for sinners such as these? Oh, how He loves you and me—sinners, just like those in the Bible. So, you see, God is not inaccessible.

He is not disinterested.

He is not distracted.

He is not too high tech; He's not too low tech, either.

He is not out of range.

He is not out of touch.

God is perfect in communicating His love to you and me.

There have been some great communications recorded throughout history:

"Following the light of the sun, we left the Old World" (Christopher Columbus). But, how about the Light and leaving the old nature? Jesus said in John 8:12: "I am the light of the world. Whoever follows Me will never walk in darkness, but will have the light of life." "Therefore, if anyone is in Christ, he is a new creation. The old is gone, the new has come!" (2 Cor. 5:17*).

"We hold these truths to be self-evident, that all men are created equal, that they are endowed by their Creator with certain unalienable

Rights, that among these are Life, Liberty, and the pursuit of Happiness" (Declaration of Independence). But, how about life which is full and everlasting, no matter the circumstances or the country? Jesus said in John 10:10: "I have come that they may have life, and have it to the full," and in John 11:25-26, Jesus said: "I am the resurrection and the life. The one who believes in me will live, even though they die; and whoever lives by believing in me will never die."

"That on the first day of January, in the year of our Lord, one thousand eight hundred and sixty-three, all persons held as slaves within any State or designated part of a State, shall be then, thenceforward, and forever free" (Emancipation Proclamation). But, how about freedom for the soul of sin and its consequences for all? Jesus said in John 8:32: "Then you will know the truth, and the truth will set you free," and in John 8:36: "So if the Son sets you free, you will be free indeed."

"This is one small step for a man, one giant leap for mankind" (Neil Armstrong). But, how about the leap of redemption for all mankind by our Savior Jesus? "For God so loved the world that he gave His one and only Son that whoever believes in him shall not perish but have eternal life" (John 3:16).

Many had fallen away from Jesus, and He looked around at His disciples, asking if they, too, would leave Him. Simon Peter spoke up and said, "Lord, to whom shall we go? You have the words of eternal life. We have come to believe and to know that you are the Holy One of God" (John 6:68).

Yes, these are the words of life, communicated to you and me throughout the ages, communicated to you and me at this very moment. Everything about God communicates to you that He loves you.

Will you listen to Him? Will you love Him?

O Lord God, I pray for the one reading this that Your communication of love and salvation would hit home, and that he or she would communicate with You in trust and obedience to Your will. In the name of Jesus, the perfect Communicator of love and salvation. Amen.

Creator versus Created

*A*re your eyes on the Creator or on the created? Do you worship created things, or do you worship the Creator? Do created things give you hope? Do created things give you peace? When we exchange the truth of God for lies, we do so at our own peril. When we exchange the glory of the living God for images and things, we are foolish.

"The wrath of God is being revealed from heaven against all the godlessness and wickedness of people, who suppress the truth by their wickedness, since what may be known about God is plain to them, because God has made it plain to them. For since the creation of the world God's invisible qualities—his eternal power and divine nature—have been clearly seen, being understood from what has been made, so that people are without excuse. For although they knew God, they neither glorified him as God nor gave thanks to him, but their thinking became futile and their foolish hearts were darkened. Although they claimed to be wise, they became fools and exchanged the glory of the immortal God for images made to look like a mortal human being and birds and animals and reptiles. Therefore God gave them over in the sinful desires of their hearts to sexual impurity for the degrading of their bodies with one another. They exchanged the truth about God for a lie, and worshiped and served created things rather than the Creator—who is forever praised. Amen" (Rom. 1:18–25).

If you are trusting in that which is created, and not trusting in your Creator, then you are being deceived. And if you are being deceived, then you are in danger.

Each of us will either end up trusting our Creator God or trusting something else. That something else could be many things, but all of them are created things, and all of them are being pushed at you by the deceiver, Satan himself.

You may not see his wicked hand in your decisions, but he is out to get you; he is out to bring you down. He desires that you be with him—outside of God's presence, outside of God's grace, and outside of God's salvation, for all eternity. And, that is exactly where you *will be* if you trust in anything created rather than trusting in the Creator.

You may be saved, and if so, Satan cannot pluck you out of God's hand. Nothing can separate you from God's love if you are trusting in Him. But, if you, even as a believer, allow yourself to be deceived, you will be trusting in something created instead of your Creator.

Look at Abraham, a man described as a man of faith. Abram, as he was called before God renamed him, grew up in pagan surroundings, an environment in which folks worshiped created things—not the Creator. Yet, this man is called by the apostle Paul as the "father of all who believe" (Rom. 4:11) and "Abraham, the man of faith" (Gal. 3:9). Faith in what, believer in what? Abram listened when the Lord spoke to him, "Go from your country, your people, and your father's household to the land I will show you" (Gen. 12:1). Mind you, this isn't a call to move to the next field, or to the next town a few miles away. How about four hundred miles? On foot. At 75 years old. With a great many possessions.

This is after their collective family had already made a six-hundred-mile move from Ur to Harran. Surely, it would have made a lot more sense to just move a few miles away if everybody in the family needed a little more space. Yes it would, if the focus was on created things, like creature comforts, familiarity, and the like. But Abram focused on the Creator and what the Creator had to say to him. And now, he was being called by his Creator to go the land occupied by the Canaanites.

He obeyed. And, when he arrived in this foreign land, "he built an altar there to the Lord, who had appeared to him" (Gen. 12:7b). The Lord had also told him, "I will make you into a great nation, and I will bless you; I will make your name great, and you will be a blessing. I will bless those who bless you, and whoever curses you I will curse; and all peoples on earth will be blessed through you" (Gen. 12:2-3).

OK, let's look at this from the logical side—the side focused on the created. A great nation through Abram? First of all, Abram and Sarai were childless. Second, she was well beyond child-bearing years. In fact, "she was not able to conceive," according to Gen. 11:30. That alone makes it impossible, right?

Then, a great nation through Abram? They had left their home country, a place where they actually had some roots, some "connections," to travel far away to a foreign place among strangers, and on top of all that—a place experiencing a severe famine!

Now, the Lord had said to Abram about this land, "to your offspring I will give this land" (Gen. 12:7a). So, how in the world would a couple who couldn't have children, in a foreign land among strangers—and one wracked with famine—possibly give birth to a great nation? Jesus teaches us from Luke 18:27, "What is impossible with man is possible with God." Now, this was in response to the question posed to Jesus regarding if a rich man, who was apparently a moral, law-abiding sort, would not inherit eternal life in his present state, then who could be saved?

This man was held up as a model citizen, one who had kept the commandments. So, if he had not done enough to inherit eternal life, then who? The focus was on the man and his works—the created—and not on the Creator. Jesus made clear that the path to eternal life for this man—same as for you and me—was choosing Jesus as Savior and following Jesus as Lord above all else in this life. We can't make a path to God. It is impossible. Only God can make the path to Himself. In fact that is exactly what He has done. Jesus is the path—the Way, the Truth, the Life (John 14:6).

God is in the habit of doing what man cannot do, creating all that is, breathing life into the unborn, sustaining our very being, breath by breath, restoring downcast souls, giving new life to the condemned, bringing hope to a hopeless world.

It sure seemed hopeless for Sarai and Abram that they would ever give birth to a son of their own, much less give birth to a great nation. Hopeless, as long as their eyes were on the created. God even helped them in the refocusing process by giving them new names—Sarah from Sarai and Abraham from Abram, so they would be mindful of God's plan for their being mother and father of many nations. Ah, but still— perhaps like you and me—they saw the limits of the created instead of the limitless nature of the Creator. So, they took matters in their own hands. They didn't do it overnight, mind you.

It had been about ten years since the Lord had told Abram that, "I will make you a great nation and I will bless you" and "to your offspring I will give this land. So he built an altar there to the Lord, who had appeared to him" (Gen. 12:2, 7). But, in that ten years, Sarai was still childless, and since she believed that the Lord had kept her from having children, their only hope seemed to be for Abram to father a child with another woman—Hagar, their Egyptian hand-servant.

So, Abram went along with this plan because their focus was on the created—not on the Creator—and Hagar bore a son named Ishmael. Now this was going to be one happy family, don't you know. Not. There was no peace, no harmony, in this household. There never is when we aren't obedient to the Lord, when we take matters into our hands, when we rely on our own wits, and when we focus on the created instead of the Creator. Surprise, surprise, Hagar despised her mistress, and Sarai blamed Abram for all the suffering and anguish. Ultimately, Hagar and Ishmael were sent away.

So, when Abram was ninety-nine years old, the Lord appeared to him again to remind him that "I am God Almighty; walk before me faithfully and be blameless" (Gen. 17:1), and to confirm His covenant that Abram, now called Abraham, would be the father of many nations. He went on in Genesis 17:15: "'As for Sarai your wife, you are no longer to call her Sarai; her name will be Sarah. I will bless her and will surely give you a son by her. I will bless her so that she will be the mother of nations; kings of peoples will come from her.'"

What would your reaction have been at this point? Well, "Abraham fell facedown; he laughed and said to himself, 'Will a son be born to a man a hundred years old? Will Sarah bear a child at the age of ninety?'" As a matter of fact, yes. That is exactly what God's message was: "Your wife Sarah will bear you a son, and you will call him Isaac" (Gen. 17:17, 19). In Genesis 18, the Lord appeared again to Abraham with this message, "I will surely return to you about this time next year, and Sarah your wife will have a son" (Gen. 18:10). God has been pretty clear about His plans, hasn't He? Still doesn't mean it looked like it was possible.

Sarah certainly saw no possibility of all this, "Now Sarah was listening at the entrance to the tent, which was behind him. Abraham and Sarah were already very old, and Sarah was past the age of childbearing. So Sarah laughed to herself as she thought, 'After I am worn out and my lord is old, will I now have this pleasure?'" (Gen. 18:10b-12). Listen to the Lord's response, "Why did Sarah laugh and say, 'Will I really have a child, now that I am old? Is anything too hard for the Lord? I will return to you at the appointed time next year and Sarah will have a son'" (Gen. 18:13-14).

Interestingly, Sarah was afraid and lied about laughing, but the Lord told her that yes, she did laugh. God didn't change His plans because these folks, like you and me, find His plans hard to understand—perhaps even unbelievable. He repeatedly made His plans clear, and He delivered. He always delivers what He promises. Do you know anyone else that does that? Nothing created delivers what it promises for very long. Only the Creator delivers what He promises, and for the long haul, for all time. In Genesis 21, we read:

"Now the Lord was gracious to Sarah as he had said, and the Lord did for Sarah what he had promised. Sarah became pregnant and bore a son to Abraham in his old age, at the very time God had promised him. Abraham gave the name Isaac to the son Sarah bore him... Abraham was a hundred years old when his son Isaac was born to him. Sarah said, 'God has brought me laughter (by the way, Isaac means "he laughs"), and everyone who hears about this will laugh with me." And she added,

"Who would have said to Abraham that Sarah would nurse children? Yet I have borne him a son in his old age."

God delivered just as He promised He would. He always does, against all logic. "For nothing is impossible with God" (Luke 1:37*), referencing the Messiah to be born of the virgin Mary. We shouldn't think we would have been any different than Abraham and Sarah. We would likely have had similar reactions of disbelief, laughter, and maybe even dismissal.

Now, let's look at this same Abraham some years later when the son God had brought to them in their old age had grown into young manhood (in Genesis 22). "Some time later God tested Abraham. He said to him, 'Abraham!' 'Here I am,' he replied. Then God said, 'Take your son, your only son, whom you love—Isaac—and go to the region of Moriah. Sacrifice him there as a burnt offering on a mountain I will show you.'" Sacrifice him? Does that seem like an impossible request to you? It does to me. Yet, Abraham obeyed. He didn't look for a way out. He obeyed. He didn't protest. He obeyed. He didn't laugh. He obeyed. Now, his focus was not on the created, his focus was on the Creator. This is overwhelming to me, isn't it to you?

"Early the next morning Abraham got up and loaded his donkey. He took with him two of his servants and his son Isaac. When he had cut enough wood for the burnt offering, he set out for the place God had told him about. On the third day Abraham looked up and saw the place in the distance. He said to his servants, 'Stay here with the donkey while I and the boy go over there. We will worship and then we will come back to you'" (Gen. 22:3-5).

What were Abraham's eyes of faith seeing? I don't know, but I do know that he was trusting his Creator God. How would he sacrifice his son Isaac and yet both of them return?

"Abraham took the wood for the burnt offering and placed it on his son Isaac, and he himself carried the fire and the knife. As the two of them went on together, Isaac spoke up and said to his father Abraham, 'Father?' 'Yes, my son?' 'The fire and wood are here,' Isaac said, 'but where is the lamb for the burnt offering?' Abraham answered, 'God himself will provide the lamb for the burnt offering, my son.' And the two of them went on together.

When they reached the place God had told him about, Abraham built an altar there and arranged the wood on it. (Do you think he arranged, rearranged, rearranged, and rearranged the wood—stalling, as I likely would have done?). He bound his son Isaac and laid him on the altar, on top of the wood. Then he reached out his hand and took the knife to slay his son. (What would have been going through his mind at that point? What anguish would he have been experiencing?). But the angel of the Lord called out to him from heaven, 'Abraham! Abraham!' 'Here I am,' he replied. 'Do not lay a hand on the boy,' He said. 'Do not do anything to him. Now I know that you fear God, because you have not withheld from me your son, your only son.' Abraham looked up and there in a thicket he saw a ram caught by its horns. He went over and took the ram and sacrificed it as a burnt offering instead of his son. So Abraham called that place The Lord Will Provide" (Gen. 22:6-14a).

So the Lord did indeed provide for this one who trusted—who obeyed—Him. And, the Lord has kept His promise to bless all who would come after Abraham, and also trust and obey the same living God, our creator God. There came a point in time some 2,000 years later when another son would be laid on an altar of sacrifice. An only son. This son had known what was coming. He would die. He had been born for this. He asked His Father if there was another way. Yet He knew there wasn't, and so He willingly became the sacrificial lamb.

This time, there would be no ram in the thicket. This time, there would be no substitute for the Son. He *was* the substitute—for me, for you. This time the grieving Father would find no relief—only pain. He would turn away from His Son in anguish no man can fathom. This time the sky would turn black. This time the sun would stop shining. This time the whole earth would shake.

The Sacrifice Himself could have stopped it at any time, but His life wasn't taken against His will. He gave His life out of love. Yes, this time the Son would die. He would die at the hands of those who mocked Him, who spat upon Him, who stripped Him, who struck Him, who taunted Him, who rejected Him, who despised Him, who didn't see that it was *His love* that brought them into creation and *His love* that offered them life and peace.

This time the Son would die—hanging on a cross—no human dignity, just divine love. This time the Son's body would be laid in a tomb, not a family tomb, a borrowed tomb. But it wouldn't be needed for long.

There sure seemed to be defeat in the air that day as Jesus's limp frame had hung lifeless on that cross, but that was only if one looked at the created, and not to the Creator. Because the Creator was not finished.

There was victory to be won on that morning when the Father breathed life into His Son, when Jesus shed the burial clothes, when Jesus arose and left the tomb, when Jesus overcame death and defeated Satan once and for all, when Jesus made good on all the promises of God that indeed He would send us the Savior. The Savior gave His life so that we have life beyond the grave. And now we have life everlasting.

The one who will only focus on the created will not see the Creator through the eyes of faith and tragically will miss the whole meaning of life. But the one who will focus on the Creator and trust Him and follow His Son Jesus will find the full and meaningful life in the here and now, and will one day enter into eternal life.

Will you choose to worship the created to your tragic doom?

Or, will you choose to worship the Creator to your eternal bliss?

O Lord, our Creator God, thank You that You have revealed Yourself in all creation, and most of all through Your Son Jesus. I pray for the one reading this for a trust in You and not in anything that You have created so that salvation and peace is his or hers. In the name of our Savior Jesus. Amen.

Damaged Goods

*A*re you damaged goods? Do you feel like you have been chewed up and spit out? Are you afraid there is no hope for you to have a brighter day? A higher purpose? Is this as good as it gets? The world has a way of using up the best we have and leaving us defeated, leaving us wanting.

What do you do with chewing gum that has lost its flavor? You spit it out, don't you? OK, actually you dispose of it properly in a garbage can, right? That chewing gum has lost its value, so you throw it away.

You may have been in a relationship with someone who did exactly that to you—used you; bled the flavor—the life—right out of you until there was nothing left; then spit you out, throwing you away. It's hard to go on when you feel cast aside, isn't it?

Often, we hear the term *damaged goods*. It typically refers to a value lowered because the quality of something has been lessened. Because it is not worth as much, the price goes down, and the buyer pays less. Now when we are considering material goods, this does make sense. But tragically, the term and the practice is also used for human beings—in particular—females. Females (but males as well) have been abused, used up, cast aside by others who were feeding their own selfish desires, regardless of who else was hurt in the process.

We live in a society where consideration for human life and human suffering has diminished. Just stop and consider that it is estimated that around 125,000 living, unborn babies are killed daily in our world, according to the World Health Organization. And over 60,000,000 living, unborn, babies have been killed—"legally"—in the U.S. since

1973. Now, we can make a case for the varying worth of *goods* as to their value to the buyer. But, can we make the same case for *human beings*— folks created in God's image?

You may believe you are damaged goods, that there is no hope for a brighter day, no higher purpose than your current level in life. You may believe that you can never get beyond this pain, this despair, this emptiness. But God says something different to you than what the world says to you. And God always speaks the truth.

You see, the world treats you like Satan treats you. No surprise there. After all, he is the prince of this world. He is all about using you up until there is nothing left, and then spitting you out. He will constantly feed you a line of bull. Nothing that he tells you is for your own good. Nothing that he tells you will make your life ultimately better. *Nothing*!

When someone lies to you, what happens to their credibility? It's shot, isn't it? At least until they prove to you otherwise. Know this: Satan is a liar. A liar is *not to be believed; not to be trusted.* A liar has *no credibility.* "for he is a liar and the father of lies" "When he lies, he speaks his native language" (John 8:44). It is not out of character for him, it *is* his character. But worse yet, he is a murderer—"He was a murderer from the beginning, not holding to the truth, for there is no truth in him" (John 8:44).

Satan is characterized in 1 Peter 5:8 as your enemy—keep that in mind always. "Your enemy the devil prowls around like a roaring lion looking for someone to devour." Is a roaring lion something to be taken lightly? Something to toy with? Satan is not to be taken lightly, not to be toyed with. He wants to destroy you. He lies to you. He destroys you if you let him.

John 10:10 says, "The thief comes only to steal and kill and destroy." Now, you and I have seen what devastation lying and murder lead to. So, keep in mind, this is what Satan is all about. It is who he is. But keep also in mind the second part of John 10:10 as Jesus assures us, "I have come that they may have life, and have it to the full." Satan's power is nothing in comparison to the power of our Creator—almighty God. Greater is the Lord Jesus in us than Satan who is of this world (1 John 4:4).

Jesus said, "I have told you these things, so that in me you may have peace. In this world you will have trouble. But take heart! I have overcome the world" (John 16:33). The Lord God is about love. He is about truth; He is about peace. He is about mercy; He is about forgiveness, and He is about grace. In fact, He *is all these in the person of Jesus, the Christ.*

You may believe, right now, that you are worth nothing to anyone, but God wants you to know that is just not true. You *are* worth everything to God in Christ Jesus. You may believe, right now, that you could never have a higher purpose in this life, but that is just not true. You *have* a higher purpose from God in Christ Jesus.

You may believe, right now, that you could never experience a full and meaningful life, but that is just not true. You *can* experience a full and meaningful life from God in Christ Jesus. And He offers that to you right now. You see, even though the amount of damage inflicted on you and me may be different, we both really are damaged goods. First of all, we are damaged because we have chosen to sin:

"We all, like sheep, have gone astray, each of us has turned to our own way" (Is. 53:6).

"For all have sinned, and fall short of the glory of God" (Rom. 3:23).

But God assures us that, in spite of our damage—our sin—He still loves us. Romans 5:8 tells us, "But God demonstrates his own love for us in this: While we were still sinners, Christ died for us." In fact, you and I are so important to Him that He paid the highest price for us that He could.

I heard the following on a Paul Harvey broadcast years ago. The story has been told about an encounter in an alley between a lad of about ten years old and a preacher.

The lad was unwashed and rather unkempt, and as he walked along, he swung at his side an old caved-in bird cage. Several tiny birds shivered on the floor of it. The preacher asked him where he got the birds, and he replied that he had trapped them. He was asked by the kindly man what he was going to do with them. He said that he was going to have some fun with them and then later feed them to his cats. The preacher asked him how much he wanted for the birds. The boy was surprised, even disbelieving, saying that these were just plain old field birds. He said that they couldn't sing, and besides, they were ugly. The preacher asked him to just tell how much he wanted. The grubby little lad squinted and said how about two dollars. He was surprised when the man pulled the money from his pocket and paid the ransom. The boy took off up the alley, and the preacher took up the birdcage. He opened the door of the cage and encouraged the little birds to fly to their freedom. One by one, they did exactly that. With that empty old birdcage sitting on the pulpit, the preacher told to his congregation a story, one in which Jesus and the devil had a conversation. Satan had boasted how he had baited a trap in the garden of Eden, and caught himself a world full of people. Jesus asked him what he was going to do with all those people in "his cage." He said that he would play with them, tease them, incite them. He would tempt them to be filled with pride, to hate, to lie, to steal, to kill, and to destroy. Jesus asked how much would he want for them. Satan laughed and said that surely they would not be worth the price for what they would do to Jesus – mock him, spit on him, beat him, even drive nails into him and crucify him. Jesus said, "How much?" Satan said, "All of your tears and all of your blood. That's the price." Jesus paid that price and the door was opened.

Satan could no longer hold us in captivity unless we rejected the grace offered in Jesus's sacrifice:

"So if the Son sets you free, you will be free indeed" (John 8:36).

"For God so loved the world that he gave his one and only Son, that whoever believes in him shall not perish but have eternal life" (John 3:16).

God wants no one to perish, but everyone to come to repentance (2 Pet. 3:9).

God does not want you to perish!

God wants everyone to be saved, and come to a knowledge of the truth (1 Tim. 2:4).

God wants you to be saved!

He didn't lower the price He would pay because of your damaged state. He didn't say, "Well, she is of so little value that I will lower the price I will pay" or "He is so used up that I cannot pay full price." You are worth the same to the heavenly Father as Moses, as Mary, as Paul, as Mother Theresa, as Billy Graham.

No, the price was still to be the same—a human life, but not just any human life—the perfect human life. There is only one. The Father paid the full price, the highest price—His perfect Son, Jesus, the Christ. How can we be worth the price He paid? We cannot, yet He paid it. He gave nothing less than the best He had for you and me. What love is this in the Father's will?

Jesus told us in John 6:40, "for my Father's will is that everyone who looks to the Son and believes in him shall have eternal life, and I will raise them up at the last day." 1 John 5:11–12 confirms this: "And this is the testimony: God has given us eternal life, and this life is in his Son. Whoever has the Son has life; whoever does not have the Son of God does not have life." You see, it's not what the world thinks you are worth that matters; it's not even what you think you are worth that matters. It is what God *knows* you are worth—to Him—that really matters.

My Mother taught me not to think more highly of myself than I should, which is wise advice. We also ought not to think of ourselves less than God thinks of us, should we? In fact, we need to see ourselves just as our heavenly Father who created us sees us, shouldn't we? God says, "You see, at just the right time, when we were still powerless, Christ died for the ungodly (the sinners, the damaged goods, you and me)...but God demonstrates his own love for us in this: while we were still sinners, Christ died for us" (Rom. 5:6–8).

You know, there's a whole lot of talk in the world today and often not much action to back it up. But know this, God doesn't just *say* the right thing—He *does* the right thing! It is His gift of love in Christ Jesus to redeem us—to purchase us—with the highest price He could pay. He doesn't ask us to *prove to Him* what our worth is—He *proves to us* what our worth is to Him.

Think of the one who lay by the side of the road in Luke 10:30–37. He had fallen into the hands of robbers. They had stripped his clothes off him; they had beaten him; they had left him for dead. Several passed by without helping him, including a religious leader and a lay leader, but there was one who did help. He was a Samaritan, a half-breed, one who was looked at with scorn, one who was rejected, despised by most. You know what he did? He not only stopped and looked, but he had pity on this poor soul.

He bandaged his wounds. He put the man on his own donkey. He took him into town, secured a room for him in the inn—he took care of him. He supplied the man's needs out of his own resources. He rescued this man. Others may talk a good game. But he walked the talk, he did the right thing.

Who has proven to you that He loves you in such a way? Who is your Rescuer? Your Deliverer?

You do have one who binds your wounds, who lifts your head, who restores your soul, who pays the price to care for you, and who shows that you are worth whatever He must give to save you. You see, like the good Samaritan, Jesus was looked at with scorn, rejected, despised of men. Did this stop Him from loving, forgiving, sacrificing? No, no, and *no*. He gave it all for you. He longs for you to spend eternity with Him in a place He prepares for His own. There will be no remnants of this sinful world there. All that hurts you and binds you will be left behind.

Think of this, *the only scars in heaven will be His.* Knowing this, what does this make you want to do? Does it make you want to embrace the one who loves you so? Does it make you want to be held by the one who is love? By the one whose hands and feet were nailed to a cross because He wanted so desperately to free us from the penalty that you and I owe because of our sin? He owed nothing, yet paid everything.

We don't have to get everything right in order to come to Him. In fact, we couldn't get everything right, even if we wanted to. You need to know that God's embrace of those who trust in Him is forever. Nothing can pluck us out of His hand, once we are there. Nothing can separate us from His love and care. He offers you a full and meaningful life in the here and now. He offers you peace and contentment in the here and now. He offers you strength for the day in the here and now. But, above all that, He offers you everlasting life in His home, His presence, His heaven if you will put your trust in Him.

If you feel cast aside, remember, the Father's arms are open wide. He reaches down to where you are; His hands are ready to pick you up, telling you "I love you. My Son died for you. I offer you everlasting life with Me in My heavenly home."

Know this, you must pass by His waiting open arms in order to go down the road to hell and destruction. You must reject His invitation to eternal life in order to choose eternal death. Like the door on that cage that was opened to free the birds, Jesus is the door that leads to everlasting life. It is only through Jesus that we come to the Father, and Jesus is hoping that you will trust Him to dwell in you forever.

Let Him show you daily what you are worth to Him.

He will.

O Lord God, I pray for the one reading this, that no matter how he or she sees themselves or how others see them, that Your message of love and value for them will come through by the power of Your Holy Spirit. In the name of the perfect one, Jesus, who loves and saves. Amen.

Arms of Jesus

I am at peace in the arms of Jesus;
He calms my soul in the midst of the storm;
His nail-pierced hands are gentle and warm;
I am at peace in the arms of Jesus.

No matter what trouble comes with each day,
No matter what trial may yet unfold,
He's faced it already, and shown me the best way,
The darkest my hour, the tightest His hold.

Pressed on all sides, confused and weary,
I find myself reeling from Satan's blows.
Then I remember my Jesus in victory;
His power renews me, my faith in Him grows.

Joy and love upon me He showers;
Contentment in Christ is forever mine.
When I am weak, by grace He empowers,
Filling my soul with His Spirit divine.

Give Us Barabbas!

The people shouted, "Give us Barabbas!" Give them Barabbas instead of whom? Instead of the one they called "the king of the Jews," Jesus of Nazareth. The story is told in John 13–19.

Jesus had been betrayed by one of His own disciples—one who had been with Jesus throughout his earthly ministry—the treasurer, in fact. Jesus had spent His last meal with these disciples, still teaching them, still loving them, still setting the perfect example for them, and still comforting them. Jesus had even knelt before each of them to wash their dirty feet, modeling for them what it really means to be a servant. Jesus had challenged them to do greater things than they had ever imagined if they would but ask the Father in the name of His Son.

These same men, as well as countless others from town to town, village to village, had seen Jesus give life to dead persons; give sight to dead eyes; give sound to dead ears; give walk to dead legs; give flight to diseases; give food to the hungry, and give water to the thirsty. But, more than all these, this same Jesus gave hope to the lost; He gave heaven to those destined to hell. He gave righteousness to the unrighteous.

Multitudes had seen the miracles and had followed Him because of them. Yet many had fallen away when this one who seemed to be in control of everything, even the elements of nature, now appeared to lose all control as he was arrested and faced trial.

Where was his control now? Had he lost control? No, not even for a nanosecond. His control had not been lost; it had not been lessened. He had set it aside—of His own free will—so that the Father's plan for you and me, and all mankind would unfold.

"No one takes it (my life) from me, but I lay it down of my own accord. I have authority to lay it down and authority to take it up again. This command I received from my Father" proclaimed Jesus from John 10:18.

You see, His plan is that you and I enter into His presence one day in a righteous state (which is the only way we can enter His Father's presence), so that we can spend eternity with Him as His family, around His table, serving Him in whatever capacity He desires. This means we would be heirs to the same fortune as the Father's true Son, Jesus. We would be heirs as adoptees, yet have the same access to the Father as His only Son.

"For those who are led by the Spirit of God are the children of God. The Spirit you received does not make you slaves, so that you live in fear again; rather, the Spirit you received brought about your adoption to sonship. And by him we cry, '*Abba*, Father.' The Spirit himself testifies with our spirit that we are God's children. Now if we are children, then we are heirs—heirs of God and co-heirs with Christ, if indeed we share in his sufferings in order that we may also share in his glory" (Rom. 8:14–17).

Co-heirs with Christ, we would be treated exactly as God's Son is treated. Can you believe it? How is this possible? Could you and I have that kind of righteousness that heaven's doors would be thrown open to welcome us alongside God's only Son? Don't think for a second that you or I could have even a speck of righteousness to make any claim to the Father's inheritance.

"There is no one righteous, not even one" (Rom. 3:10).

"We all, like sheep, have gone astray, each of us has turned to his own way, and the Lord has laid on him the iniquity of us all" (Is. 53:6).

"for all have sinned and fall short of the glory of God" (Rom. 3:23).

"Therefore no one will be declared righteous in God's sight by the works of the law; rather, through the law we become conscious of our sin" (Rom. 3:20).

So, how can we have hope? We can't on our own. We can't apart from Jesus. Yet, the people cried out—same as today—"No, not him!" Not Jesus, What were they saying when they asked for Barabbas instead of Jesus? Perhaps it had more to do with what Jesus wasn't than it did with what Barabbas was.

What wasn't Jesus? He wasn't a military leader, even though He would win the greatest battle of all time—resurrection from the grave.

Death lost. Life everlasting won.

Hate lost. Love won.

Earth lost. Heaven won.

The people wouldn't receive the deliverance they wanted from the oppressive slavery under the Roman rulers, yet all who would believe on Him would receive *a deliverance far greater* than that, deliverance from sin and its power, deliverance from the author of all sin—Satan.

Jesus wouldn't give them all that would satisfy their worldly desires, but, instead, Jesus would give them that which they needed most, forgiveness, peace, contentment. Would Barabbas give them what they wanted? Of course not. Yet, the people cried, "Give us Barabbas!"

As Jesus stood on the balcony next to Pilate—who could find no basis for any charge against Jesus—the choice before the people was the one from heaven—the life giver, or the one from earth—the life taker (murder was one of Barabbas' crimes). They chose the created one over the Creator. They chose the world over heaven.

When we choose the world over heaven, we don't end up with the world. We end up with hell. "What good will it be for someone to gain the whole world, yet forfeit their soul?" taught Jesus from Matt. 16:26. The world and the things of the world can seem like the right path to choose—a popular path with plenty of folks alongside us. "There is a way that appears to be right, but in the end it leads to death" (Prov. 14:12).

You see, it isn't your opinion or my opinion about the path that matters. It is what God says that carries the day, and, in fact, carries all days throughout eternity. Jesus and the ways of Jesus can seem like a narrow path—a less-traveled path with not so many folks alongside. That is exactly what God says to you and me.

We are instructed to "Enter through the narrow gate. For wide is the gate and broad is the road that leads to destruction, and many enter through it. But small is the gate and narrow the road that leads to life, and only a few find it" (Matt. 7:13–14).

A person needs to fully understand what she or he is saying when they ask for Barabbas. Because Barabbas isn't really what they want. They just don't want Jesus. They are asking for *anything but Jesus.* They are asking for anything but what our loving heavenly Father offers. They are asking for anything but peace and fulfillment. They are asking for anything but forgiveness and hope. They are asking for anything but everlasting life.

No one comes to the Father except through His Son. "I am the way and the truth and the life. No one comes to the Father except through me" were Jesus's words from John 14:6. So, is Jesus our only hope? Is Jesus our only way? Is Jesus our only Savior? Yes, yes, and yes. There is no hope apart from Jesus.

You mean there aren't many ways of truth? Correct.

You mean there aren't other paths to heaven? Right.

You mean there aren't numerous religions that lead us home? God said it.

Jesus made it clear that no one knows the Father—or ultimately will see the Father—unless first they see Jesus through the eyes of faith in Him. "I and the Father are one," said Jesus in John 10:30. The Father did not send many into the world as Saviors, as Messiahs, as Lights of the world. He sent one. He sent the only one. He sent His one Son.

"For God so loved the world that he gave his one and only Son, that whoever believes in him shall not perish but have eternal life. For God did not send his Son into the world to condemn the world, but to save the world through him. Whoever believes in him is not condemned, but whoever does not believe stands condemned already because they have not believed in the name of God's one and only Son" (John 3:16-18).

There is only one Son of God; only one Lamb of God; only one perfect sacrifice for our sins; only one Bread of Life; only one Good Shepherd; only one Door; only one who is in the Father, and in whom the Father is.

Jesus is the Messiah.
Jesus is the Christ.
Jesus is the anointed one.

"In the beginning was the Word, and the Word was with God, and the Word was God. He was with God in the beginning. Through him all things were made; without him nothing was made that has been made. In him was life, and that life was the light of all mankind" (John 1:1–4).

"The Word became flesh and made his dwelling among us" (John 1:14a).

"Yet to all who did receive him, to those who believed in his name, he gave the right to become children of God" (John 1:12).

You see, we have no way to become children of the Father except that we receive Jesus, except that we believe in His name, except that we follow Him as Lord.

Couldn't the people see that Barabbas was deserving of punishment? He had been convicted of crimes—even murder. He was guilty. He hadn't given them any reason to trust him. He hadn't shown love and compassion toward them. He hadn't sacrificed for their good.

Jesus had committed no crime. His arrest was without basis. His trial was a mockery. His accusers were liars. There was no foundation for any legal proceeding against Jesus. It was a sham. Yet, all of this would lead to the place where Jesus once and for all would show all mankind for all eternity what love is, what love really is.

Heavenly love covers all our faults; heavenly love covers all our warts; heavenly love covers all our sins. Heavenly love flows through the shed blood of God's only Son. It is this blood that cleanses. You and

I will not be cleansed by any other means. You and I will be cleansed only by His blood, through His blood.

Why would we cry out for anyone or anything but Jesus? Why would we settle? We warn our sons and daughters not to settle. We even warn our friends and acquaintances not to settle. So, why would you settle for anything but Jesus? Jesus is the best. There is none like Him. He has shown only love for you. He has done for you what no one else has ever done or could ever do: atone for your sins. You could never do enough to pay for your sins, but Jesus can and has.

Would you be righteous? Do you want to be righteous? You can, but only in repenting of your sins and taking on the righteousness of the only Perfect One—Jesus. In our sins, we die. In His sinlessness, we live.

"For the wages of sin is death, but the gift of God is eternal life in Christ Jesus our Lord" (Rom. 6:23).

"Unless you repent, you too will all perish," said Jesus (Luke 13:3).

But God wants you. He wants you to repent, and He wants to save you.

So, would you choose anything or anyone—Barabbas—over Jesus?

Or, will you choose Jesus who alone can satisfy and save you?

O Lord God, You have made our choice clear. How could any of us, including the reader of this message, choose anything or anyone but Jesus? Thank you for Your perfect gift, Your Son and our Savior Jesus. Amen.

God Chooses the Weak

*A*re you mighty in strength? Do you stand out in wisdom? Are you wealthy? Are you powerful? Do you come from an influential family? When you are spoken of by others, do they say, "You know who she is," and then cite a great accomplishment of yours. Or, do they say "You know who he is," and then they point to some organization you founded or one that you run. Or, maybe you are known because of your family's leadership or philanthropy in the community. Are you tops in your field? The cream of the crop? Were you voted most likely to succeed? Were you destined for greatness? Or, are you pretty average?

Do you not really stand out from others? Are you not one of whom others stop and take notice? Does it seem that you don't really have much power, much influence, much control? Join the club, the same club of which most of us are members. But know this, you may be exactly who the Lord is calling to greatness. You may be primed and ready for the Lord to work in you and through you if you will be one who boasts not about yourself, but instead boasts about Him.

What if an angel of the Lord appeared to you today—in your present circumstances—and said, "The Lord is with you, mighty warrior"? You might look in the mirror to see if some miraculous physical change has taken place—a Bruce Banner to the Incredible Hulk kind of transformation—for example. You might check your outfit to see if a Wonder Woman belt or Superman cape has suddenly appeared. You might pinch yourself to make sure this isn't some kind of dream.

You might question the Lord as Moses did at the burning bush, "Who am I that I should go to Pharaoh and bring the Israelites out of

Egypt?" (Ex. 3:11) and, as Gideon did, when, in fact, he heard those very words, "The Lord is with you, mighty warrior" (Judg. 6:12). You see, Gideon was not on the ladder to success. He was not engaged in some lofty pursuit. There was no applause as he went about his day. What was he doing? He was threshing wheat. Nothing wrong with that; it was a pretty ordinary daily task. What was different about it was that he was doing it at the floor of a winepress, essentially hiding. Why? So, he wouldn't be seen by the enemies, who would destroy the crop and maybe even Gideon himself. Let's see what was going on around Gideon and his people.

"The Israelites did evil in the eyes of the Lord, and for seven years he gave them into the hands of the Midianites. Because the power of Midian was so oppressive, the Israelites prepared shelters for themselves in mountain clefts, caves, and strongholds. Whenever the Israelites planted their crops, the Midianites, Amalekites and other eastern peoples invaded the country. They camped on the land and ruined the crops all the way to Gaza and did not spare a living thing for Israel, neither sheep nor cattle nor donkeys. They came up with their livestock and their tents like swarms of locusts. It was impossible to count them and their camels; they invaded the land to ravage it" (Judg. 6:1–5).

So, here was Gideon, keeping out of sight, trying to salvage some small measure of his wheat crop, and he was being told, "The Lord is with you, mighty warrior." The enemy was all around, too numerous to count, ruthless, ever at the ready to wreak havoc and destruction. We can be certain that Gideon was feeling like anything but a mighty warrior. But understand...the people had cried out for help, and God had heard. "Midian so impoverished the Israelites that they cried out to the Lord for help" (Judg. 6:6). Over and over again throughout God's Word we read that His people cried out to Him in their anguish, their despair, their oppression, and over and over again, God responded with His mighty hand.

So, the angel of the Lord appeared to Gideon to tell him that the Lord was with him, and then called him "mighty warrior." His response:

"'Pardon me, my lord', Gideon replied, 'but if the Lord is with us, why has all this happened to us? Where are all his wonders that our ancestors told us about when they said, 'Did not the Lord bring us up out of Egypt?' But now the Lord has abandoned us and put us into the hand of Midian'" (Judg. 6:13).

I appreciate Gideon's honesty before God, don't you? Can you be that honest with your heavenly Father? It has been a long learning process for me.

Do you think that our loving Father, who knows all our thoughts and knows our hearts inside and out, is ever going to be fooled by our dishonesty or lack of candor? Is He ever going to be unprepared for our questions or complaints? We don't fly under God's radar, as much as we might fool ourselves into thinking so. So, Gideon is assured of God's presence and God's plan.

What a great reminder that even though we may feel abandoned, we can rest assured that we are not... "for the Lord your God goes with you; he will never leave you nor forsake you." Those were Joshua's words to the Israelites as they were about to enter the Promised Land in Deuteronomy 31:6, Joshua 1:5, and cited again in Hebrews 13:5.

It sure didn't seem like the Lord was with Gideon and his people. Yet, that is exactly what He told Gideon, "Go in the strength you have and save Israel out of Midian's hand. Am I not sending you?" (Judg. 6:14). Maybe you and I would have thought, well, that's a battle that's going to last about a minute and a half. At least this will all be over quickly! Maybe you and I would have protested, as Gideon did, "but how can I save Israel? My clan is the weakest in Manasseh, and I am the least in my family" (Judg. 6:15).

You may identify with Gideon here. You may say that you or your family have no influence, no power, no resources to pull off some great victory. And you are right. That's the point. It was the point for Gideon. It is the point for you and me. Then, how could a victory be won? "The Lord answered, 'I will be with you, and you will strike down all the

Midianites, leaving none alive" (Judg. 6:16). "Some trust in chariots and some in horses, but we trust in the name of the Lord our God" (Ps. 20:7).

What did God say to Moses in response to his protest? "I will be with you... I AM Who I AM" (Ex. 3:12, 14). I AM was sending Moses. I AM was calling Gideon and sending him out. I AM is calling you today to send you out. God sees what we cannot. God's ways are not our ways—His are higher than ours. "'For my thoughts are not your thoughts, neither are your ways my ways,' declares the Lord. 'As the heavens are higher than the earth, so are my ways higher than your ways and my thoughts than your thoughts'" (Is. 55:8–9).

I am constantly reminded that it is God's thoughts that I need, not mine, what about you? It was God's thoughts that Moses and Gideon needed, not theirs. They needed His ways, not theirs. It won't likely be an instant transformation for you or me, nor was it for Moses or Gideon.

Moses protested enough about his difficulty with speech that God responded in His grace and had Aaron go with him to do the speaking. Gideon kept asking for a sign that this was the real deal, and God responded in His grace to give Gideon assurances.

God will likely listen as you protest, and likely respond in His grace to address your doubts, but still call you to do what He asks. That has been my experience. I really just need to say yes to whatever He asks me to do, even before He asks me. So do you. I am trying to be more obedient, more faithful. How about you?

So what about Gideon? After he finally became convinced that the Lord was in this, he called all his fighting men together for battle—32,000 soldiers. Big army, huh? Not so much when compared to 135,000—the coalition of Midianite armies. Then God said something that we—in our way of thinking—find absurd. God told Gideon he had too many men. Okay, has somebody miscounted here?

God's ways are not our ways, and we thank Him for it. His ways are always right. His way was for Gideon to send all who trembled with fear back home. There went 22,000. So, 10,000 versus 135,000—now those are great odds, huh? Uh, for the Midianites.

Then God said something that we—in our way of thinking—find even more absurd. God told Gideon that he still had too many men. So in the next test, Gideon was to observe how the men drank water from the stream, and select only those who drank from their cupped hands, and not down on their knees to drink. That left 300 men. That's more like it—300 versus 135,000! Really, it is. Because it is not in our own might, our own strength, our own resources, that the victory is won. It is in God's own might, God's own strength, God's own resources, that the victory is won.

"The Lord said to Gideon, 'With the three hundred men that lapped I will save you and give the Midianites into your hands. Let all the others go home'" (Judg. 7:7).

What does it take for you and me to win the important victories in life? What does it take for you and me to aspire to greatness in life? Submission to Almighty God, and humility before Almighty God. He is the one who is the most powerful in all of creation—His creation. He is the one who is in control of our destiny. He is the one who calls us to believe Him, trust Him, obey Him. Moses did, and he led the Israelites out of 400 years of bondage—by God's hand. Gideon did, and would win the victory over the cruel enemy—by God's hand.

The cruel enemy was large. "The Midianites, the Amalekites and all the other eastern peoples had settled in the valley, thick as locusts. Their camels could no more be counted than the sand on the seashore" (Judg. 7:12). But, before the battle, God, in His grace, encouraged Gideon against such a powerful enemy by allowing him to get close enough to their camp to hear the following conversation between of the soldiers.

"'I had a dream,' he was saying, 'A round loaf of barley bread came tumbling into the Midianite camp. It struck the tent with such force that the tent overturned and collapsed.' His friend responded, 'This can be nothing other than the sword of Gideon son of Joash, the Israelite. God has given the Midianites and the whole camp into his hands'" (Judg. 7:13–14). "When Gideon heard the dream and its interpretation, he bowed down and worshipped" (Judg. 7:15). Would that you and I would bow down and worship every time God encourages us and assures us.

"He returned to the camp of Israel and called out, 'Get up! The Lord has given the Midianite camp into your hands.' Dividing the three hundred men into three companies, he placed trumpets and empty jars in the hands of all of them, with torches inside" (Judg. 7:15–16). Now there is some firepower for you: trumpets, jars, torches. Don't tell me that the Lord lacks a sense of humor. Did anyone raise their hand to ask where were the swords, spears, even slings, for goodness sake? Doesn't matter when the Lord is in control, does it? His ways are not our ways, and we should ever thank Him for that.

"'Watch me,' he told them. 'Follow my lead. When I get to the edge of the camp, do exactly as I do. When I and all who are with me blow the trumpets, then from all around the camp blow yours and shout, 'For the Lord and for Gideon'" (Judg. 7:17–18). They did exactly that, they blew their trumpets and broke the jars and they shouted. The Lord caused the enemy to turn on themselves with their swords. Then they fled, only to be met by more Israelites from the hill country, and the Midianite forces were completely defeated.

Just as the Lord had said.

Just as the Lord had said.

Just as the Lord had said.

Why is that so hard for us? God always does what He says He will do. God is faithful. He doesn't leave us out to dry. He doesn't toy with us. He delivers us. "Not by might nor by power, but by my Spirit, says the Lord Almighty" (Zech. 4:6). Gideon had no might. Gideon's 300 men had no power compared to the 135,000 troops of the enemy. Gideon's army didn't even have any weapons of war. But none of those were needed. All that was needed was the Spirit of the Living God. Praise Him!

"Brothers and sisters, think of what you were when you were called. Not many of you were wise by human standards; not many were influential; not many were of noble birth. But God chose the foolish things of the world to shame the wise; God chose the weak things of the world to shame the strong. God chose the lowly things of this world and the despised things—and the things that are not—to nullify the things that are, so that no one may boast before him. It is because of him that you are in Christ Jesus, who has become for us wisdom from God—that is, our righteousness, holiness, and redemption. Therefore, as it is written: Let the one who boasts boast in the Lord" (1 Cor. 1:26–31).

Think of it. Maybe you are not all that wise, all that influential, all that noble, all that strong. What does that really mean? It means that you are primed and ready to be used by Almighty God. He chooses folks like you and me through whom to show His might, His power.

So we will boast in Him, and not of ourselves. Even those in this world who have the most to boast about in human terms, really have nothing to boast about because they would be nothing without the blessings of the Almighty God. No one should boast about anything other than what God is doing.

He alone is worthy of our boasting.
He alone is worthy of our praise.
He alone is worthy of our obedience.
He alone is worthy of our attention.
He alone is worthy of our surrender.

O Lord God, thank You that You can overcome all odds in our lives, and I pray for Your power upon, and within, the one reading this, as well as myself, to be used of You for greatness in accordance with Your plan. In the name of the mightiest of all warriors, Jesus. Amen.

God Says, "I Will"

Psalm 91:14–16...
"I will rescue him,"
"I will protect him,"
"I will answer him,"
"I will be with him in trouble,"
"I will deliver him,"
"I will honor him,"
"I will satisfy him,"
"I will show him My salvation."

To whom is God speaking? "I will *rescue* her" and "I will *rescue* him." Rescue: To free from confinement or danger; to recover. Have you ever been rescued? Can you recall those times when you were rescued? Were you rescued by a parent? By a friend? By an unseen hand? By your heavenly Father? Was it from physical harm? From death even? From heartache of some kind? From tragic consequences of some sin you committed?

I have logged well over a million miles on the highway. I have been rescued many times from tragedy on those highways. From severe injury, even death, numerous times from sixteen years old to now. Rescued with my wife from our capsized canoe in the French Broad River. We thank God for His working our rescue through these near disasters, as well as countless others.

Many times has God rescued me and mine that I know about. But, I also know, without a shadow of doubt, that there were many more times I don't even know about. Being rescued assures us, and gives us hope, doesn't it? It shows us that someone is watching out for us. Who doesn't want to be rescued? Who doesn't want a Rescuer? "Rise up and help us; rescue us because of your unfailing love" (Ps. 44:26).

"I will *protect* him...I will *protect* her." Protect: Shield from injury or destruction; guard. Have you ever been protected? By parents or guardians? By a friend? By an older sister or brother? What about the heroes in our military? By our police or firefighters? By an unseen hand? By your heavenly Father? Being protected gives us security, doesn't it?

Folks, just like you and me, spoke and wrote words, recorded in the Psalms: "The Lord is my strength and my shield; my heart trusts in him, and he helps me" (Ps. 28:7). Who doesn't want to be protected? To be shielded? To be guarded? God will guard us on our path if we will but trust Him. "for he guards the course of the just and protects the way of his faithful ones" (Prov. 2:8).

"I will *answer* her...I will *answer* him." Do you want answers to your questions? In order to answer someone, you must do what? Listen and hear what they say, right? Interestingly, one of the definitions of answer is "correct response." There are multitudes of answers given in our world today, yet how many are accurate? How many are actually *correct* responses? Has God ever answered you? God is listening; God hears. Do you call upon Him? Have the answers always been what you wanted to hear? Probably not.

Are you still waiting for an answer? Maybe you are in God's waiting room, which seems a tough place to be sometimes. But think of this, if you are in God's waiting room, then you want to hear from Him, and you will hear from Him, and someday, you will see Him. If you are not in His waiting room, then you have no expectation of hearing from Him, no hope of seeing Him.

Having our questions answered gives us guidance, doesn't it? And, when God answers, it *will* be the correct response. And, He has answered many of our questions (before we ever ask or think to ask) in His Word—His personal letter to you and to me.

Jesus said this: "Ask and it will be given to you; seek and you will find; knock and the door will be opened to you. For everyone who asks receives; the one who seeks finds; and to the one who knocks, the door will be opened" (Matt. 7:7–8). "If you seek him, he will be found by you" (wise counsel from David to his son Solomon) (1 Chr. 28:9). "You will seek me and find me when you seek me with all your heart" (Jer. 29:13).

"I will *be with* him in *trouble.*" I will *be with* her in *trouble.*" Have you ever been in trouble? Had troubles? So have I. What does trouble cause? Trouble causes worry, anxiety, distress, confusion, unrest, and frustration.

I remember the first time that I soiled my diaper, and my Mother was not immediately there to take care of this problem. And I thought what's up with this? (good memory, huh?). You see, trouble starts when we are young, and it follows us all our days. Even Jesus said, "In this world, you will have trouble" (John 16:33).

Is it comforting to have someone with you when you are in trouble? Their presence can be reassuring, comforting, can't it? In the hospital, at the funeral home, at the police station… having someone present who loves you is a good thing, isn't it? Who doesn't want the presence of someone who cares for you?

Jesus *did* say, "In this world, you will have trouble," but He *also* said, "but take heart! I have overcome the world" (John 16:33). God assures those who trust in Him that they will never be forsaken or left behind. In Hebrews 13:5, right after instructing us to keep away from love of money, God says, because I will never leave you; never will I forsake you. Over and over in the accounts of Psalm 107, folks who were in trouble—even at their wits' end—cried out to the Lord for His unfailing love, and you know what? He was there to bring them out of their trouble.

"I will *deliver* her…I will *deliver* him." Have you ever been delivered? Every one of you has, because you are here. Someone delivered you out of your mother's womb into this world. Deliver: Set free; carry to an intended destination. Deliverance is from one place to another place, isn't it? Such as to family or friends far away from home. Or, deliverance unto a desired place to a vacation spot by car, plane, train, or boat. Who doesn't want to be delivered? "I love you, Lord, my strength. The Lord is my rock, my fortress, and my *deliverer*" (Ps. 18:1–2). There is an eternal deliverance to the most desired place of all: heaven. We cannot deliver ourselves there, no matter what we do, who we are, how we are, or how hard we try. We can only be delivered by the Deliverer—the Lord Jesus. Without Him, there is no deliverance.

"I will *honor* him...I will *honor* her" Honor: To esteem, recognize; give privilege or attach worth; give a good name. Have you ever been honored? If anyone ever thanked you for something you said or something you did, then you have been honored in a way. If you have ever been recognized for some accomplishment—received a diploma, degree, certificate, raise, promotion, trophy, or award, you have been honored. It is rewarding to be honored, isn't it? Who doesn't want to be honored, to have a good name, to be thought worthy? Think about the honor of being one of God's chosen children.

God gives the right to become his children, children of the King, to all who receive His Son Jesus, who believe on His name. Whoever believes in the Lord Jesus is reckoned righteous as Jesus is righteous. Then, we are joint heirs with Christ Jesus to all the Father has to offer (John 1:12; Rom. 3:22; Rom. 8:17).

Have you noticed how much attention we pay to those who are heirs to earthly thrones and to earthly fortunes? TV shows and movies often depict the fortunes and possessions of the earth's wealthiest persons. Those pass away. Those pass away. Those pass away.

Jesus didn't leave a will to disperse of His earthly belongings—in fact, there was only one—the garment he wore. Yet, you see, He owns it all anyway. But what He does leave to those who follow Him is eternal treasure from the one who created all that is. Now that is something to pay attention to—that is something to desire. More importantly, it is something to receive, and it is something that we *can* receive in Christ Jesus.

"I will *satisfy* her...I will *satisfy* him." Satisfaction: Being fulfilled; being assured; having enough; having our doubts erased. Have you ever been satisfied? Have you been fulfilled after a good meal? After something particularly uplifting or rewarding? After some good work? Satisfaction comes through a desired result, doesn't it? Who doesn't want to be satisfied, assured, to have enough? Jesus said, "I came that they may have life, and have it to the full" (John 10:10).

How about this for satisfaction, being filled to the measure of all the fullness of God, so that we can escape the corruption in the world caused by evil desires (Eph. 3:19; 2 Pet. 1:3)? "And my God will meet all your needs according to the riches of his glory in Christ Jesus" (Phil. 4:19). Is there really any fulfillment apart from Jesus?

What about traditions? First Peter 1:18 calls it the "empty way of life," and calls to our attention that neither traditions, silver, nor gold will redeem us from this empty way of life, but only the most precious gift of all—the precious blood of the perfect Sacrifice—Jesus—redeems us and brings us fulfillment.

What about salvation? "I will show him *My salvation*...I will show her *My salvation*." Salvation: Deliverance from the power and effects of sin; preservation from destruction, harm, risk, loss. How many salvations are there? According to the world's literature, philosophy, and music, there are many salvations obtained through knowledge, through good works, through pleasure, through drugs, through religions. Yet, God has instructed us in this matter of salvation, and it is He alone who has instructed us correctly that there is one—and only one—way to salvation: through His Son, Jesus the Christ.

"Salvation is found in no one else, for there is no other name under heaven given to mankind by which we must be saved" (Acts 4:12). "God our Savior, who wants all people to be saved and to come to a knowledge of the truth. For there is one God and one mediator between God and mankind, the man Christ Jesus, who gave himself as a ransom for all people" (1 Tim. 2:3–6a).

Now, who is it that receives all the blessings we have discussed by the hand of Almighty God? Who is it that is rescued; that is protected; that will be answered; that has God's presence in trouble; that is delivered; that is honored; that is satisfied; that is saved? Verse 1 of Psalm 91 says, "Whoever dwells in the shelter of the Most High will rest in the shadow of the Almighty." Ain't nobody gonna dwell in the Lord's house that don't want to be there. You see, you must *desire* His presence in order to *dwell* in His presence. Jesus put it like this—"Anyone who loves me will obey my teaching. My Father will love them, and we will come to them and make our home with them" (John 14:23).

If a person does not want God's presence, then that loving, personal relationship with Him will not develop, will it? We come to the Father through Jesus—"I am the way and the truth and the life. No one comes to the Father except through me" (John 14:6). We cannot experience the fullness of that relationship with the heavenly Father except through the Lord Jesus.

Do you love God? How do you show it? Do you call upon God only when you are in trouble? I can't speak for you, but I have done that, many times. I have made wrong choices and then asked God to keep me from the consequences. Some, He did. I praise Him for that. Some, He did not. I praise Him for that.

Are you afraid of what will happen to you if you submit to the Father's will? Are you afraid to trust Him? Are you afraid you will lose your friends?

It is good to remember that if someone isn't interested in your long-term good, then maybe that person isn't really your true friend. Are you afraid that you will have to give up everything that's fun or tastes good? Would a loving Father who cares for you beyond your wildest imagination want you to live a life of misery and same old, same old? You see, outside of the relationship with God through the Lord Jesus, there is no meaning in life. Jesus desires that we have joy, that our joy may be complete, and it is only in Him (John 15:11).

Why are you here? What is life all about? God has made it clear that He put us here to love us. God has made it clear that He put us here to love Him. Life to the max, to the full. Because he loves me, says the Lord, "I will not forget you! See, I have engraved you on the palms of my hands" (Is. 49:15–16).

Psalm 48:14 tells us, "For this God is our God for ever and ever; he will be our guide even to the end." Psalm 33:18–21 assures us that His eyes are upon us; He is our help, protecting us like a shield. In Him, our hearts rejoice, for we are trusting in His holy name.

How do you begin? How do you begin when you first love someone? You began to date, to spend time with each other, to talk with each other, to learn to love each other. You grow to love as you spend time with. God already loves you to the max. Would you decide to spend time with Him and learn to love Him more and more as He loves you?

O Lord God, thank You for offering to this reader all these benefits and blessings of being Your child, and I pray it be so according to Your lovingkindness. In the name of Loving Jesus. Amen.

He Who Overcomes

*W*hat do you do when you face opposition? What do you do when you are being pressured to go along with those around you? What do you do when doing the right thing is going to cost you something? What do you do when you *have* done the right thing, yet it still seems to be working against you? What do you do when you are getting no encouragement to do the right thing, to believe God and to trust Him?

The Lord God speaks much about overcoming. "He who *overcomes* will not be hurt at all by the second death" (Rev. 2:11*). "To him who *overcomes* and does my will to the end, I will give authority over the nations" (Rev. 2:26*). "He who *overcomes* will, like them (the ones deemed worthy—deemed righteous), be dressed in white. I will never blot out his name from the book of life, but will acknowledge his name before my Father and his angels" (Rev. 3:5*). "To him who *overcomes,* I will give the right to sit with me on my throne, just as I *overcame* and sat down with my Father on his throne" (Rev. 3:21*). "He who *overcomes* will inherit all this (home in heaven, God's home, where is no death, mourning, crying, or pain—where every need is already met—where everything is new), and I will be his God and he will be my son" (Rev. 21:7*). "You, dear children, are from God and have *overcome* them (the spirits of the anti-Christ), because the one who is in you is greater than the one who is in the world" (1 John 4:4*). "For everyone born of God *overcomes* the world. This is the victory that has *overcome* the world, even our faith. Who is it that *overcomes* the world? Only he who believes that Jesus is the Son of God" (1 John 5:3*).

Jesus teaches and assures us, "I have told you these things, so that in me you may have peace. In this world you will have trouble. But take heart!

I have *overcome* the world" (John 16:33*). Jesus said, "I have given you authority...to *overcome* all the power of the enemy; nothing will harm you. However, do not rejoice that the spirits submit to you, but rejoice that your names are written in heaven" (Luke 10:19*).

Who is it who overcomes? Do you believe it is possible to be an overcomer? Or, do you believe that for you, it is impossible to be an overcomer? Do you believe that it only is true for a select few? Do you believe that it only is true for ones who have a "special connection" to God? Let's look at some folks—ordinary folks—from the Bible who inspire us because they overcame in the face of utter defeat.

Hananiah (meaning the Lord shows grace), Mishael (Who is what God is?), Azariah (the Lord helps)—young Israelite men had been carried off from their homeland in Jerusalem to a foreign land, Babylon, when the armies of Nebuchadnezzar besieged Jerusalem.

You may now live in a different area from your childhood, so perhaps you can identify with being away from home. Maybe the language and the local practices are foreign to you. We are told that these three were handsome, intelligent, well-spoken, quick to listen, quick to learn, and showing aptitude to apply their learning. King Nebuchadnezzar commanded that these men be taught his language, be trained in his ways, be fed food and wine from the king's table for three years; then, they would be fit for service to the king. Hmmm, fit for service to which king?

But, led by Daniel, they decided they would not eat the food and wine of the pagan king—why? Because they believed it would defile them— it was contaminated, unclean. The first portion was offered to idols and poured out on the pagan altar.

Now, at this point, I would like to say that it didn't matter what they looked like, what their backgrounds were, what their educational level was. What mattered was that they had convictions regarding God Almighty, and they *stood* on those convictions. So should you and I.

Instead, Daniel asked that they be fed only vegetables and water for ten days, and compare their appearances with the others in training, and then render judgment based on their condition at that time. Do you think they would have been encouraged by those around them to do this? Do you think their peers would have said, "Aw yeah, that's a great idea, go for veggies and water instead of steak, wine, and all the feast of the king; aw yeah, that makes a lotta sense, guys."

Don't you think they were probably warned what could happen, maybe even laughed at for what sounded so ridiculous? But at the end of the ten days, who looked healthier? At the end of the ten days, who looked better nourished?

Daniel, Hananiah, Mishael, and Azariah, all looked healthier and better nourished than the ones who had eaten and drank from the royal table. So, they were allowed to eat and drink as they chose, and God gave knowledge and understanding to them of all kinds of literature and learning (Dan. 1).

He does the same for you and me: "If any of you lacks wisdom, you should ask God, who gives generously to all without finding fault, and it will be given to you" (James 1:5).

Do you hear that?—the part about not finding fault. God doesn't say, "Well, you should have studied harder, or you should have been listening before." I can tell you that I am still learning lessons that God has been trying to teach me for many years. I am stubborn and selfishly motivated, and some lessons sink in slowly. But God gives wisdom to this sinner when I ask, and I ask often. I ought to be much wiser than I am, but that is not God's fault. I can tell you that He has given me wisdom in areas where I am void of knowledge or expertise. You see, He knows everything. He knows how everything works.

Many times I have prayed when visiting a customer who has a problem. I prayed that I would understand what the problem is and prayed to know what options we had to solve the problem. Many times, I have had no particular knowledge about what the customer was doing, but God gives wisdom and enables me to help find a solution or a resolution. Glory be to the Lord God of all, who understands it all.

Daniel could understand visions and dreams of all kinds. How did he do that? Because God had the understanding and wisdom, and He imparted it to Daniel. So, these three young men entered into Nebuchadnezzar's service, and they excelled in every way.

God had not stayed behind in Jerusalem. He was with them every step of the way—every minute of the day. God has not stayed behind somewhere in your past. He is with you now, ever ready to guide your life on the path of righteousness.

Now Nebuchadnezzar—not really a humble sort—made an image of gold, ninety feet high and nine feet wide, to stand on the plain there in Babylon, for all to bow down and worship. Everyone was commanded—as soon as the sound of the horn, flute, zither, lyre, harp, pipes, and all kinds of music was heard—to fall down and worship the image of gold that King Nebuchadnezzar had set up. If anyone did not fall down and worship, then they would be immediately thrown into a blazing furnace (Dan. 2).

Now, I am believing that some of the folks who knew Shadrach, Meshach, and Abednego were speculating about what they would do. OK, it's one thing to not eat from the king's table, but to defy a command of the king and risk your life? Don't you think that these three were probably warned by their peers, even urged to not go ahead with this? C'mon now fellas, be realistic; it isn't worth dying for, is it? You can bow down physically, but not in your heart, right? This guy, Neb, is serious, he's got thugs all around who would just as soon step on you as look at you. C'mon, just go along. It will be over in a few minutes, and you will get to keep on living. What would you do? What would I do? I've sold out before, haven't you? I've justified bad behavior, disobedient behavior, before, haven't you?

I wonder how these three made their decision. I wonder if they discussed all their options, and then decided. Maybe they had already determined that nothing would cause them to compromise their trust in the Almighty God.

It is interesting to note that they had been assigned new names – the ones we hear most often–which related to pagan meanings, but that did not alter their commitment to the living God, their God.

Well, Hananiah (Shadrach—probably related to command of Aku, a moon-god), Mishael (Meshach—probably who is what Aku is?), and

Azariah (Abednego—servant of Nebu) refused to bow down and worship the idol. They were ratted out to the king, and he was furious. He had them brought before him and asked them if this was true. He even swung the big stick—the one about being burned alive—reminding them that they would be immediately thrown into the blazing furnace.

He then asked this question—"Then what god will be able to rescue you from my hand?" He really thought that he was in control, didn't he? *What God indeed?*

How many powerful world leaders get to believing that they are the ones in control, that they are the ones calling all the shots, that no one can stop them from anything they want to do? Hitler, Mussolini, Hussein, Qaddafi, Amin, Kim, Mao, Stalin, Ahmadinejad, Un? But who has the final say, who is really in control? Our heroes knew. Here is their reply:

"King Nebuchadnezzar, we do not need to defend ourselves before you in this matter. If we are thrown into the blazing furnace, the God we serve is able to deliver us from it, and he will deliver us from Your Majesty's hand. But even if he does not, we want you to know, Your Majesty, that we will not serve your gods or worship the image of gold you have set up" (Dan. 3:16–18).

Who did they believe was in control? Their God was more powerful than all the gods that Nebuchadnezzar worshipped, and certainly more powerful than he himself. And even if God has another plan, that's OK, too. They will submit to *His will* and not Nebuchadnezzar's. Well, old Neb was furious. Who are these peons to stand up to him?

So, he had the furnace heated seven times hotter than before and commanded the strongest soldiers in his army to throw them in the blazing fire. Now, would it have taken his strongest soldiers to subdue these three? But it was important for Neb to display a show of strength, to display his power, to display who is in control here. So what happened to the strong men?

Now the three were fully clothed, turbaned, and tied—thrown into the blazing furnace. The furnace was so hot that the flames of the fire killed the soldiers who had thrown them in. So, who could hope to survive inside the furnace? Nobody—on their own. But they were not on their own; they were not alone.

Someone was with them; Neb looked and saw four in that furnace, and they weren't crying out in anguish; they weren't being consumed by the flames; they weren't screaming for help; they weren't perishing. They were walking around in the fire—unbound and unharmed, the fourth looked like what? A God! This time, Neb has a different tone—he is singing a different tune—he shouted "Shadrach, Meshach, and Abednego, servants of the Most High God, come out! Come here!" (Dan. 3:26).

And, they did come out—not harmed, not a hair singed, no clothes scorched, not even the smell of fire was on them.

"Then Nebuchadnezzar said, 'Praise be to the God of Shadrach, Meshach, and Abednego, who has sent his angel and rescued his servants! They trusted in him and defied the king's command and were willing to give up their lives rather than serve or worship any god except their own God. Therefore, I decree that the people of any nation or language who say anything against the God of Shadrach, Meshach and Abednego be cut into pieces and their homes be turned into piles rubble, for no other God can save in this way!" (Dan. 3:28–29)

"Trust in the Lord with all your heart, and lean not on your own understanding; in all your ways submit to him, and he will make your paths straight" (Prov. 3:5–6). Straight through the fiery trial, straight through the temptation, straight through it all... behind the Lord Jesus. These men overcame in the Lord.

So can you. If you are following the Lord Jesus, then you are on the right path—the path of righteousness, and that path leads you home. Where else would you want to go?

How else can you overcome?

Only in Jesus.

Only in following Him as Lord.

O Lord God, thank You that we truly can overcome in Your power. Jesus overcame in the face of the worst that evil could offer, and I pray that so will the reader of this message. In the name of Jesus, The Overcomer. Amen.

And The Three Bowed Not

Their names were Hananiah, Mishael, and Azariah.
Along with Daniel, they were carried off to Babylon.
But they'd not defile themselves with food and wine of the pagan king,
And the Lord God made them wise over others ten-fold.

The image of gold to the king reached high, and the people bowed low.
Except God's three who disobeyed by standing tall;
Sentence of death pronounced, they were bound and thrown into
the flame,
And the fire was turned up seven times hotter than before.

Immanuel led His own unharmed right through their trial;
Not even a hair was singed, nor a thread had smell of smoke.
What God indeed can save like this? Only one true and living God
For the ones who'll follow Him in faith to the very end.

And the three bowed not to Nebuchadnezzar
Though facing death, they would not swerve.
He will deliver us through the blazing fire;
But even if not, the Lord God only we will serve.

If It Is The Lord's Will

*W*hat will your life be like in ten years? What will your life be like in five years? What will your life be like this time next year? What will your life be like an hour from now? Truth is, you don't know, do you? Neither do I. None of us do.

How often our lives change in the twinkling of an eye. Companies downsize, jobs are eliminated, and what seemed to be a secure position now is no more. Marriages seem to be secure, but then one partner seeks comfort or pleasure elsewhere, and homes are shattered. Children have accidents, and security within the family changes dramatically. Loved ones die, and days are filled with grief. Doctors speak many words, but cancer is the one in caps—and louder than all the rest—and our health security is in doubt. Bank accounts and portfolios shrink, and financial security slips away. Listen to these words from James 4:13–17...

"Now listen, you who say, 'Today or tomorrow we will go to this or that city, spend a year there, carry on business and make money.' Why, you do not even know what will happen tomorrow. What is your life? You are a mist that appears for a little while and then vanishes. Instead, you ought to say, 'If it is the Lord's will, we will live and do this or that.' As it is, you boast in your arrogant schemes. All such boasting is evil. If anyone, then, knows the good they ought to do and doesn't do it, it is sin for them."

Maybe you've heard this phrase used when plans are being made, "Good Lord willin' and the creek don't rise." Truth is, there is much over which we have no control, isn't there? So, what do we do? Fret and wring our hands in worry? Be nonchalant...after all, what will happen will happen. Trust in the Eternal One? The one who does know what will happen, who does know what is best, who does—*always does*—what is best for you and me? Does God understand what we face? Does God care? Does God act on our behalf in the midst of uncertainty? Well, it is He who created us. It is He who created time, space, life, and death. Yes, He understands!

It is He who loves, Who, in fact, is love defined, love complete, who is love.

It is He who wants you and me to experience the best life possible here on earth.

It is He who wants you and me to spend eternity with Him.

It is He who gives us the only security we could ever know.

It is He who offers us peace and forgiveness.

Yes, He cares! It is He who focuses all His attention on our well-being. There are no surprises to the Almighty.

He is never caught off guard.

He is never in doubt.

He is never out to lunch.

He is never out of touch.

He is the same yesterday, today, and tomorrow.

He is our strength, our stay, our rock, our refuge.

One of my favorite passages is Psalm 18:1–3*...

"I love you, O Lord, my strength. The Lord is my rock, my fortress, and my deliverer. My God is my rock, in whom I take refuge. He is my shield, and the horn of my salvation, my stronghold. I call to the Lord who is worthy of praise, and I am saved from my enemies."

Look at all the descriptors of our Creator God – my Strength; my Rock; my Fortress; my Deliverer; my Refuge; my Shield; my Salvation. Hallelujah! When we are in the midst of uncertainty, we would do well to reflect on how our God is for us! We look for that which is sure in this life, that on which we can count, that in which we can be secure. The world offers little security.

Do you think the disciples came to understand this? Absolutely, and in ways that you and I will likely never fathom. The security they had in their families, in their jobs, in their hometowns, was disrupted by the one called Jesus of Nazareth. He called them to follow Him, and they left these earthly securities for the unknown. They were drawn to this one who was so different from anyone they had known, but they had no idea what awaited them. Their world was turned upside down at Calvary. Their leader, their friend, their teacher wasn't supposed to be tortured and crucified, or was he? Actually, he had told them it would be this way, but they were not ready to see that.

So, as Jesus surrendered his spirit, nothing seemed sure anymore to his followers. For sure, there had been a lot to keep them off balance moment by moment in those ministry years with Jesus. He was casting out demons in one moment, giving sight to the blind in another. He was speaking life lessons to the multitudes in the morning, multiplying a few fish and loaves of bread to feed thousands later in the day. He was healing a woman of a life-draining disease one moment, raising a dead girl to life the next.

He was warning the religious leaders about their hypocrisy one moment, giving hope to a woman caught in adultery in another. He was sleeping peacefully in the midst of a violent storm on the lake, calming the winds and the waves in the next moment with just his words. He was teaching all who would listen to him in the synagogues, driving the money-changers and greedy merchants from the temple grounds afterward. He was enabling paralyzed legs to walk again in one moment, then, in another, holding up a mustard seed to illustrate the power of faith.

He was teaching a Pharisee about being born again, then teaching a Samaritan woman about true worship. He was in the cities; He was in the countryside. He was in the homes of the temple leaders; He was in the homes of tax collectors. He was preaching from a boat; He was preaching on the hillside. He was reclined at the supper table one evening; He was being arrested before the next dawn.

He was laughing with them one day; He was being flogged on another. He was calling them to follow him and become fishers of men one day; then He was being mocked by those He came to save. He was praying in their midst for his disciples' welfare; then He was praying for forgiveness—for his executioners—while nailed to the cross. He was riding into Jerusalem to Hosanna choruses; then He was falling under the weight of the cross among jeering crowds.

They were never sure what would be next in this journey with their Master, Jesus. But, of this they could be sure: Jesus would always do the right thing, Jesus would always do the best thing for all around him, and Jesus would lead them on the right path always.

They had experienced a security in his presence that they had never known, one that the world does not offer. Yet, how could all this lead to his arrest, to all those false accusations, to that mockery of a trial, to the crowd crying out for release of a convicted murderer over the gentle Son of God, to his crucifixion between two criminals, to his last breath, to his death?

He had told them what was coming, but who could blame them for not seeing it? Would we have been any different? But, just as real as all they had experienced with their Savior when He was alive, would be the reality of His victory over death. Just as sure as He would be buried in a tomb behind a sealed stone, would be His leaving the tomb to appear to His followers and many others as the resurrected Savior. Just as sure as anything in this life were His words spoken to them about his coming, their following Him, and their purpose in this life. Just as sure are all His words to you and me. Do you believe His words?

Do you believe that He is "the resurrection and the life?" Your resurrection and your life (John 11:25)?

Do you believe that He is "the good shepherd," and that you are a lost sheep without Him (John 10:14)?

Do you believe that He is "the Son of the Most High" (Luke 1:32)?

Do you believe that He is "the light of the world?" The Light of your life (John 8:12)?

Do you believe that He is "the gate?" Your gate into God's family (John 10:7, 9)?

Do you believe that He is "the true vine?" and that unless you are joined to Him, you can do nothing (John 15:1–5)?

Do you believe that He is "the way and the truth and the life," and the only hope you have for heaven (John 14:6)?

Do you believe that He is standing at your door, knocking, wanting you to let Him in so you can be in right relationship with your Maker (Rev. 3:20)?

Do you believe that He gave His life for you (John 3:16)?

His followers had heard these words and so many other words of truth, and they came to know that all He said came true (Matt. 24:35). On Jesus you can count (Heb. 13:8).

If it is the Lord's will. A phrase used a lot today. A phrase often misunderstood. We want to live by our own will. We want to believe that we are in control. Yet, would we want to be accountable for the results? The fact is that we will all be accountable for whose will we choose. We can choose our own will in disobedience to His... and suffer eternal separation from God and all that is good. We can choose His will, which gives us security in the here and now with His Spirit within us, and in the hereafter—in His presence, where nothing will ever cause us pain and grief and sorrow again. The Lord has given us this testimony...

"And this is the testimony: God has given us eternal life, and this life is in His Son. Whoever has the Son has life; whoever does not have the Son of God does not have life. I write these things to you who believe in the name of the Son of God so that you may know that you have eternal life" (1 John 5: 11–13).

Now, there is the security we all need, the security we all long for, the security we all have available to us in Christ Jesus.

The disciples who followed Jesus, who trusted in Jesus, who obeyed Jesus, experienced this security, this peace. Even though they gave up their earthly securities to move from town to town with their Teacher, their Lord, their Savior, they found real security and peace that they had never known.

It is this security and peace in the Lord Jesus that sustained each one that was martyred in His name, and apparently each one, except John, sacrificed his life in such a way for their Lord and Savior.

What is God's will for you and me? Trust and obey the Lord Jesus.

Thank You, O Lord our God, for Your will. Oftentimes we have thought—mistakenly—that Your will is cumbersome, draining, and impossible. Please forgive us—please forgive the one reading this, and me for wrong thinking and wrong believing. Please guide us to believe in Your will, Your good, pleasing, and perfect will, unto our good and our usefulness to You. In the name of Your perfect representation Jesus. Amen.

If the Lord Is God, Follow Him

1 Kings 17–18

*W*hat do we know about Ahab? He was an Israelite—from God's chosen people, chosen to be ones through whom God would reveal His plan of love and redemption for all mankind. Ahab reigned as king of Israel for twenty-two years. Ahab married Jezebel, who was from outside Israel, from the Tyre and Sidon region. She brought Baal worship—worship of a false god, in opposition to worship of the living God—with her to Israel.

Guess who began to participate also in Baal worship? Ahab—no big surprise there, is it? He even set up an altar for Baal in the temple of Baal that he built in Samaria. He made an Asherah pole—in the image of the goddess Asherah. Jezebel not only worshiped a false god but sought to *kill* the prophets of the one true Lord God. Ahab did more to provoke the Lord God of Israel to anger than did all the kings of Israel before him, as revealed in scripture. Did he intend to establish so much Baal worship? Maybe not, there are indications that he didn't intend to replace the worship of the Lord God with worship of Baal but probably to worship both. Yet he turned his back on the Creator of the universe to worship an imaginary creature who was made up by the people. The Israelites followed their king's lead and worshiped Baal also.

Is this really a big deal? God says it is. God says, "You shall have no other gods before me" (Ex. 20:3). God says, "You shall not make for yourself an image in the form of anything in heaven above or on the earth beneath or in the waters below. You shall not bow down to them or worship them" (Ex. 20:4–5). "Our ancestors possessed nothing but false gods, worthless idols that did them no good" (Jer. 16:19). So, can we worship the Lord God and also worship any created thing?

We are warned in Romans 1:22: "Although they claimed to be wise, they became fools and exchanged the glory of the immortal God for images made to look like a mortal human being and birds and animals and reptiles," and in 1:25, we are told: "They exchanged the truth about God for a lie, and worshiped and served created things rather than the Creator—who is forever praised. Amen."

So, what can we learn from Ahab? Ahab didn't guard his heart; he didn't obey God; and his influence over his people was misguided. We are told in Proverbs 4:23: "Above all else, guard your heart, for everything you do flows from it." We mustn't let anything creep in that will draw us away from worship of the one True God. Others will watch what you do, and you can influence them in the right way, or you can influence them in the wrong way.

Now, Elijah was a hero for the folks who loved God because he confronted Ahab and his false gods. To those who followed Ahab and worshiped Baal, he was an enemy. Elijah, the Tishbite, whose name means "The Lord is my God," stood in opposition to Ahab, and I mean vigorous, bold opposition, not only in word but also in deed. Elijah stood before Ahab and told him, "As the Lord, the God of Israel, lives, whom I serve, there will be neither dew nor rain in the next few years except at my word" (1 Kin. 17:1).

God does not delight in making his people suffer, but He sent the drought to get their attention. They were being led astray by Ahab, Jezebel, and the false prophets. He wanted them to see that there is one true God, that only He is Lord, so that they would turn and follow Him.

After many weeks, the plants began to wither and die. After many months, the streams and rivers dried up. Animals were dying, and soon the people would die. The drought lasted over three years, and during that time God took care of Elijah's needs every single day. God told him to go hide in the Kerith Ravine, east of the Jordan. There, Elijah was fed by ravens who brought him bread and meat in the morning, and bread and meat in the evening. He drank from the brook until it finally dried up.

Can we ever learn a lesson in trust from Elijah! Is it always going to look like we want it to look? No, it isn't. Are we always going to be in our comfort zone? No, we aren't. But the important thing is learning to trust in the Almighty, the Lord of all.

God then told him to go to Zarephath of Sidon where God had commanded a widow to supply him with food. So he went, found the widow, who was gathering sticks. Elijah asked her to bring him a little water in a jar so he may have a drink, and also a piece of bread.

Her response, "'As surely as the Lord your God lives,' she replied, 'I don't have any bread—only a handful of flour in a jar and a little oil in a jug. I am gathering a few sticks to take home and make a meal for myself and my son, that we may eat it—and die'" (1 Kin. 17:12*). Elijah told her not to be afraid (words right out of the Lord's mouth to you and me as we trust Him). He told her to go home and do as she had planned, except make a small cake of bread for him first, and then make something for herself and her son. "For this is what the Lord, the God of Israel, says, 'The jar of flour will not be used up and the jug of oil will not run dry until the day the Lord gives rain on the land'" (1 Kin 17:14*). She did what Elijah requested (as God commanded), and God did what He said He would do.

We can always count on God. God always keeps His promises. There was food every day as God promised, and the jar of flour was not used up, and the jug of oil did not run dry. Elijah trusted—the Lord provided. The widow trusted—the Lord provided. Are you trusting the Lord right now? Now, a crisis arises—another opportunity to trust or not to trust.

The son of the widow became ill. He grew worse and worse and finally stopped breathing. She said to Elijah, "What do you have against me, man of God? Did you come to remind me of my sin and kill my son?" (1 Kin.17:18*). She was having a crisis of faith. Likewise, Elijah was having a crisis of faith. So will you have crises of faith, and what will you do? Let's see what Elijah did:

"'Give me your son,'" Elijah replied. He took him from her arms, carried him to the upper room where he was staying, and laid him on the bed. Then he cried out to the Lord, 'O Lord my God, have you brought tragedy also upon this widow I am staying with, by causing her son to die?' Then he stretched himself out on the boy three times and cried to the Lord, 'O Lord my God, let this boy's life return to him!'" (1 Kin. 17:19–21*).

"The Lord heard Elijah's cry, and the boy's life returned to him, and he lived. Elijah picked up the child and carried him down from the room into the house. He gave him to his mother and said, 'Look, your son is alive!'" (1 Kin. 17:22-23*). His faith in the Lord Almighty was strengthened. Her faith was strengthened as well, "Now I know that you are a man of God and that the word of the Lord from your mouth is the truth" (1 Kin. 17:24*). Crises should drive us to our knees—crying out to the Lord God of all, and then, He who is faithful will hear our cries, and strengthen our faith in Him.

Now, there was coming a day of reckoning for the people. Elijah asked Obadiah, his friend and a devout follower of the Lord to ask for a meeting with Ahab. By the way, Obadiah was the head of Ahab's household affairs, and he also had saved the lives of one hundred of God's prophets by hiding them from Jezebel. So, Ahab went to meet Elijah, and upon seeing him said, "Is that you, you troubler of Israel?" (1 Kin. 18:17). Elijah's response,

"'I have not made trouble for Israel,' Elijah replied, 'But you and your father's family have. You have abandoned the Lord's commands and have followed the Baals. Now summon the people from all over Israel to meet me on Mount Carmel. And bring the four hundred and fifty prophets of Baal and the four hundred prophets of Asherah, who eat at Jezebel's table'" that is, who are supported by Jezebel (1 Kin. 18:18–19).

Talk about overwhelming odds! Have you ever been one against 850? Really, it was much worse than that because many of the people opposed Elijah, as well.

They gathered as requested, and Elijah stood before them, and said, "How long will you waver between two opinions? If the Lord is God, follow Him, but if Baal is God, follow him" (1 Kin. 18:21). Reminds me of Joshua when he told the Israelites to choose this day whom you will follow, gods that are no gods at all, or the Lord God of all (Josh. 24:15). The people's response? There was none. They said nothing (1 Kin. 18:21).

So, Elijah laid out the day's activity. The Baal prophets would choose first—one of two bulls to sacrifice, and Elijah would take the other one. The Baal prophets would go first in preparing the altar on which to sacrifice their bull, except they would not set fire to it. Elijah would do the same.

Then, the Baal prophets would call on their god, and Elijah would call on the name of the Lord, and "the god who answers by fire—he is God" (1 Kin. 18:23–24). So, the Baal prophets called upon the name of Baal from morning till noon, shouting and dancing to arouse their god to respond. They shouted louder, and bled freely as they cut themselves—not uncommon in their efforts to be heard by their god, who could not hear at all.

We are reminded in Jeremiah 10:5* "Like a scarecrow in a melon patch, their idols cannot speak; they must be carried because they cannot walk. Do not fear them; they can do no harm nor can they do any good." Do you know the Lord God of heaven requires no such ritualism or self-mutilation from you and me? Far from it! Everything He does is born out of love for our good.

Elijah taunted them by suggesting that maybe their god was busy, sleeping, or just unavailable. By evening, it was apparent that there would be no response, no one to answer, no one to pay attention (1 Kin. 18:27–29). Then Elijah summoned the people to himself, and began to repair the altar, which had been in ruins. He took twelve stones—one for each of the twelve tribes of Israel—and built the altar in the name of the Lord. He dug a trench around it, large enough to hold a moat of water. He had water poured on the offering and the wood, not once, but three times until water filled the trench. Have you ever tried to light a wet piece of wood, let alone tried to light meat, stones, and water?

"Answer me, O Lord, answer me, so these people will know that you, O Lord, are God, and that you are turning their hearts back again" (1 Kin. 18:37*). "Then the fire of the Lord fell and burned up the sacrifice, the wood, the stones and the soil, and also licked up the water in the trench" (1 Kin. 18:38*). Hallelujah! Is there any god like the living God, the Lord God Most High, the Lord God of all creation, our creator God, the Lord God Almighty? "When all the people saw this, they fell prostrate and cried, 'The Lord—he is God! The Lord—he is God!'" (1 Kin.18:39*). That is what you and I need to do right now—cry out from our hearts, The Lord—He is God! The Lord—He is God!

They had the false prophets of Baal seized and put to death. God is serious about any force that leads His people astray. Now, Ahab went off to eat and drink—at Elijah's request—but Elijah went off to pray, and he prayed, and he prayed, and he prayed. Gradually the clouds formed, and the sky grew black, and the wind rose, and heavy rains came down. Ahab rode off on his chariot, but Elijah tucked his cloak into his belt, ran under the power of the Lord, and guess who won that race? He ran ahead of Ahab all the way to Jezreel. Is the Lord God awesome?

Are you putting anyone or anything before the Lord God? Know this—it will do you no good. Good will only come, salvation will only come, as you put your trust in the one true God. He alone deserves our worship, our obedience, our trust. So be it today, in you and me, through Christ Jesus.

Surely, if the Lord is God, follow Him, but if anyone or anything else is God, follow him. The Lord God has made clear in the person of His Son, Jesus the Christ, that He is Lord over all creation, over life, over death, over heaven and earth, over the past, the present, and the future, over all powers.

The Lord is God, follow Him.

O Lord our God, thank You for making our choice clear between You, the true living God, and all else -which are no gods at all. I pray for the one reading this to choose You to follow and to serve, in the name of the true Savior Jesus. Amen

Elijah Summoned

Elijah summoned the people that day to witness the power of God.
For too long they had wavered, and now was the time
To declare who they'd follow as Lord.

It was one man of God and 450 of Baal
Who would call out to the heavens that day.
The altars were made ready for each sacrifice
To the God who would rain fire from above.

Morning to night, the false prophets shouted and danced;
They cut themselves, still no answer came forth.
Their god could not hear, could not speak, could not save;
All their efforts were expended in vain.

But when Elijah stepped forward and prayed to the Lord,
Fire consumed even waters in the trench.
The people saw anew that the *Lord, He is God,*
As they fell prostrate in worship and praise.

In the Beginning, God

*I*f you stumble on these first four words of the Bible, then the rest of God's words will be problematic for you. If you don't believe the first four words of the Bible, "In the beginning, God," then you will likely have trouble believing many of the words that follow. Keep in mind that which God tells us in 1 John 5:10, "Whoever does not believe God has made him out to be a liar, because they have not believed the testimony God has given about his Son."

All of God's Word is about your and my redemption. It is about how you and I have sinned against God, how He calls us to repent of that sin, and put our faith in the only one who can save us—His perfect Son, Jesus—the one who gave His life so that you and I can have life, full, meaningful, everlasting. You see, God *is* from everlasting to everlasting. God has no beginning, and God has no end.

But there was a beginning for our world, our solar system, the galaxies, and the universe. There was a beginning for the animals of the field, the air, and the sea. There was a beginning for man. Do we know that God created all this? In the beginning, God created. I believe it. Do you? Do we know how God did it? Do we need all the answers for how God did it? I say no, we don't. We need only know that God did it.

I am reminded of a few of the passages in Job 38:4–6, 12, 18–21 and 42:1–3 when Job was reminded that his understanding of God and the ways of God were limited. We cannot fathom how God did it. It is ours to believe or not to believe. God truly is the Creator. He truly makes something out of nothing.

Man often credits himself with creating something, when, in fact, man takes something that is already created, and reshapes, reformulates, resomethings it, but he does not create. Only God can take nothing, only God can take a void, and only God can take emptiness and create something out of it. And He does just that.

From where did God come? I don't know; I do know that God always *is*. Yesterday, today, and tomorrow, and forever, God *is*. How do we know that? In Exodus 3:13-14, Moses was called by God to go to Egypt and ask the pharaoh to release God's people. "Moses said to God, 'Suppose I go to the Israelites and say to them, The God of your fathers has sent me to you, and they ask me, What is his name? Then what shall I tell them?' God said to Moses, 'I AM WHO I AM. This is what you say to the Israelites. I AM has sent me to you.'" God goes on to say that this is His name forever.

God never changes, never slumbers, and never sleeps (Mal. 3:6, Ps. 121:3). Hebrew 13:8 says that "Jesus Christ is the same yesterday and today and forever." Scripture leaves no doubt about the relationship between our Creator God and Jesus Christ. Jesus said, "I and the Father are One" (John 10:30).

John 1:1 tells us "In the beginning was the Word, and the Word was with God, and the Word was God. He was with God in the beginning. Through him, all things were made; without him nothing was made that has been made. In him was life, and that life was the light of all mankind." Hebrews 1:3 tells us, "The Son is the radiance of God's glory and the exact representation of his being."

Now, were you the same years ago as you are today? Will you be the same years from now as you are today? Ever known anyone like that?

You and I were different years ago than we are today. You and I will be different years from now than we are today. We change in appearance. We change in body. We change in spirit. We change in mind. We change in circumstance. We change in relationships. We are not the same yesterday as today, nor today as tomorrow. We are finite human beings. We are created human beings. Not so with God. He is not a created being.

He *is* the Creator. And scripture makes clear to us that Jesus was with the Father at the beginning of it all. Through Him, all things were made—without Him, nothing was made that has been made.

Colossians 1:16* says, "He is the image of the invisible God, the firstborn over all creation. For by him all things were created; things in heaven and on earth, visible and invisible, whether thrones or powers or rulers or authorities; all things were created by him and for him. He is before all things, and in him all things hold together."

You see, without God's active hand on you and me every day, every hour, every minute, every second, we come apart; we cease to exist. God has not just put us here to sit back in some cosmic recliner to see what happens. He actively keeps our planet in right relationship to the sun and other planets so we can continue to live.

One minute change in our relationship to the sun, and we all die. He is actively sustaining life as we know it continuously. It takes much greater blind faith to believe that all this that we are a part of just came into being by chance. It takes much greater blind faith to believe that at one point there was nothing, and then at another point there was—somehow—something, without there being Someone who caused it to be. That it just somehow happened by chance.

Like the analogy of the watch. Can you look at the inner workings of a watch with its wheels, gears, springs, and pins, that all work together to move an hour hand, a minute hand, and a second hand in harmony from which to tell the time of day—and believe for a second that all those individual components could just somehow fall into place and be a working timepiece by themselves?

Most anyone would appreciate the fact that engineers designed all those individual components to work together, and then a watchmaker took the design, and perhaps even made some changes to the design from his own expertise to fit them all into place, and produce the finished product. It took all the individuals working together toward a common goal. Yet, they didn't create. They didn't make something out of nothing. They made something out of that which was already created.

How did God create in the beginning? He spoke it into being. What did He say? "Let there be light, and there was light. . . . Let the water under the sky be gathered to one place, and let dry ground appear, . . . Let the land produce vegetation, . . . Let there be lights in the vault of the sky, . . . Let the water teem with living creatures, . . . Let the land produce living creatures,... Let us make mankind in our image, in our likeness" (Gen. 1).

He spoke it all into being. But, why? Why did God create all this, and you, and me? You see, we were created to be like God—conformed to the likeness of His Son, Jesus, the Christ (Rom. 8:29). We were created to be in fellowship with Him. He created us to love us. He created us to love Him. He created us to make something out of us spiritually.

Like the void and emptiness out of which God created, we are void and empty—dead in our sins—nothing of any value until God's Holy Spirit indwells us and makes something of us. We can do nothing apart from the Spirit of the Lord Jesus.

So, God formed man from the dust of the ground and breathed into his nostrils the breath of life, and the man became a living being. Man was *not* at one point, and then *was* at one point because our Creator willed it to be. God is sovereign, above and superior to all others. Greatest. Supreme. Ruler over all.

He is not sovereign because we deem it to be so. He is not sovereign by popular vote. He is *sovereign*!

He can do anything He wants to do.

He can make it rain; He can stop the rain.

He can make the wind to blow; He can make the wind stop.

He can give life; He can take it away.

What does this mean for you and me? Well, first of all, if we believe that all life is from our Creator God, then we need to understand why He created us. He makes that clear all throughout scriptures. We know from all those that have gone before us and in our own lives, that man is rebellious and wants his own way. You and I have sinned and fallen short of what God desires from us (Rom. 3:23 and Is. 53:6). There is a penalty for that sin—death (Rom. 6:23).

There is a remedy. God knew that we would not live up to the standard He created in the Ten Commandments. He knew that He would have to do something to save us from ourselves and our sinfulness. He knew that it would be the ultimate sacrifice on His part, yet He was willing to redeem us from our fallen state by offering His sinless Son as the perfect sacrifice.

Jesus came to earth to live among us—being tempted in every way just as we are, but, unlike us, He didn't give in to the temptation, as we do. He lived the perfect life in order that He be crowned , with what? A royal crown fit for a king? Not on this earth. Instead—a crown of thorns, pressed into His skin, releasing a flow of blood down His face. He lived the perfect life in order that He be wrapped in a king's robe? Not on this earth. Instead—a purple robe of mockery. In order that He be bowed down to as the only One ever to live without committing a single sin? No, not on this earth, with few bowing down to His majesty, and most spitting, jeering, striking Him with their fists, and flogging Him.

In this world, what awaited Jesus after living a life of love, of compassion, of mercy, of forgiveness, of sacrifice, of healing, of encouragement? Calvary's cross. Jesus earned the right to take your place and my place on the cross—to save us. No one else could ever be worthy of that place on Calvary's cross.

How could He create such beings who would turn our backs on Him, reject Him, ignore Him? Because He is what love is all about. He is what forgiveness is all about. He is love. He is forgiveness. The only way we know about love, forgiveness, and salvation is through Jesus.

In the beginning, God...

"In the beginning was the Word; the Word was with God; the Word was God" (John 1). Jesus said, "I am the way and the truth and the life. No one comes to the Father except through me" (John 14:6).

Where will you be in the end? That will be decided by what you do in the here and now. God has done all He needs to do to save you from an eternal hell and unto an eternal home with Him. God calls you to put your trust in Him and receive everlasting life that only He offers. God calls you to Himself to take your nothingness and create a new person to serve Him as a follower of the Lord Jesus.

Only the Creator can create. And create He will do. Out of your nothingness, He can create someone really special—His own child.

Will you start at the beginning: that the Lord He is God?

Will you stay with Him until the end, until He takes you home?

O Lord our God, our Creator God, who loves us from everlasting to everlasting. Would You touch the one reading this by the power of Your Holy Spirit to draw him or her to You for a new beginning of the life You offer through the risen Christ Jesus? Amen.

In the Lion's Den

*D*aniel was a Jew, likely of royal blood, from Jerusalem, but lived most of his life in a foreign land, about 1000 miles from home. He served the Lord God all his days, striving for excellence in all he did. He served kings in pagan governments, yet did not compromise his integrity, remaining true to the Lord God in word and deed.

During Daniel's life, this ancient world would be subject to domination by world power after world power. When Daniel was eighteen years old, there was one such world power emerging out of Babylon. The armies of Babylon invaded Jerusalem several times, and around 606 BC, Daniel was captured and taken to Babylon. Taken along with Daniel were most of the cream of the crop from among the Israelites.

"Then the king ordered Ashpenaz, chief of his court officials, to bring into the king's service some of the Israelites from the royal family and the nobility—young men without any physical defect, handsome, showing aptitude for every kind of learning, well informed, quick to understand, and qualified to serve in the king's palace" (Dan. 1:3–4).

King Nebuchadnezzar wanted the best and the brightest from among the Jewish captives. He commanded that these men be taught the language, be trained in his ways, and be fed the food and wine from the king's table for three years; then they would be fit for service to the king, an earthly king, that is.

Now, Daniel (Belteshazzar—probably rooted in the name of one of their gods—Baal or Bell) along with his friends, Hananiah (Shadrach), Mishael (Meshach, and Azeriah (Abednego), decided they would not eat the food and wine of the pagan king. Why? Because they believed it would defile them—it was contaminated, unclean. The first portion was offered to idols, and poured out on the pagan altar.

Now, at this point, I would like to say that what is important isn't what they looked like, what their backgrounds were, or what their educational level was; what mattered was that they had convictions from God Almighty, and they *stood* on those convictions. So, then, should you and I.

So, Daniel asked that they be fed only vegetables (also called pulse, which is food grown from seeds) and water for ten days, and have their appearances compared with the others in training, and base the decision on what was then observed. Daniel had consideration for the chief official, probably recognizing that if the king found out that some of the captives weren't following his directions, they would all be in serious trouble.

Do you think Daniel and his friends would have been encouraged by those around them to do this? Do you think their peers were cheering them on? Or do you think they were warned what might happen to them? Or maybe even made fun of? But, at the end of the ten days, what happened?

"At the end of the ten days, they looked healthier and better nourished than any of the young men who ate the royal food. So the guard took away their choice food and the wine they were to drink and gave them vegetables instead" (Dan. 1:15).

There is a great lesson here for you and me... decide beforehand what you will do when faced with a tough decision. Who will be your guide? Will you purpose to trust God and obey Him even when you are being pressured otherwise?

Daniel didn't know for sure how this was going to turn out—he might be thrown in prison or he might be put to death—but he trusted God to take care of him.

"At the end of the time set by the king to bring them into his service, the chief official presented them to Nebuchadnezzar. The king talked with them, and he found none equal to Daniel, Hananiah, Mishael, and

Azariah; so they entered the king's service. In every matter of wisdom and understanding about which the king questioned them, he found them ten times better than all the magicians and enchanters in his whole kingdom" (Dan. 1:18).

He does the same for you and me. "If any of you lacks wisdom, you should ask God, who gives generously to all without finding fault, and it will be given to you" (James 1:5).

Daniel could understand visions and dreams of all kinds. How did he do that? Because God had the understanding and the wisdom, and He imparted it to Daniel. So they entered into Nebuchadnezzar's service, and they excelled in every way. God had not stayed behind in Jerusalem. He was with them every step of the way—every minute of the day. God has not stayed behind somewhere in your past. He is with you now, ever ready to guide your life on the path of righteousness.

Now, those of us who are followers of the Lord Jesus should be what? We should be good parents. We should be good spouses. We should be good citizens. We should be good neighbors. We should be men and women of our word. We should pay our bills. We should do right by our employers. Daniel was such a man. He lived his life above reproach. He lived his life with integrity, true to the one True God.

"In the second year of his reign, Nebuchadnezzar had dreams; his mind was troubled and he could not sleep. So the king summoned the magicians, enchanters, sorcerers, and astrologers to tell him what he had dreamed. When they came in and stood before the king, he said to them, "I have had a dream that troubles me and I want to know what it means." Then the astrologers answered the king, 'May the king live forever! Tell your servants the dream, and we will interpret it.' The king replied to the astrologers, 'This is what I have firmly decided: if you do not tell me what my dream was and interpret it, I will have you cut into pieces and your houses turned into piles of rubble. But if you tell me the dream and explain it, you will receive from me gifts and rewards and great honor. So tell me the dream and interpret for me.' Once more they replied, 'Let the king tell his servants the dream, and we will interpret it.' Then the king answered, 'I am certain that you are trying to gain time, because you realize that this is what I have firmly decided; If you do not tell me the dream, there is only one penalty for you' (Dan. 2:1-8).

The astrologers answered the king, 'there is no one on earth who can do what the king asks! No king, however great and mighty, has ever asked such a thing of any magician or enchanter or astrologer. What the king asks is too difficult. No one can reveal it to the king except the gods, and they do not live among humans'" (Dan. 2:10-11).

They are right—aren't they—about the gods? There is only one true God who does live among men: the Lord Most High, the Lord of all creation. They are right—aren't they—about no man on earth being able to do what the king asks? The problem for them is that Nebuchadnezzar sentenced all the wise men of Babylon to be executed. And they would have been except for the one among them who walked with the one true God.

You know what Daniel did when he heard about this? He asked the king for time so that he might meet the king's demands, and then he asked Hananiah, Mishael, and Azariah to pray for mercy from the God of heaven. You know what God did? He revealed the dream and the interpretation to Daniel in the night.

"Praise be to the name of God for ever and ever; wisdom and power are his. He changes times and seasons; he deposes kings and raises up others. He gives wisdom to the wise and knowledge to the discerning. He reveals deep and hidden things; he knows what lies in darkness, and light dwells with him. I thank and praise you, God of my ancestors: You have given me wisdom and power, you have made known to me what we asked of you, you have made known to us the dream of the king" (Dan. 2:20-23).

Oh how we need to learn that God will use us in ways beyond our comprehension to make Him known in this world. God will call on you to do things which you cannot do on your own. Praise be to God. Doesn't that inspire you—that God would want to use You for His purposes?

Daniel asked to be taken before the king:

"The king asked Daniel (also called Belteshazzar)), 'Are you able to tell me what I saw in my dream and interpret it?' Daniel replied, 'No wise man, enchanter, magician, or diviner can explain to the king the mystery he has asked about, but there is a God in heaven who reveals mysteries'" (Dan. 2:27-28).

So, Daniel revealed, in detail, what the world scene would look like in years to come, Nebuchadnezzar's current reign would end, replaced by a second world power (the Medo-Persian Empire set up by Cyrus), to be replaced by a third world power (the Greek Empire set up by Alexander the Great), to be replaced by a fourth world power (the Roman Empire). But, over and above all that, the Kingdom that would eventually come is the one which will endure forever, never to be destroyed or replaced, the one established by the God of heaven. The king fell prostrate before Daniel and paid him honor. "Surely your God is the God of gods and the Lord of kings and a revealer of mysteries, for you were able to reveal this mystery" (Dan. 2:47).

He then placed Daniel in a high position: Ruler over the entire province of Babylon, over all the wise men. Then, Nebuchadnezzar had a second dream, one which caused Daniel to be perplexed because it revealed that the king would be brought low—even to the point of grazing in the grass like cattle until he would praise the Most High God. From Daniel 4:27-32, we read Daniel's plea to Nebuchadnezzar and God's judgment:

"Renounce your sins by doing what is right, and your wickedness by being kind to the oppressed. It may be that then your prosperity will continue."

"All this happened to King Nebuchadnezzar. Twelve months later, as the king was walking on the roof of the royal palace of Babylon, he said, 'Is not this the great Babylon I have built as the royal residence, by my mighty power and for the glory of my majesty?' Even as the words were on his lips, a voice came from heaven, 'This is what is decreed for you, King Nebuchadnezzar: Your royal authority has been taken from you.

You will be driven away from people and will live with the wild animals; you will eat grass like the ox.'"

This came to pass until finally Nebuchadnezzar acknowledged the Most High God and His sovereignty over the kingdoms of men, and when he did this, and then praised the Most High God, his sanity was restored and his kingdom was reestablished. God is Sovereign.

Now, we move forward to Nebuchadnezzar's successor, his son Belshazzar, and Daniel's serving the Lord under him. From Daniel 5:1-6*...

"King Belshazzar gave a great banquet for a thousand of his nobles and drank wine with them. While Belshazzar was drinking his wine, he gave orders to bring in the gold and silver goblets that Nebuchadnezzar his father had taken from the temple in Jerusalem, so that the king and his nobles, his wives and his concubines might drink from them. So they brought in the gold goblets that had been taken from the temple of God in Jerusalem, and the king and his nobles, his wives and his concubines drank from them. As they drank the wine, they praised the gods of gold and silver, of bronze, iron, wood, and stone. Suddenly the fingers of a human hand appeared and wrote on the plaster of the wall, near the lampstand in the royal palace. The king watched the hand as it wrote. His face turned pale and he was so frightened that his knees knocked together and his legs gave way."

So the king called out for all the enchanters, astrologers, and diviners and he told them all that whoever could read this and interpret it would be clothed in purple; a gold chain would be put around his neck; and he would be the third highest ruler in the kingdom. None could do it.

The queen remembered Daniel and what he had done during Nebuchadnezzar's reign, so he was summoned. Belshazzar made him the same promise as the others, to which Daniel responded, "You may keep your gifts for yourself and give your rewards to someone else. Nevertheless, I will read the writing for the king and tell him what it means" (Dan. 5:17).

He recounted how Nebuchadnezzar had become arrogant and hardened with pride, and then how he was humbled until he acknowledged the Most High God as sovereign. Then, Daniel told Belshazzar that even though he knew all this, he had not humbled himself, but instead set himself up against the Lord of heaven by praising the gods of silver, gold, bronze, iron, wood, and stone, as he and those around him were drinking from goblets stolen from the temple. Therefore, God had sent this hand to write:

"MENE, MENE, TEKEL, PARSIN" meaning NUMBERED, NUMBERED, WEIGHED, DIVIDED.

"Mene: God has numbered the days of your reign and brought it to an end.

Tekel: You have been weighed on the scales and found wanting.

Parsin: Your kingdom is divided and given to the Medes and Persians."

That very night Belshazzar, king of the Babylonians, was slain, and Darius the Mede took over the kingdom, at the age of sixty-two" (Dan. 5:26, 30-31).

Daniel would serve under yet another ruler. Darius found Daniel to have an excellent spirit within him, and trusted him so, that he planned to set him over the whole kingdom. Those around Daniel were jealous and sought to bring him down. When we serve the Lord, we will be met with opposition. In fact, it may be that some will look for every opportunity to do us damage.

So, these opposing Daniel concocted a plan and duped Darius into signing a decree that no one in the kingdom could pray to any god or man except to Darius for the next thirty days. If anyone disobeyed this decree, they would be thrown into the lions' den, that is, the death sentence.

What did Daniel do? He remained true to the Lord in his daily walk, which was getting down on his knees three times daily, upstairs in his home where the windows opened toward Jerusalem. He wasn't putting a show—this was his normal daily habit. He didn't alter it because of this decree. It would cost him his life, so thought his enemies who told on Daniel to the king.

"When the king heard this, he was greatly distressed; he was determined to rescue Daniel and made every effort until sundown to save him. Then the men (who plotted against Daniel) went as a group to King Darius and said to him, 'Remember, Your Majesty, that according to the law of the Medes and Persians no decree or edict that the king issues can be changed.' So the king gave the order, and they brought Daniel and threw him into the lions' den. The king said to Daniel, 'May your God, whom you serve continually, rescue you!'" (Daniel 6:14-16).

A stone was placed over the mouth of the den, and Daniel was alone with the man-eaters, or was he?

Darius spent the night awake, alone, and fasting. At the first light of dawn, he hurried to the lions' den, and "called to Daniel in an anguished voice, 'Daniel, servant of the living God, has your God, whom you serve continuously, been able to rescue you from the lions?' Daniel answered, 'May the king live forever! My God sent his angel, and he shut the mouths of the lions. They have not hurt me, because I was found innocent in his sight. Nor have I ever done any wrong before you, Your Majesty" (Dan. 6:20-22).

Daniel was not alone with the lions. The God he served sent His protecting angels to deliver Daniel. Even the earthly king Darius was overjoyed that Daniel was not killed, in fact, not even wounded. Will you or I ever be in the lions' den? You and I *are* in the lions' den daily. "Your enemy the devil prowls around like a roaring lion looking for someone to devour" (1 Pet. 5:8).

You may think that you can handle the temptations—the devil—you face this day all by yourself.

Reminds me of the wasp clinging to my truck window. As I drove 20 mph, 30 mph, 40, and 50, he hung on there and hung on there, a long time...but finally he was overcome and couldn't hang on any longer. Finally, he was overcome by the more powerful wind.

So, too, will the devil overcome you in your power alone. So, how do you and I combat him—Resist him, standing firm in your faith, humble yourselves, therefore, under God's mighty hand, claim Jesus as Lord of your life; then greater will He be in you than the devil, the roaring lion, of this world.

You see, just like Belshazzar who was weighed and found wanting, so you and I are weighed and found wanting. We probably haven't raised stolen goblets to gods of gold, silver, and the like. But, we have sinned against Holy God in ways equally condemning. So, we must humble ourselves and call upon the only one who can save us: Jesus, the Christ. We are found wanting. He is not. We are imperfect. He is perfect. He gave his perfect life for our imperfect lives so that we can be joint heirs in the kingdom of God with Him. Hallelujah!

Will you humble yourself before the Lord God, as Daniel did? Will you submit yourself to the Almighty God, resisting the devil, as Daniel did? Will you then excel as the Lord God's servant, as Daniel did?

O Lord God, You who are most excellent in every way, please make this reader and me excellent in Your service as You have done for Daniel and others before us. In the name of Mighty Jesus. Amen.

I Look Up; There's Jesus

The waters swirl 'round me, threatening to drown,
My fears overwhelm me, taking me down.
I look up, there's Jesus;
He heard my prayer, now He is there to rescue me.

Burdensome pressures, schedules to meet,
Victories few, more often defeat.
Who can I please, no one it seems;
Nothing is right, except in my dreams.

In this world, I'll have trouble, temptation to fall;
Jesus said, "Take heart—I o'rcame them all."
He's conquered all that I'll ever face,
Even death on a cross when He hung in my place.

Here am I again, Lord, in need of Your grace;
Here are You again, Lord, You lift up my face.
I'm sorry I've been here so often before.
Cleanse me, fill me, Lord, teach me to soar.

In What Will You Find Contentment?

*A*re you putting your trust in religion? You have been a Baptist, a Catholic, a Presbyterian, a Methodist, or whatever denomination all your life, and you believe that is all that's needed. Or, you are one who doesn't believe in denominations, so you are a member of a nondenominational church, and you are trusting that this is the way. Or, for you, it is the interdenominational church that is the way. Are you content because of your church membership? After all, what is wrong with church membership?

Maybe you are one who was baptized as an infant and believe that the Almighty will punch your ticket on this basis. Perhaps you practice religion religiously, giving the tithe without fail, attending every church service, quoting scripture at every opportunity, and praying at the appointed times. Are you content because of your "devoutedness?"

Maybe you have a family history of those who weren't just religious but actually served the Lord. Your family includes those who have been priests, pastors, elders, deacons, missionaries, Sunday school teachers, and leaders. You are hoping that all they have done will give you security with the heavenly Father.

Maybe your family has been influential in other ways. Your family name commands respect. Those in your family have done much for the community. They have helped many and contributed to many worthy causes. Perhaps they are pillars of your city or model citizens, and folks want to know what they think or even want to be like them. You are proud that your family name is _____.

Does your contentment lie in this? What is wrong with having a good family name?

Maybe success *hasn't* been characteristic of *your* family, but you changed all that. You were the first to graduate high school or to earn a college degree or to own your own business or to blaze some other kind of trail. It is you who are influential. It is you to whom folks look for leadership. It is you who is "self-made." No one else did it for you. You have controlled your own destiny.

Maybe your success is in religion; maybe you are an expert in your trade; maybe your success is in business; maybe your success is in education; maybe your success is in entertainment; maybe your success is in sports. Do you have contentment because of your success?

Are you content because of all the things that you have accomplished in this life? Will your track record stand you in good stead before the Father? What is wrong with accomplishment and success?

Maybe, you have been blessed materially with all that you could ever have imagined, and then some. Your income is far beyond your goals. Your house is bigger than you ever dreamed. Your family is Norman Rockwell worthy. You are enjoying the good life. Is this where your contentment is found?

What is wrong with the comforts of this world?

Some believe the good life revolves around pleasure. Is this you? You just want to eat, drink, and be merry. You want to have fun with your friends and your family. What is wrong with laughter, parties, and entertainment? What is wrong with traveling, fine wine, and fine food?

Solomon epitomized all of the above. He was from prime stock. He was the son of a king, and not just any king.

King David was popular, handsome, talented. After all, he was a boyhood hero, slayer of lions, bears, and even the giant Goliath (of course, it was God who gave David the victory in each battle, but David was given more than his share of the glory by the people). David was a leader—spiritually, emotionally, politically, and militarily. His Psalms bring us comfort, strength, and guidance yet today.

Solomon had reason to take pride in his heritage. But, could he find contentment in this?

Solomon was learned. In fact, he asked the Almighty for wisdom, and his prayer was granted. First Kings 3:12 records God speaking to Solomon: "I will do what you have asked. I will give you a wise and discerning heart, so that there will never have been anyone like you, nor will there ever be." He had "wisdom and very great insight, and a breadth of understanding as measureless as the sand on the seashore... He was wiser than anyone else" (1 Kin. 4:29, 31).

Solomon declared, "I devoted myself to study and to explore by wisdom all that is done under heaven" (Eccl. 1:13*). He was a prolific writer—3000 proverbs and 1005 songs (1 Kin. 4:32). The queen of Sheba traveled far to meet Solomon and to put him to the test, and after he had answered all her questions, the conclusion was, "nothing was too hard for the king to explain to her" (1 Kin. 10:3). Could he find contentment in this knowledge, this insight, this discernment?

Solomon was accomplished. "I undertook great projects: I built houses for myself and planted vineyards. I made gardens and parks and planted all kinds of fruit trees in them. I made reservoirs to water groves of flourishing trees" (Eccl. 2:4–6). It sounds like an enchanted surrounding, doesn't it? He was the largest employer in the land, recruiting tens of thousands of workers for his various projects. He oversaw the building of the temple to the Lord God—perhaps close to 200,000 workers, taking seven years. (Now, it should be noted here that the construction of his own palace took thirteen years.) Could he find contentment in houses, grounds, gardens, or in building the Lord's temple?

What about livestock? "I also owned more herds and flocks than anyone in Jerusalem before me" (Eccl. 2:7). Just to give you an idea, 1 Kings 8:63 records at the dedication of the newly completed temple that Solomon's fellowship offering was 22,000 cattle and 120,000 sheep and goats, for the vast number of people who participated in this fourteen-day ceremony.

Solomon amassed wealth unimaginable: "silver and gold for myself, and the treasure of kings and provinces" (Eccl. 2:8). "Solomon accumulated chariots and horses; he had fourteen hundred chariots and twelve thousand horses" (1 Kin. 10:26). Income? Do you measure yours by weight? Maybe you earn about five pounds of dollars a month or whatever. "The weight of gold that Solomon received yearly was 666 talents, not including the revenues from merchants and traders and from all the Arabian kings and the governors of the territories" (1 Kin. 10:14–15). So, let's see. That amounts to about twenty-five tons of gold annually (well over $1 billion at today's $1500 per ounce), not including the chump change from outsiders, which alone would provide great wealth. Could he find contentment in his income and wealth?

Was the man a lover? How about "seven hundred wives of royal birth and three hundred concubines" (1 Kin. 11:3). There must have been a few "lookers" in the lot. But alas, "his wives led him astray" (1 Kin. 11:3b). "His heart was not fully devoted to the Lord his God" (1 Kin. 11:4). Not really shocking, is it? Was Solomon's contentment going to come from his wives and lovers?

In Proverbs, there is wisdom from above through Solomon. In Ecclesiastes, there is only Solomon's earthly wisdom, which is foolishness apart from God. We have the ultimate look into the human philosophy of life and its end result. In Ecclesiastes, we see man's pursuit for contentment in all the wrong places. In Ecclesiastes, we see the futility of man's striving for contentment in this life apart from a right relationship with our heavenly Father.

What did Solomon conclude from all this? "So I hated life." Many people would look at Solomon's life and say, "You what?? You hate life?? Give me some of that, and I bet I can be content!" God says otherwise. "So I hated life, because the work that is done under the sun was grievous to me. All of it is meaningless, a chasing after the wind. I hated all the things I had toiled for under the sun, because I must leave them to the one who comes after me" (Eccl. 2:17–18).

"Whoever loves money never has enough; whoever loves wealth is never satisfied with their income" (Eccl. 5:10). "I denied myself nothing my eyes desired; I refused my heart no pleasure. My heart took delight in all my labor, and this was the reward for all my toil. Yet when I surveyed all that my hands had done and what I had toiled to achieve, everything was meaningless, a chasing after the wind; nothing was gained under the sun" (Eccl. 2:10-11). Note how many references to I and my are in this statement. It is in vain when it is only of our doing. It is purposeless when Christ Jesus is not our guide and our purpose. Our Lord God has put eternity in our hearts. The void in our souls can only be filled by Jesus, and without Him, there will be a void.

Without Him, I would be nothing; without Him, I'd surely fail; without Him, I would drifting like a ship without a sail. (*Without Him* by Mylon LeFevre)

There are roads that take you anywhere but where you need to go.

There are roads that don't go anywhere.

And there is one that leads you home. (*The Man With the Nail Scars* by David Meece)

The One is Jesus. He alone leads us home. He, it is, who is the Way, the Truth, and the Life. The world is too big for us, yet its satisfactions are too small. Solomon learned this through all his accumulations and accomplishments, all too small to satisfy, all too inadequate to bring contentment. So, is there wisdom, true wisdom, from Solomon in all this?

"Now all has been heard; here is the conclusion of the matter; Fear God and keep His commandments, for this is the whole duty of man" (Eccl. 12:13). Fear God, and obey His commands. That was true in Solomon's day. It is true in our day.

"Trust in the Lord with all your heart and lean not on your own understanding; in all your ways submit to him, and he will make your paths straight" (Prov. 3:5–6). So, in what are you trusting to bring you contentment? Has anything you have tried done it? Is there anything wrong with church membership? Certainly not. God teaches us to worship and serve alongside fellow believers. Is there anything wrong with a good family name? Certainly not. A good reputation and respect in the community is to be desired. Is there anything wrong with accomplishment and success? Certainly not. We should strive for excellence in all we do. Is there anything wrong with enjoying the comforts of this world? Certainly not. We should enjoy and share with others. But, if you are trusting in any or all of these, then your trust is misplaced. If you believe the contentment that your heart longs for will be found in any or all of these, then you will be found empty on the last day.

Now, you may think that you will be the one to figure it all out. You will do it all differently than ones who have gone before. You won't make the same mistakes that others have made before you. It will be different for you. But, my friend, that grip that you have on the things of this life will weaken in time, and eventually, you will release it all in death.

Jesus asked this question, "What good will it be for someone to gain the whole world, yet forfeit their soul? Or what can anyone give in exchange for their soul?" (Matt. 16:26). Our souls are only content in Jesus. Our fulfillment is only realized in our following the Lord Jesus. He said that He came to give us life to the full—full and meaningful, fulfillment, contentment (John 10:10).

Please know that there is another who will offer you false contentment and satisfaction. He will offer you the things of this world, temporary, perishable, corruptible. That one is Satan, who is nothing more than a liar, nothing more than the father of lies. Lying is his native language; he is nothing more than a predator—a murderer—ever seeking whom he can lead astray and devour (John 8:44; 1 Pet. 5:8).

Please pray to see the truth, and when you do, you will see Jesus. You will see that He is the Truth, and that in Him, you will be free (John 8:32, 36). Jesus offers us that which is not temporary, not perishable, not corruptible, "For you know that it was not with perishable things such as silver and gold that you were redeemed from the empty way of life handed down to you from your ancestors, but with the precious blood of Christ, a lamb without blemish or defect" (1 Pet. 1:18-19).

He offers us the covering of His own blood, which cleanses us from all our sin.

He offers us His righteousness; we have none on our own.

Apart from Jesus, there is no freedom. In Jesus, there is true freedom.

In Jesus, in God's plan for your life, there is contentment like none other.

O Lord God, thank You for the contentment that is mine, and I pray that it is, as well, for the reader of this message through Christ Jesus. In the name of Jesus, Contentment Himself. Amen.

It's Too Late

It's too late.

*T*hose are sad words. It's sad when your team scores what would be the winning points, but time expired. It's too late. It's sad when the plane or train takes off before you arrive. You've missed it; it's too late. It's sad when you need to mail an important letter, but you don't get to the post office in time to go out that day. It's too late. It's sad that you had a job to do, but you delayed, and then you were told that it was too late. It's really sad that you didn't do right by your son or daughter, and finally you attempted to make things right, but you were told that it was too late.

Maybe you blew your marriage up because of adultery or abuse, and you asked for another chance, but the words came to you: you're too late. Opportunities were missed because you delayed doing something that needed to be done, and then, it's too late. Words that needed to be said, but you did not speak them when the time was right, and then, it was too late. Sometimes, the opportunity comes again. There is another game, another flight, another mail run, another conversation. But, what about when there is death? Death shuts the door on opportunities to make decisions in this life.

Decisions to forgive.
Decisions to reconcile.
Decisions to thank.
Decisions to give.
Decisions to embrace.

Decisions to love.

"It's too late" can be the most haunting words in this life, especially when the opportunity will be no more. Many have stood in the funeral parlor, staring at the body of a loved one, wishing it was not too late to say things left unsaid; to make right things left all wrong, but now, it was too late.

Many remember face-to-face times with loved ones when words that should have been said weren't; when apologies that should have made weren't; when confessions that should have been forthcoming weren't, but now, it was too late.

What would you say, given the opportunity again? What would you do, given the opportunity again? All the above are sad, heartbreaking for sure. But think on eternity. Think on the most important decision you will ever make—what will you do about Jesus?

Will you stand before your Creator one day in eternity, knowing that you rejected His Son here on earth, and now face the reality that it's too late? There can be nothing more tragic than having the opportunity to follow Jesus into His eternal home prepared for you, but choosing hell instead.

There are not many paths to heaven. There are not two paths to heaven. There is but one path to heaven: one way—Jesus. He stated as clearly as He could, "I am the way and the truth and the life. No one comes to the Father except through me" (John 14:6). There can be no fence-sitting on this one. Jesus left no doubt.

Maybe you haven't really seen God as He is, like Philip, who said, "Lord, show us the Father and that will be enough for us." Jesus answered him, "Anyone who has seen me has seen the Father" (John 14:8, 9). If you would see God, you must see Jesus. God, our Father, has shown us Jesus throughout His Word and by the power of His Holy Spirit within us. Jesus told us that He and the Father are one (John 10:30). God has not made us as robots, programmed to do this and do that. God has given us free will to choose life or to choose death. But, understand this, there is a choice to be made, and you will make it.

In the Old Testament, Joshua's words reminded the Israelites that there was a choice to be made, "then choose for yourselves this day whom you will serve" (Josh. 24:15). Would it be the Lord, who had been, and still was, their Deliverer? Or would it be any other gods that are no gods at all? Joshua made clear his choice, "But as for me and my household, we will serve the Lord" (Josh. 24:14–15).

The prophet Micah declared his choice, "But as for me, I watch in hope for the Lord, I wait for God my Savior; my God will hear me" (Mic. 7:7). All throughout scripture, men and women have made the choice to follow the Lord God. All throughout history, men and women have made the choice to follow the Lord God. Men and women are still making the choice to the follow the Lord God in our day.

Jesus made clear that there was a choice to be made: following Him or following the ways of the world. He told all will listen, "Whoever wants to be my disciple must deny themselves and take up their cross and follow me. For whoever wants to save their life will lose it, but whoever loses their life for me will find it. What good will it be for someone to gain the whole world, yet forfeit their soul? Or what can anyone give in exchange for their soul?" (Matt. 16:24–26).

Jesus showed that you are more important to Him than anything in this world. What in the world is more important than Jesus? Would gaining the whole world be more important than Jesus? It is a sorry exchange to give up one's soul to gain even the whole world. To save, Jesus said, we must give up. We must lose our lives in His—in the here and now—in order to save them in the hereafter. Who is it that can be saved? Anyone—and everyone—who will trust in, believe in, and follow, the Lord Jesus.

"God our Savior, who wants all people to be saved and to come to a knowledge of the truth. For there is one God and one mediator between God and mankind, the man Christ Jesus, who gave himself as a ransom for all people" (1 Tim. 2:4). There is hope for anyone who still has breath. It is not too late for anyone still here on earth. Each of us still alive has the opportunity to choose Jesus, to choose life, to choose hope, and to choose forgiveness and peace. Before it is too late. Nothing can be sadder than the soul unsaved—destined for an eternal hell—because this life passed without choosing Jesus. Then, it's too late.

It may seem right now that it is already too late for you. You have made too many mistakes. You carry too much baggage from your past. You are in such a deep hole that there is no way out. The mountain in front of you is so overwhelming that you could never climb it. There is no hope. You have missed your chance. It is too late. But look, the disciples of Jesus thought that it was too late when Jesus was dying on the cross.

There was nothing more that they could do. Apparently, there was nothing more Jesus could do. After all, he had just stood there, in the Garden of Gethsemane, as Judas betrayed him with a kiss, and then he allowed the soldiers to arrest him. He had just stood there as false accusations were made about him. He had just stood there as the blows pounded his body and the whips ripped away at his flesh; as the spittle spewed from the mouths of his tormenters, and ran down his face; as the thorns—the crown of thorns—tore into his scalp, releasing the flow of blood about his head; and as the fists smacked his face repeatedly. He had just stood there as he was mocked, as he was ridiculed, as he was derided, as he was rejected. He just stood there as the people cried out for him to be crucified–not the guilty one, the murderer–but Jesus, the innocent one who had never committed the first crime, never broken any of the rules, never hurt anyone, who only loved anyone and everyone.

He had just willingly picked up the cross to carry it to the place of his execution. He hadn't stopped them from stripping his clothes off. He had just laid there as they drove the nails into his hands and his feet. And he had just hung there on that cross. He had just hung there. And he had died. It was too late. Their hope was gone. Surely, they could have done something.

Jesus had always done something. He had been there for anyone who needed him. He had been there for them—to teach them, to comfort them, to show them, to save them—yet, they had turned their backs on him, even abandoned him, in his hour of need, all but John. It was now too late.

His body had been taken down from the cross. His body had been cleansed and wrapped for burial. His body had been laid in a tomb. In fact, the tomb had been sealed so no one could get in, and certainly no dead man would be coming out. But there was a *live man* coming out. There was a *live Son of God* coming out because *it wasn't too late.* God is never too late.

God the Father had breathed the Spirit of life into His dead Son, and His Son arose to conquer death—once and for all—and live forever. It wasn't too late for Jesus's disciples, except for the betrayer, Judas, who had taken his own life. And it is not too late for you.

"Come to me, all you who are weary and burdened, and I will give you rest," Jesus beckons us. (Matt. 11:28). Do not put off until tomorrow the decision that you need to make today. Remember missed opportunities because you delayed. Remember the lingering pain caused by your not doing the right thing when you had the chance. Remember these words: "Now is the time of God's favor, now is the day of salvation" (2 Cor. 6:2). You can choose Jesus right now—"Salvation is found in no one else, for there is no other name under heaven given to mankind by which we must be saved" (Acts 4:12).

There have been many who chose Jesus as they faced death's door, maybe in a foxhole, maybe in hospital, or even on a cross. Don't forget, there were two other men crucified that day at Calvary. Of course, unlike Jesus, they *were* criminals. So, was there hope for one who had been sentenced to die for crimes he actually had committed? That would sure seem to be a hopeless situation, wouldn't it?

Listen to the sneering of the people on the ground.

Listen to the mocking of the soldiers at the foot of the cross.

Listen to the one criminal hurling insults at Jesus as he was dying right next to him.

But, above all that noise, listen to the rebuke of the other, "'Don't you fear God,' he said, 'since you are under the same sentence? We are punished justly, for we are getting what our deeds deserve. But this man has done nothing wrong.' Then he said, 'Jesus, remember me when you come into your kingdom'" (Luke 23:40-42). Was it not too late?

"Jesus answered him, 'I tell you the truth, today you will be with me in paradise'" (Luke 23:43).

You see, even for this one—who, in only a matter of moments—would stand before his Maker to give account for his life, it wasn't too late. He chose Jesus; he chose life everlasting. Yes, he made his choice at the eleventh hour. But he made it while he had a breath in him. There will be no eternal regrets for him, only peace and forgiveness forevermore.

Will you choose Jesus; will you choose him now before it is too late?

O Lord God, thank You that You never give up on us as long as we live. I pray for the one reading this message for understanding that it is not too late to do the right thing unto salvation and everlasting peace. In the risen Christ Jesus. Amen.

Job: God Is Almighty, and God Is Just

*H*ow do we look at others who seemingly have it all—good looks, wealth, family, big income, attractive spouse? Whatever they do seems to work out for them. All that the world affords is at their disposal.

Have you ever thought about such a someone as this?

Perhaps that someone had been characterized as a Christian, as a religious person, and, just maybe you thought, "No wonder! If I had everything he or she had going, I would be religious too."

It may be that Job was such a man. He may have been envied because of what all he possessed. I don't know about his looks or how attractive his wife was, but we are told that he had a big family and great wealth. Satan picked up on this and decided to use all that against him.

Job lived around 3,000 years ago in a land far away from here, and yet we can learn from his life, his trials, his faith, and his faults.

We are told that Job "was blameless and upright; he feared God and shunned evil. He had seven sons and three daughters, and he owned seven thousand sheep, three thousand camels, five hundred yoke of oxen, five hundred donkeys, and had a large number of servants. He was the greatest man among all the people of the East" (Job 1:1–3).

Does this mean that Job was perfect? No, but he did fear God and did desire to lead his children to do the same. A man who was spiritually and morally upright. He believed in doing the right thing, and tried to do it consistently. His family would regularly host feasts for one another in each other's homes for special occasions. These might last up to a week. Job even cared about his family so much that at the end of the feasts, he would offer a sacrifice for each of them so that they would be purified, just in case they had "sinned and cursed God in their hearts" (Job 1:5). He went before the Lord on behalf of his children continually, a good lesson for those of us who are parents. We need to intercede for our own out of our love for them, and out of our concern for what happens to them.

Now, we are told Job and his life were brought up in heavenly conversations as the angels came to present themselves before the Lord. Satan—the accuser—not only Job's accuser, but your accuser, my accuser, also appeared before the Lord with them.

Remember, Satan was created by God—like all angels—to serve and to glorify God. However, he chose instead to rebel against his Creator, and to seek glory and power for himself. He is prideful—in fact, the epitome of pride. He is a liar, and the father of lies. He is a murderer, a thief, and a destroyer. He is characterized in 1 Peter 5 as a lion prowling around looking for someone to devour. He will do everything he can to use your weaknesses against you—and he knows what our weaknesses are, and he will bring you and me down to his level if we let him. Nothing he does is for your good or mine.

He desperately desired to bring Job down and believed he could do it by taking away some of his earthly security, his family, his creature comforts, and his health.

"Then the Lord said to Satan, 'Have you considered my servant Job? There is no one on earth like him; he is blameless and upright, a man who fears God and shuns evil.' 'Does Job fear God for nothing?' Satan replied. 'Have you not put a hedge around him and his household and everything he has? You have blessed the work of his hands, so that his flocks and herds are spread throughout the land. But now stretch out your hand and strike everything he has, and he will surely curse you to your face" (Job 1:8, 9).

Isn't it likely that Satan had already been working on Job—perhaps for some time—but without success so far? So Satan complained to God about a hedge He had placed around Job.

Do you have a hedge around you? Scripture teaches us that we, in fact, who are followers of the Lord Jesus, do have a hedge of protection around us. We are not exposed to anything and everything that Satan wants to do to us, else we would all be destroyed at his whim. He hates you. He hates me.

He wants to destroy you and me. However, the one who is greatest—the Lord Himself—will not allow Satan to thwart His purpose in our lives. Satan can do nothing to you or me that the Father doesn't allow. And whatever the Father allows is for our own good and for His glory.

Can we understand this? Can we explain it? Perhaps not, but God is Almighty, and God is Just.

"And we know that in all things God works for the good of those who love him, who have been called according to his purpose" (Rom. 8:28). Love Him; serve Him; and He works for your good in all things.

We see in Job 1:12, "The Lord said to Satan, 'Very well, then, everything he has is in your power, but on the man himself do not lay a finger.' Then Satan went out from the presence of the Lord."

Satan had made the claim that Job's godliness was really evil and self-seeking. He was righteous only because it paid well. Break that link between righteousness and blessing, and Job would be exposed. In other words, take down the hedge and let me at him, said Satan, and he will curse You, God. Many are like that. Job wasn't. God knew that. Satan did not. So, God allowed Satan to take away some of that on which Job leaned—all his possessions.

Satan believed he could prove that if God didn't "pay" Job, then Job would neither love Him nor serve Him. God knew Job's heart better than that.

The attack—the disasters—came fast and furious at Job as we see in 1:13–19: First, all his oxen and donkeys were stolen, and those taking care of them were killed. Second, all his sheep and those tending them were burned up in a fire. Third, all his camels were stolen, and those caring for them were killed. Just like that, all his livestock and servants were gone. Fourth, all his children were killed as a mighty wind collapsed the house in which they were feasting. Just like that, all that were left were Job and his wife. What would you do? Curse God? Many have done just that—in far less tragic life experiences than this. Satan believed Job would curse God. He didn't.

"At this, Job got up and tore his robe and shaved his head. Then he fell to the ground in worship and said: 'naked I came from my mother's womb, and naked I will depart. The Lord gave and the Lord has taken away; may the name of the Lord be praised.' In all this, Job did not sin by charging God with wrongdoing" (Job 1:20–22).

Where does everything we have that is any good come from anyway? "Every good and perfect gift is from above, coming down from the Father of the heavenly lights" (James 1:17). Job recognized this truth. Job recognized that God is Almighty.

Whatever we have has been gifted to us—entrusted to us—by our Creator God. And we take nothing with us out of this world. Once after a wealthy man had died, his accountant was asked how much did he leave? His response was, "He left it all." We brought nothing into this world. We take nothing out of this world. Job recognized this to a greater degree than most. What matters above all else is our relationship with Almighty God—our Creator, and the Lover of our souls.

Job wept loudly, I have no doubt. Job mourned in his suffering. Job's heart was breaking, yet in all this, he did not curse God. But it got worse because Job's testing increased, if that is possible. Satan had failed in his first attack against Job, so he came before the Lord again. Verses 2:3-6:

"Then the Lord said to Satan, 'Have you considered my servant Job? There is no one on earth like him; he is blameless and upright, a man who fears God and shuns evil. And he still maintains his integrity, though you incited me against him to ruin him without any reason.' 'Skin for skin!' Satan replied. 'A man will give all he has for his own life. But now stretch out your hand and strike his flesh and bones, and he will surely curse you to your face.' The Lord said to Satan, 'Very well, then he is in your hands; but you must spare his life.'"

God affirmed Job's reverence for God, but Satan now believed that an attack on Job's body would cause him to give up and curse God. God knew Job. Satan didn't.

Verses 2:7–10: "So Satan went out from the presence of the Lord and afflicted Job with painful sores from the soles of his feet to the crown of his head. Then Job took a piece of broken pottery and scraped himself with it as he sat among the ashes. His wife said to him, 'Are you still maintaining your integrity? Curse God and die!' He replied, 'You are talking like a foolish woman. Shall we accept good from God, and not trouble?' In all this, Job did not sin in what he said." (before we throw his wife out on her ear, let's be mindful that her heart was pierced by these tragedies, as well).

In all this, Job did not sin in what he said. He did not curse God. God is almighty and God is just. How bad was Job suffering? Throughout the book, we learn he had festering sores over his whole body. The scabs peeled and turned black. His pain was constant, day and night. He suffered from nightmares. He had a fever. He was excessively thin. He had bad breath. He was disfigured and revolting in appearance. He was alone in this world.

Then, his friends came—Eliphaz the Temanite, Bildad the Shuhite, and Zophar the Naamathite. When they had "heard about all the troubles that had come upon him, they set out from their homes and met together by agreement to go and sympathize with him and comfort him. When they saw him from a distance, they could hardly recognize him; they began to weep aloud, and they tore their robes and sprinkled dust on their heads. Then they sat on the ground with him for seven days and seven nights. No one said a word to him, because they saw how great his suffering was" (Job 2:11-13). That is true friendship, true consideration, true compassion. When we are in the deepest valley, sometimes all we want is someone's presence, someone's compassion.

The story is told about a little girl who cried out from her bedroom during a thunderous storm, and her dad came in to check on her. He told her not to be afraid, and that God was with her there in her room.

She replied, "I know, but right now I just want somebody with skin on." Doesn't God use folks around us—with skin on—to bring comfort to us in our trouble, our sorrow?

"Praise be to the God and Father of our Lord Jesus Christ, the Father of compassion and the God of all comfort, who comforts us in all our troubles, so that we can comfort those in any trouble with the comfort that we ourselves have received from God" (2 Cor. 1:4).

Job finally broke the silence and cursed the day he was born. He cried out that he had no peace, only turmoil. Then, one by one, his friends orated. They were now going to "teach" Job, to "clarify" for Job why he was in this mess, to "solve" his problems. There were three cycles of speeches, "friend" speaks, Job replies, "friend" speaks, Job replies, and so on. Their logic may have been flawless, but their words were wounding.

They undertook to debate—exactly what Job didn't need. They spoke in clichés and platitudes. They were condescending in tone. They were accusatory and not the least bit compassionate. Their words were hurtful, even brutal. They drew on tradition, experience, and legality, but not out of the well–the deep, deep well–of Almighty God's mercy and grace, carried by His Spirit into our hearts. Much of what they said was true but not helpful. Job calls them "miserable comforters" in 16:2. Some examples:

Eliphaz. Verse 5:17: "Blessed is the man whom God corrects; so do not despise the discipline of the Almighty" (this wasn't about discipline). Verse 15:20: "All his days the wicked man suffers torment, the ruthless through all the years stored up for him" (this wasn't about the wicked suffering). Verse 22:15: "Will you keep to the old path that the wicked have trod?" (Job hadn't trodden the wicked path).

Bildad. Verse 8:4: "When your children sinned against him, he gave them over to the penalty of their sin" (this wasn't about penalizing Job and his children). Verse 18:5: "The lamp of the wicked is snuffed out; the flame of his fire stops burning" (this wasn't about Job being punished for wickedness). Verse 18:21: "Surely such is the dwelling of an evil man; such is the place of one who knows not God" (this wasn't about an evil man). Verse 25:6: "How much less a mortal, who is but a maggot—a human being, who is only a worm!" (comforting words there, huh?).

Zophar. Verse 11:11: "Surely he recognizes deceivers; and when he sees evil, does he not take note?" (this wasn't about Job being deceitful). Verse 20:29: "Such is the fate God allots the wicked, the heritage appointed for them by God" (Job had not shown himself to be wicked).

But their being in the wrong doesn't make Job be in the right. There was much yet for Job to learn about His Creator. But, first, another would speak. The fourth speaker to Job was Elihu, who was younger than the others, and who had listened quietly to the previous discourses. He finally spoke, and spoke in anger at Job for justifying himself rather than God.

Elihu. Verse 32:8: "But it is the spirit in a person, the breath of the Almighty, that gives him understanding." While he offered no comfort for Job's suffering, he did cite Job's own words which showed a problem of pride. Verse 33:8: "But you have said in my hearing—I heard the very words—'I am pure, I have done no wrong; I am clean and free from sin.'" Verse 34:5: "Job says, 'I am innocent, but God denies my justice.'" He also reminds us that God uses trouble to get our attention, and draw us to Himself. Verse 34:12: "It is unthinkable that God would do wrong, that the Almighty would pervert justice." Verse 36:10–12: "He makes them listen to correction and commands them to repent of their evil. If they obey and serve him, they will spend the rest of their days in prosperity and their years in contentment. But if they do not listen, they will perish by the sword and die without knowledge." Verse 37:23: "the Almighty is beyond our reach and exalted in power; in his justice and great righteousness, he does not oppress."

Job Answers. Job didn't understand God, nor did he understand himself. He was conscious of God, fearful of God, somewhat trusting of God, but he could find nothing wrong with himself. He wanted to defend himself before God, but the truth of the matter is that none of us has any defense before God Almighty. Job was righteous in his own eyes, but Job was not righteous before God. All that Job could do—all any of us can do—is plead guilty, and fall before the Almighty seeking mercy and grace. He had expressed his hope in the Almighty but still was looking to defend himself. Verse 13:15: "Though he slay me, yet will I hope in him; I will surely defend my ways to his face. Indeed, this will turn out for my deliverance, for no godless man would dare come before him!"

Job believed—in his heart of hearts—that one day he would see God beyond this life, a great statement of faith that encourages us to this day. Verse 19:25–27: "I know that my redeemer lives, and that in the end he will stand upon the earth. And after my skin has been destroyed, yet in my flesh I will see God; I myself will see him with my own eyes—I, and not another. How my heart yearns within me!" Yet, Job needed to repent. Each of us needs to repent. Verse 40:4: "I am unworthy—how can I reply to you? I put my hand over my mouth" (a lesson we can all learn). Verse 42:3, 6: "Surely I spoke of things I did not understand, things too wonderful for me to know...Therefore I despise myself and repent in dust and ashes."

God Asks Job What Power He Has. You see, God had made some truths known very clearly to Job. Verse 41:11: "Who has a claim against me that I must pay. Everything under heaven belongs to me." God is Almighty. Verse 38:2–5: "Who is this that obscures my plans with words without knowledge? Brace yourself like a man; I will question you, and you shall answer me. Where were you when I laid the earth's foundation? Tell me, if you understand. Who marked off its dimensions? Surely you know! Who stretched a measuring line across it?" Verse 38:8: "Who shut up the sea behind doors when it burst forth from the womb," Verse 38:12: "Have you ever given orders to the morning, or shown dawn its place,"

Verse 38:16: "Have you journeyed to the springs of the sea or walked in the recesses of the deep? Have the gates of death been shown to you?" Verse 38:19: "What is the way to the abode of light? And where does darkness reside?" Verse 38:21: "Surely you know, for you were already born! You have lived so many years! Have you entered the storehouses of the snow or seen the storehouses of the hail," Verse 38:28: "Does the rain have a father? Who fathers the drops of dew?" Verse 38:31-33: "Can you bind the chains of the Pleiades? Can you loosen Orion's belt? Can you bring forth the constellations in their seasons or lead out the Bear with its cubs? Do you know the laws of the heavens? Can you set up God's dominion over the earth?"

Verse 38:36*: "Who endowed the heart with wisdom or gave understanding to the mind?" Verse 38:41: "Who provides food for the raven when its young cry out to God and wander about for lack of food?" Verse 39:19: "Do you give the horse its strength or clothe its neck with a flowing mane?" Verse 39:27: "Does the eagle soar at your command and build its nest on high?" Verse 40:2: "Will the one who contends with the Almighty correct him?" Verse 40:8-9: "Would you discredit my justice? Would you condemn me to justify yourself? Do you have an arm like God's, and can your voice thunder like his?"

Verse 41:1-2, 5: "Can you pull in Leviathan with a fishhook or tie down its tongue with a rope? Can you put a cord through its nose or pierce its jaw with a hook?...Can you make a pet of it like a bird or put it on a leash for the young woman in your house?"

First, Job learned to be silent. So, too, do you and I need to be silent—to "be still, and know that I am God" (Ps. 46:10). Next, Job learned to be submissive. Likewise, you and I need to be submissive—"Submit yourselves, then, to God. Resist the devil, and he will flee from you. Come near to God and he will come near to you" (James 4:7). Finally, Job learned to be a servant. As well, you and I need to be servants, after our Lord Jesus—"For even the Son of man did not come to be served, but to serve, and to give his life as a ransom for many" (Mark 10:45).

When gold is refined, it is being heated up increasingly until the dross is removed from the top. Finally, the image of the refiner is seen in the pure gold. So it is with God's own, as He refines us. He is ever working us—refining us—in order to see His image in our character and through our lives. "But he knows the way I take; when he has tested me, I will come forth as gold" (Job 23:10).

Trust God through suffering. We have often heard of Job's patience, but in James 5:11, we read of the "patience of God and endurance of Job." We can learn from Job's experiences, his suffering, his endurance. Through all of Job's testing, God proved to be almighty, and God proved to be just.

We will have trials, but God is just. He will be our Strength, our Shield, our Refuge. His grace will be sufficient for us. His grace will be made known in our weakness (Ps. 18:1–3; 2 Cor. 12:9). We can learn from these trials that God is almighty. Satan cannot contend with God hand to hand, so he attempts to alienate the ones God loves from God.

Job was robbed of every sign of God's favor, yet he knew in his heart of hearts that his godliness had been authentic and well-placed in the Almighty, and that he would be vindicated one day. What pained him most was his alienation from God. But his alienation from God was not caused by his suffering—it was caused by his pride. In the end, Job learned that he needed to rely upon God in all things—for all things. So do we. We need to be humble and submissive before God.

Like Jesus, just like Jesus, who, similar to Job, was alienated from His heavenly Father in great suffering, unimaginable to you and me, suffering through being nailed to a cross. You drive nails through boards to build things. You don't drive nails through a human being to hang him up to suffer an excruciating death, and publicly for all to see. Yet, mankind did that to Jesus. He allowed it. He didn't want it. How could anyone? But He allowed it.

"Christ Jesus: Who, being in very nature God, did not consider equality with God something to be used to his own advantage; rather, he made himself nothing by taking the very nature of a servant, being made in human likeness. And being found in appearance as a man, he humbled himself by becoming obedient to death—even death on a cross! Therefore God exalted him to the highest place and gave him the name that is above every name, that at the name of Jesus every knee should bow, in heaven and on earth and under the earth, and every tongue acknowledge that Jesus Christ is Lord, to the glory of God the Father" (Phil. 2:5b–11).

Through Job's suffering, he learned to trust in God, the one who is almighty and just. He didn't know what the future held for him here on this earth, but he did know Who held the future. And in the end, Job was blessed with family—seven sons and three daughters, and more livestock, "The Lord blessed the latter part of Job's life more than the former part...And so Job died, an old man and full of years" (Job 42:12, 17).

So, we are blessed beyond measure through suffering—Christ Jesus's suffering—because we are reconciled to God, our Father, through it. God's plan for you and me is not an idea, a proposition, a dogma. His plan for you and me is a Redeemer—Jesus.

"I am the way and the truth and the life. No one comes to the Father except through me" said Jesus, recorded in John 14:6.

"For there is one God and one mediator between God and mankind, the man Christ Jesus, who gave himself as a ransom for all people" (1 Tim. 2:5).

The very redeemer in which Job hoped is the very Redeemer who saves our souls—Job's, yours, mine.

May it be so in your life, my friend, in the name above all names— Jesus, the Christ, the Sufferer, the Savior for you and me.

O Lord God, Almighty and Just... thank You for showing us in the life of Job how You are ever working to prove us out to be faithful to You, and showing us that we are worth more than anything in this world. Thank You for showing Yourself through Your Son to be our Redeemer. I pray that You redeem the reader of this message. In the Name of Jesus. Amen.

Leave the Past in the Behind

Exodus 14:19

*G*od stands between you and me and our past, our painful past, our hurtful past, our sinful past. He leads us into the future. He delivers us from the past. What helps you escape from your painful past? What brings you relief? Does anything ease the pain? Does it give you hope, or is it a temporary diversion? Can you even put the past in the be-hind, or is it bigger than you?

The Israelites had been in bondage for 430 years in the foreign land of Egypt. And, even though they had grown in number to 600,000 men—plus all the women and children, they were yet powerless. They were slaves to the cruel Pharaoh and his merciless taskmasters. They had lost sight of their identity as God's chosen people and had become accustomed to the Egyptian ways. They had eaten the food of this foreign people and had been influenced by the worship of their many gods. The resultant pain and despair was deep and abiding. Their oppression was 24/7.

What haunts you from your past? What were you a slave to? Or, are you still? Alcohol? Gossip? Drugs? Dishonesty? Pornography? Theft? Adultery? What was more important than God in your life? What kept you from being the person that deep down you aspired to be? Or, are you still there? Do you need rescuing?

The Israelites' backs had been broken. They cried out to the heavens for help. Would anyone hear? Would anyone care? Could anyone deliver them? God heard. God cared. God would deliver them.

Are you crying out? Do you believe anyone hears? Do you believe anyone cares? Do you believe that you have a deliverer? God called a deliverer for His enslaved people...

"The Lord said, 'I have indeed seen the misery of my people in Egypt. I have heard them crying out because of their slave drivers, and I am concerned about their suffering. So I have come down to rescue them from the hand of the Egyptians and to bring them up out of that land into a good and spacious land, a land flowing with milk and honey'" (Ex. 3:7–8).

Have you been rescued and delivered to the land of milk and honey, the place of hope and promise where you commune with the living God, the one who created you for His purpose? Or, are you still in bondage to the merciless taskmaster, in a place far from home, far from where you long to be, and far from where God intends you to be?

The Israelites had had enough. Have you? They cried out for help. Have you? God would send one to lead them out of their hellacious predicament. God will do the same for you. Moses would lead the Israelites out. Jesus will lead you out. Who says so? I AM says so.

"So now, go. I am sending you to Pharaoh to bring my people the Israelites out of Egypt. . . . And God said, 'I will be with you'" (Ex. 3:10, 12).

"Moses said to God, 'Suppose I go to the Israelites and say to them, The God of your fathers has sent me to you, and they ask me, What is his name? Then what shall I tell them?' God said to Moses, 'I AM WHO I AM. This is what you are to say to the Israelites: I AM has sent me to you'" (Ex. 3:13–14).

Jesus says to you, "I am the way and the truth and the life. No one comes to the Father except through me... Then you will know the truth, and the truth will set you free" (John 14:6; John 8:32). The Israelites had to put their trust in God and His deliverer, Moses. They would, and he would lead them out of bondage but not without a struggle, well, struggles.

The one who keeps others in bondage does not give them up easily. He does not surrender without a fight. He is hard-hearted. He is ruthless. He is evil. The same one who would keep you and me in bondage.

He is the evil one—Satan. He is prince of darkness, prince of this world. He is powerful, and not be taken lightly. He "prowls around like a roaring lion, looking for someone he can devour" (1 Pet. 5:8b). He would keep you in bondage, in the past, in whatever it is that keeps you from what God offers you.

God brings peace. Satan brings turmoil.

God brings forgiveness. Satan brings condemnation.

God brings freedom. Satan brings oppression.

The Israelites knew all about turmoil, condemnation, oppression. They had suffered them all at the hands of Satan's agents. So probably have you. And if you have, know this—it isn't God's way. It's Satan's way. God's way leads you to contentment. Satan's way leads you to torment. Oh, Satan's lures may yield some temporary pleasure, some temporary escape from the pain but never freedom. His lures always are attached to the deadly hook, which pulls you further and further away from freedom.

Freedom is only found in God's way, God's will.

So, the Israelites listened to Moses delivering God's message to them, and they obeyed the instructions of the one who would rescue them. God would rescue His people because, ultimately, He was in control. Pharaoh thought that he was in control. Pharaoh was wrong. Time and time again, the mighty hand of God came over Egypt, through the plagues, in order to lead Pharaoh to submit to His will for His people, yet Pharaoh continued to harden his heart until there was no turning back. Finally, with all his kingdom collapsing around him and amid the wailing of his people as death pierced every household in his land, Pharaoh released God's people—actually urged them to go, and their deliverance began.

Satan would have you harden your heart as Pharaoh did, so you will not listen and obey Almighty God, your heavenly Father. It didn't go well for Pharaoh. It won't go well with you either. That is what Satan is working toward—your demise, your destruction. And, just because you have become a follower of the Lord doesn't mean Satan will give up trying to tempt you, to entice you off the right path. So, it was with the Israelites.

"So God led the people around by the desert road toward the Red Sea...By day the Lord went ahead of them in a pillar of cloud to guide them on their way and by night in a pillar of fire to give them light, so that they could travel by day or night. Neither the pillar of cloud by day nor the pillar of fire by night left its place in front of the people" (Ex. 13:18, 21–22).

God would lead you if you will but follow Him. He will never leave His post watching over you. You see, He never slumbers, never sleeps. (Ps. 121:4).

He was watching over me even when I was not submitted to His will. He was protecting me and rescuing me even when I was ignoring Him until I cried out for help, sometimes at the last minute. You may be able to reflect on when He was doing the same for you, even when you weren't acknowledging Him. He has promised us: "Never will I leave you; never will I forsake you" (Heb.13:5). He also never changes, "Jesus Christ is the same yesterday and today and forever" (Heb. 13:8). What assurance God's presence offers us if we will but "Be still and know that I am God" (Ps. 46:10).

We can be confident that the Israelites found assurance in God's presence in the pillar of cloud by day and the pillar of fire by night. But trouble was on the horizon. Surely Egypt had long disappeared from the rearview mirror, hadn't it? Well, yes, Egypt had, but not Egyptians— Egyptian soldiers, Egyptian chariots, In fact, they were looming larger by the minute.

"The Egyptians—all Pharaoh's horses and chariots, horsemen and troops—pursued the Israelites and overtook them as they camped by the sea... As Pharaoh approached, the Israelites looked up, and there were the Egyptians, marching after them. They were terrified and cried out to the Lord" (Ex. 14:9–10).

Wow, all the pain of the past was coming back to haunt them...no, not only to haunt them, but to destroy them. There they were—between a sea they couldn't cross and an army they couldn't defeat. Have you been in that place? Are you there now? Where is your deliverer?

This looked like the end. "What have you done to us by bringing us out of Egypt?... It would have been better for us to serve the Egyptians than to die in the desert!" said the Israelites to Moses (Ex. 14:11–12). They just couldn't yet see their deliverance, but Moses could.

"Moses answered the people, 'Do not be afraid. Stand firm and you will see the deliverance the Lord will bring you today. The Egyptians you see today you will never see again. The Lord will fight for you; you need only to be still" (Ex. 14:13–14).

Can you see that God will deliver you? Would you stand firm, being still, believing that the Lord will fight for you, and deliver you? Think of it, that stuff from the past that haunts you, plagues you, debilitates you—you will never see again—if, if you only be still, submitting to His will, and let the Lord fight for you.

"Then the angel of God, who had been traveling in front of Israel's army, withdrew and went behind them. The pillar of cloud also moved from in front and stood behind them, coming between the armies of Egypt and Israel. Throughout the night the cloud brought darkness to the one side and light to the other side; so neither went near the other all night long" (Ex. 14:19–20).

What is it you need between you and your painful past, even your sinful past? You don't need diversion, you need the Deliverer. You don't need things, you need the Creator. God is our Deliverer. He is the one who stands between us and that which would overtake us and bring us down. He is the one who stands between us and the one who would bring us down and destroy us.

"Because the one who is in you is greater than the one who is in the world" (1 John 4:4).

Is the Spirit of Jesus in you right now? He will be if you repent of your sins and submit to His will for your life. Then all the power of heaven will be in you for His will. God is always where we need Him to be. Just as God's angel moved to where he was needed most between His people and their enemy, so God moves His angel to where you need him most—between you and your enemy.

Do you believe that? You should. God always tells the truth. God always does what He says He will do.

God is faithful, and He loves you far more than you can imagine. He doesn't want the pain from the past to plague you; He wants only that it bring you to Him. It may be a process, slower than you are comfortable with. We would rather be beamed out of the mess, wouldn't we? But just because we can't see more than a step or two ahead of us in the deliverance process, it doesn't mean that the deliverance is any less of a reality. If God assures us that He is delivering, then, my friend, He is delivering.

The Israelites weren't beamed from one side of the Red Sea to the other, nor was the Egyptian army zapped instantaneously. Yet, deliverance was assured.

"Then Moses stretched out his hand over the sea, and all that night the Lord drove the sea back with a strong east wind and turned it into dry land. The waters were divided, and the Israelites went through the sea on dry ground, with a wall of water on their right and on their left" (Ex. 14:21–22).

No words or special movie effects can adequately capture the power of One who could hold back the walls of the sea in order for His people—a million or so—could move through en masse on dry ground. Not a muddy river bed, dry ground! It wasn't instant deliverance, but it was deliverance.

"The Egyptians pursued them, and all Pharaoh's horses and chariots and horsemen followed them into the sea. During the last watch of the night, the Lord looked down from the pillar of fire and cloud at the Egyptian army and threw it into confusion. He jammed the wheels of their chariots so that they had difficulty driving. And the Egyptians said,

'Let's get away from the Israelites! The Lord is fighting for them against Egypt'" (Ex. 14:23–25).

Even the nonbelieving Egyptians saw the mighty hand of the Lord—a God greater than all their gods—in this—the mighty hand of the Lord on behalf of His people, the mighty hand of their Deliverer.

"Then the Lord said to Moses, 'Stretch out your hand over the sea so that the waters may flow back over the Egyptians and their chariots and horsemen.' Moses stretched out his hand over the sea, and at day-break the sea went back to its place. The Egyptians were fleeing toward it, and the Lord swept them into the sea. The water flowed back and covered the chariots and horsemen—the entire army of Pharaoh that had followed the Israelites into the sea. Not one of them survived" (Ex. 14:26–28).

That which haunts you from your past will not survive God's mighty hand either. No, the deliverance for the Israelites was not instant, but it was real.

"The people feared the Lord and put their trust in him and in Moses, his servant" (Ex. 14:31).

There it is. Will you fear the Lord and put your trust in His servant—His Son Jesus, your deliverer?

O Lord God, thank You for deliverance that is ours for the asking. I pray for the one reading this, that she or he be delivered from whatever in the past, and that You stand between this one and all that binds her or him from the past, that they can walk with You in freedom and peace. In the name of Jesus, our Deliverer and our Future. Amen.

His Blood is on my Doorpost

The sacrifice was offered, its blood smeared on their door;
They'd soon be out from under the oppressive hand.
Now, death would pass them over, and the Promised Land in store
For God's own people held captive in a foreign land.

Bound by sin's dread shackles, myself I could not free.
The prince of darkness tempted me, I fell.
All my works and goodness summed up, enough they would not be
To save me from the fiery pits of hell.

Then the sacrificial Lamb gave up His life for me;
Only the perfect Son of God could be the one.
His blood is on my doorpost, it's my identity,
With Jesus who became my redemption.

The Lord is keeping vigil, His eye is on all who
Are needing His deliverance from Satan's hold.
The Lord already fought for you, Jesus paid your due.
Now He's calling you to come into His fold.

Letter from Home

*W*hat do you think of when you think of home? Do you think of the place of your childhood? Do you think of the place where you are raising a family? Do you think of a place that never technically was your home, but it seemed like home? Do you think of something positive when you think of a letter from home?

Were you ever away from home at camp and got homesick? Were you ever away from home at school and got homesick? Were you ever away from home serving in our armed forces and got homesick? When you were away, did you ever receive a letter from home? From your mother? From your dad? From your grandmother or aunt? From your brother or sister? From your spouse? From your child? Do you ever receive a letter from home now? How does it make you feel?

I remember when I was away at college, the one who wrote me most was Nanny, my Grandmother. It was always a thrill to receive mail that was encouraging, and Nanny's mail was always that way. Do you like receiving encouraging mail? How much of our mail today is encouraging? Have you ever just had your fill of encouragement? You know, I have never heard anyone just say, "Well that is about all the encouragement I can stand." Or, "Please, don't give any more of that encouragement—I am full up."

In truth, we long for encouraging words, uplifting words, words of truth. We may not act like it, but deep down we want that. Now, I don't mean phony words or sarcastic words that really aren't encouraging at all. I mean the real thing—genuine, heartfelt encouragement. Real love, real truth.

When was the last time you received a letter from home that made you smile? Made you warm inside? Made you want to go on? Maybe even straightened you out about some things and made you want to do better? Made you feel loved? Made you realize that you had meaning in this life? Reminded you that you mean something to someone in this life? Gave you hope?

There is a letter from home for you today.

Your childhood home may have been full of good memories. Your childhood home may have been full of bad memories: of heartache, of pain, of abuse, of abandonment, or of loneliness. Regardless of the home of your childhood, there was a home before that. It was a home far away from this earth. It was a home with the heavenly Father. You see, He thought of you long before you were born. He knew that He would create you. He knew that He would create you in His image. He knew that you would have a purpose in this life. He knew that you would be right here, right now, at this point in your life. He knew from the beginning that He was going to love you, no matter what. And you see, He knew whether you were going to love Him at this moment. He wants you to love Him. He longs for you to love Him. You need to love Him.

And, He has written to you a letter of love so that you will know, so that you will be assured, that He does loves you with all His divine Being. He wants you to know all the ways that He has made clear how much He loves you, and wants you to be in right relationship with Him. Are you in right relationship with Him at this moment? If not, He calls you to Himself in a supernatural way, through the power of His Spirit.

On our own, we are hopeless.

On our own, we are helpless.

On our own, we are doomed.

On our own, we perish.

But the good news is, that is not the way our heavenly Father wants it to be. He desires that you not perish, but instead, come to repentance. He desires your salvation. He waits patiently for you. "The Lord is not slow in keeping his promise, as some understand slowness. Instead, he is patient with you, not wanting anyone to perish, but everyone to come to repentance." (2 Pet. 3:9)

He calls us to live in "all godliness and holiness. This is good, and pleases God our Savior, who wants all people to be saved and to come to a knowledge of the truth. For there is one God and one mediator between God and mankind, the man Christ Jesus, who gave himself as a ransom for all people" (1 Tim. 2:4). You see, His desire for you is so great that He made the greatest sacrifice He could so you would not perish; so you would come to repentance; so you would know the truth; so you would have everlasting life.

In this letter from home, God, the Father, tells you about His Son coming to earth to live as one of us. John 1:14 tells us the Word—Jesus—became flesh and made his dwelling among us. He tells you how His Son faced every temptation that we face, yet He didn't sin. Hebrews 4:15 says, "For we do not have a high priest who is unable to empathize with our weaknesses (have you ever tried to relate what you were going through, but the one listening clearly had no clue about what you were experiencing?), but we have one who has been tempted in every way, just as we are—yet he did not sin." Jesus knows what you are going through. He understands. He cares. He has already done something about it.

You and I have sinned. You and I have fallen short of the standard— the perfect standard—that Jesus set (John 3:23). That's bad news, because the wages of that sin is death (John 6:23). We deserve death, and forgiveness of our sin is only possible through sacrificial death. But whose? Your death or my death wouldn't satisfy. Why? Because that is what we deserve. It would be just. It would pay the penalty we owe. It just wouldn't save us.

But what if someone who was perfect would become the sacrifice and satisfy justice but also extend grace and mercy to us, the undeserving? This letter from the Father tells us that this is exactly what happened. God, the Father, sent His only Son, Jesus, the perfect One, into this sin-sick world, to show us how to live, and to show us how to die for others–how He would die for others. In His death, and in

His resurrection from death, Jesus atoned for you and me. You know what atonement means? It means turning aside wrath, taking away sin. Hallelujah!

He ransomed us—paid for our release. He made it possible for you and me to have life, full and meaningful, on this earth. Jesus even said, "I have come that they may have life, and have it to the full" (John 10:10). He made it possible for you and me to have life everlasting, in the perfect home with God, the Father, and Jesus, the Son. First John 5:11–12 states: "God has given us eternal life, and this life is in his Son. Whoever has the Son has life; whoever does not have the Son of God does not have life."

You see, He is the one who created you, and He is the one who wants you to come home. You and I came from Him, in the beginning. Each one of us came into being because He willed it to be. He has a plan for each one of us. And I can tell you, for sure, it is not to harm us. It is not to leave us or forsake us. It is not to do anything that is not for our good.

Maybe you are like the Psalmist, who wrote, "I am poor and needy, and my heart is wounded within me" (Ps. 109:22). You know what God, the Father, says to you: "For he stands at the right hand of the needy one" (Ps. 109:31).

Here is what the Psalmist wrote in this letter: "For you created my inmost being; You knit me together in my mother's womb. I praise you because I am fearfully and wonderfully made; your works are wonderful, I know that full well" (Ps. 139:13–14).

Just as to Jeremiah, the Lord says to you and me, "I have loved you with an everlasting love; I have drawn you with unfailing kindness" (Jer. 31:3). Does God, the Father, want anything but good for you? How clear is His message about what He wants for you?

He has written to you that He loves you; that He knows everything about you, and still He loves you; that He knew you would sin and turn your back on Him, and still He loves you; that He would send His Son to take all the sins that you have committed, are currently committing, and will ever commit—same as me—upon Himself to a torturous, unimaginable death on Calvary's cross.

Jesus looked upon you and me with eyes of love, even when the pain was unbearable; even when most had turned their backs on him (perhaps the same as you and I would have done), still He loved us. And, He loves us even today.

"The Lord is compassionate and gracious, slow to anger, abounding in love. He will not always accuse, nor will he harbor his anger forever; he does not treat us as our sins deserve or repay us according to our iniquities. For as high as the heavens are above the earth, so great is his love for those who fear him; as far as the east is from the west, so far has he removed our transgressions from us" (Ps. 103:8–12).

How many letters have you ever received that tell you of your great worth; that tell you that you are loved from everlasting to everlasting; that tell you of someone who gave his life for you; that tell you that in spite of all the mistakes you have made, you are still loved and desired; that tell you how your father has compassion, mercy, and grace for you; that tell you how your father wants to spend time with you – even eternity? One letter does. God's letter to you. It is enough.

In Psalm 107, the Lord speaks of danger on the high seas, where "in the peril their courage melted away. They reeled and staggered like drunkards; they were at their wits' end. Then they cried out to the Lord in their trouble, and he brought them out of their distress. He stilled the storm to a whisper; the waves of the sea were hushed. They were glad when it grew calm, and he guided them to their desired haven. Let them give thanks to the Lord for his unfailing love."

Are you at your wits' end?

If you were ever a soldier on the battlefield, far from home, you would take heart in encouragement communicated from a loved one, in a letter from home that would speak of love, that would tell you that you matter, and that they long to see you again.

You and I are on the battlefield of this world, being tempted, being tried on a regular, seemingly relentless, basis. There is a letter from home, encouragement, love, assurance that you matter, beckoning you to come home... to the "desired haven."

If you are without Jesus, then I pray you are at your wits' end. Because it is there, that you will turn to Him, and see that He is everything that God, the Father, says He is. He is the Savior, the Lord of all, the Messiah, the Anointed One, the Bread of Life, the Door, the Way, the Truth, the Life, and the only Hope for you and me.

What more can God say to you, or show to you, but what He has already done?

The time is now for you to act in response to His love and the calling of His Holy Spirit to you.

O Lord our God, thank You for Your love letter to this reader and to each of us. Thank you for making Your love clear to us in all of creation, in Your Word, in Your Son, and in Your Holy Spirit. In the name of Jesus, the Word. Amen.

Lord's Prayer

Matthew 6:9–13**

*T*he disciples had watched as Jesus spoke with authority time
after time.

> The wind and waves were made still at His Word.
> The lame were made to walk at His Word.
> The deaf were made to hear at His Word.
> The blind were made to see at His Word.
> The lepers were made clean at His Word.
> The dead even rose to live again at His Word.

And, Jesus said this, "Very truly I tell you, whoever believes in me
will do the works I have been doing, and they will do even greater things
than these, because I am going to the Father. And I will do whatever
you ask in my Name, so that the Father may be glorified in the Son. You
may ask me for anything in my name, and I will do it" (John 14:12–14).

Is He serious? Greater things than what He has done? That *is*
what He says.

OK, how? Can we just speak the words that Jesus spoke, and the
same results will follow? Anyone out there care to speak to the wind outside to be calm and believe that it will? Anyone out there care to speak
to one around you with an affliction, believing that it will go away?

How did Jesus speak? Was it the words He used? Would He teach us some mystical phrases? Was there some secret code He used that He would reveal to us? A formula, perhaps, that we could learn?

No. The power and the authority come not in the correct recitation of the words, nor in repetition of phrase, nor in anything mystical. The power comes in learning not how to say, but in learning how to pray. The power comes from above, from the Creator of all that is, and for you and me to tap into this power, we must submit to the Giver of this power.

We are instructed in Romans 12:2, "Do not conform to the pattern of this world, but be transformed by the renewing of your mind. Then you will be able to test and approve what God's will is—his good, pleasing and perfect will."

What did Jesus say...ask in His name? Do you think asking in His name relates to asking according to God's will? There is no question about that.

So, the disciples had watched as authority and power flowed out of their Master and Friend—Jesus—day after day after day. Then, "One day Jesus was praying in a certain place. When he finished, one of his disciples said to him, 'Lord, teach us to pray, just as John taught his disciples'" (Luke 11:1).

Jesus's prayer that follows is what we call the Lord's Prayer. However, before that, Jesus had been giving instruction about praying and giving. Matthew 6:1–4 says the following:

"Be careful not to practice your righteousness in front of others to be seen by them. If you do, you will have no reward from your Father in heaven. So when you give to the needy, do not announce it with trumpets, as the hypocrites do in the synagogues and on the streets, to be honored by others. Truly I tell you, they have received their reward in full. But when you give to the needy, do not let your left hand know what your right hand is doing, so that your giving may be in secret. Then your Father, who sees what is done in secret, will reward you."

Isn't it in our nature to want others to know when we help someone? Don't we want some recognition when we "sacrifice" for others? Truth be known, we like certificates, plaques, trophies, accolades.

Schools, hospitals, cities, streets, buildings, and so on, are named for folks because of monies they have given or deeds they have done. Now, the point isn't about what others do in honor of someone who has given. The point is about you and me and how we give. Do you give in hopes that the camera is rolling, or do you give as anonymously as you can so as not to draw attention to yourself? In other words, do you give in your name, or do you give in the name of Jesus, and in the same way He gives? Matthew 6:5–8 says the following:

"And when you pray, do not be like the hypocrites, for they love to pray standing in the synagogues and on the street corners to be seen by others. Truly I tell you, they have received their reward in full. But when you pray, go into your room, close the door and pray to your Father, who is unseen. Then your Father, who sees what is done in secret, will reward you. And when you pray, do not keep on babbling like pagans, for they think they will be heard because of their many words. Do not be like them, for your Father knows what you need before you ask him."

So much around us is vain repetition, idle chatter. Just listen to talk radio or sports radio. You leave a particular program, come back after thirty minutes, and guess what: they are oftentimes still on the same point, and nothing new.

Say it long, say it loud, say it over and over again in our world, and many will believe. But those who will follow Jesus must learn that it is not in saying it long, not in saying it loud, not in saying it repetitiously; it is about our learning to pray after our Lord Jesus, and in His Name. Just as the disciples, who were with Jesus continually, needed to learn how to pray, so much more do you and I.

The Lord's prayer—sixty-six words, as recorded here—has been spoken countless times, individually, congregationally. There are millions who have spoken it, but how many have actually prayed it? Millions? Thousands? Hundreds?

Jesus said, "This, then, is how you should pray: Our Father in heaven, Hallowed be Your name" (Matt. 6:9**).

Who is our Father? He is God. He is the Lord Most High. He is the one who created you, first of all, in His mind, and then in your mother's womb.

He knew that He would love you—*no matter what.*

He is the one who knew everything about you before you drew your first breath.

He knew He would love you—*no matter what.*

He knew beforehand what you would be good at and what would cause you problems.

He knew that He would love you—*no matter what.*

He knew whether you would reject Him or whether you would trust Him.

He knew He would love you—*no matter what.*

The word *Father* may conjure up for you negative images of an earthly one who was not loving, not kind, not protective, and not forgiving as our Heavenly Father is. It may bring up memories of abuse, of laziness, of apathy—all unlike our Heavenly Father. It may be hard for you to see anything good in the concept of Father.

But Jesus wasn't putting before us any Father, wasn't praying to any Father, but only to His heavenly Father—to our heavenly Father. Our focus is to be on the one and only heavenly Father. For Jesus to refer to our heavenly Father isn't to place Him far away in heaven—He is as near as the air we breathe, as close as we want Him to be. Jesus identifies our Father with perfection, because heaven is a perfect place. It is a perfect home, where all those whose trust is in the Lord will reside for all eternity.

Our Father symbolizes authority over all His children. Our Father symbolizes love for each and every one of His children.

Just think, "Yet to all who did receive him, to those who believed in his name, he gave the right to become children of God—children born not of natural descent, nor of human decision, or a husband's will, but born of God" (John 1:12–13).

So, as His children, we are then assured in Romans 8:17 "we are heirs—heirs of God and co-heirs with Christ." Jesus would share all the glories of heaven with you and me? Well, He only gave all He had for you and me on the cross! How much more can the Father love us than by giving us His Son to take our place on the cross and then opening up all of heaven for us to enjoy for all eternity.

Prayer, however, is not a way to cash in on God's goodness, as if He were some sugar daddy to bail us out. Neither is prayer a means to activate God—He is always active, sustaining our lives continually.

Could we ever mine the depths of all the wonders of prayer? Could we ever fully appreciate what a privilege it is to have an audience with the living God, to have communion with Almighty God?

We are urged to pray without ceasing, to pray in everything. Of course, that doesn't mean we do nothing all day long but stay on our knees praying. We have responsibilities, jobs, duties.

But it does mean that we commune with our heavenly Father all throughout the day about what we can praise Him for, about needs around us, hurts around us, opportunities around us, and in everything, we are to look for God to be glorified. Our purpose in life is not that we be honored or glorified; it is that God be glorified through you and me.

And, He is our Father, for each and every one who is trusting in the Lord Jesus—no matter what you look like; no matter in what country you were born; no matter what your family history is; no matter what your educational level; no matter what sins you have committed... if you are putting your trust in the Lord Jesus for your salvation, then you can pray our Father.

"Said the robin to the sparrow, I really would like to know why those anxious human beings rush around and worry so.

Said the sparrow to the robin, I think it surely must be that they have no heavenly Father, who watches over you and me."

153

Jesus then teaches us about God's name, "Hallowed be Your name" (Matt. 6:9b**). We are to have respect and reverence for God's name. One of the Ten Commandments is not to misuse God's name. Sadly, and to our harm, God's name is misused more and more in our society. How often do you hear God's name used in vain? How often do you hear and see OMG? I don't think that folks are intending to be disrespectful oftentimes, but nevertheless, it is exactly that—disrespectful and misuse. You see, names have meanings. My name Larry means victorious, so one of my favorite verses is "But thanks be to God! He gives us the victory through our Lord Jesus Christ" (1 Cor. 15:57).

Jesus means "the Lord saves." Immanuel means "God with us." We are told in Hebrews 1:3 "The Son is the radiance of God's glory and the exact representation of his being." The majestic, powerful, all-knowing God of all creation is who our heavenly Father is, and Jesus makes that known to us so that we will have the proper image and proper respect. Jesus said, "I and the Father are one" (John 10:30). As we know Jesus, we know our Heavenly Father.

"Those who know your name put their trust in you, for you, Lord, have never forsaken those who seek you" (Ps. 9:10). "Some trust in chariots and some in horses, but we trust in the Name of the Lord our God" (Ps. 20:7).

So, in order for God's name to be hallowed, as we pray, we must submit to our Father—our heavenly Father—seeking His kingdom and His righteousness first. Jesus said that if anyone will come after Him and follow Him, we must deny self, and trust that all the things we need will be added. For God's name to be hallowed, He would have us know Him for who He really is.

"Your kingdom come, Your will be done on earth as it is in heaven" (Matt. 6:10**). There are natural laws that are constantly in effect all around us—put in place by our Creator. His laws govern the universe with absolute authority. But there is a spiritual kingdom, unseen, that is at work all around us, as well. Jesus taught from the outset, and all throughout His ministry, that the kingdom of God was at hand. If we truly want to serve the Lord, we pray for His kingdom to come in us and through us. It would be easier to pray that His kingdom go, in the sense that others go out to far-away places to establish His kingdom. But He calls you and me to establish His kingdom wherever we are. He calls us to obedience.

The story is told of a man whose faithful dog had died a few moments earlier in a great forest fire because he would not desert his master's dinner pail, which he had been told to watch. With tears running down his face, the old man said, "I always had to be careful what I told him to do, cause I know he'd do it."

One of the most effective preachers ever was Jonathan Edwards who said this: "I go out to preach with two propositions in mind. First, every person ought to give his life to Christ. Second, whether or not anyone else gives Him his life, I will give Him mine."

That is what our heavenly Father should be able to say about me and you. Here am I, Lord God, send me. Your name be glorified; Your kingdom come. Your will be done in me and through me on earth as it is in heaven. This is to be like Jesus, to do the things that Jesus did, to love the people that Jesus loved, to serve the heavenly Father that Jesus served.

Now, having honored God by recognizing our rightful place in submission to His will, Jesus taught us to bring our petitions before Him. What are the things we need most? Provision, forgiveness, and deliverance. "Give us this day our daily bread. And forgive us our debts, as we forgive our debtors. And do not lead us into temptation, But deliver us from the evil one" (Matt. 6:11-13**).

First of all, do we not need food in order to survive? Jesus understood the need for food, and provided food enough for thousands on the hillside when they were hungry; provided breakfast for his disciples by the seashore before He ascended to heaven. Our Father made our bodies, and He wants us to bring before Him our needs, our concerns for physical well-being. Has He not provided what you need so that you would have life and continue life? And remember, when Jesus gave thanks for the Father's provision to feed the multitudes, He gave thanks for what they could not see, for all that was apparent were five loaves and two fishes. Yet, they all ate until full, and there were leftovers. Our heavenly Father is our provision.

Forgiveness, one of the many realities that sets Christianity apart from other religions. Jesus taught us to pray for forgiveness, as He taught us to forgive others. It isn't that God withholds His forgiveness until we forgive others, it is that until we are forgiving others, we are not ready to receive God's forgiveness. An unforgiving spirit puts an resistant roof over our heads to block the forgiveness pouring down from our heavenly Father, already appropriated at Calvary through the shed blood of Jesus. You see, a clenched fist is not open to receive any gift, let alone the divine gift of forgiveness.

If forgiveness of another is a problem for you, remember that Jesus prayed for the Father's forgiveness for even those who betrayed Him and nailed Him to the cross. "'It is mine to avenge; I will repay', says the Lord" (Rom. 12:19). Just remember, you are not God. Don't you think it is worth not holding others' sins against them in order for you to be able to receive God's forgiveness of your own sins?

And, now, lead us not into temptation, but deliver us from evil. The evil one, Satan, knows our weaknesses. What my weaknesses are may not be yours at all, and vice versa. We must pray that ever how we are prone to be tempted, that God will lead us away from that temptation. Temptation so often grows from our thought pattern. Our thoughts are not to be taken lightly, not to be played with. We are taught as children not to play with fire, but then how often as adults we do exactly that. We allow those thoughts to creep in without praying for God's Spirit to remove them.

It can be said that we watch out for where we are weak, but not so much where we are strong. We take chances on our strengths—take Samson, for example. We allow ourselves to be in the company of those who would lead us down the wrong path instead of praying for the strength to stay away. We allow ourselves a taste of that which will deaden our will to follow the Lord, instead of praying for God's power to resist. We should know by now that Satan is called a roaring lion, seeking to devour those who will not resist him in the name of Jesus. What did Jesus do when tempted? He stood strong on God's Word, God's truth, which sets us free from the temptation. He did not do battle on earthly terms, He brought heaven down to combat the enemy. We are all in danger of falling to temptation, and our only hope for victory is in the Lord's power. And, when God delivers us, we gain new strength in Him. "I can do everything through him who gives me strength" (Phil.4:13*).

And Jesus closed with, "For Yours is the kingdom and the power and the glory forever. Amen" (Matt. 6:13b**).

You and I have come from the Creator of all that is, and you and I will each stand before Him one day to give account of ourselves. Are you trusting in the only one who can give you hope and salvation... Jesus, the Christ; Jesus, God's only Son; Jesus, the perfect sacrifice; Jesus, the Way, the Truth, the Life?

Or, are you trusting in anything else to save your soul? God forbid!

Would you trust in the only one who can save you?

The only one that our loving Heavenly Father sent to lead you home?

Would you trust in Jesus, the Christ?

"To him who is able to keep you from stumbling and to present you before his glorious presence without fault and with great joy—to the only God our Savior be glory, majesty, power and authority, through Jesus Christ our Lord, before all ages, now and forevermore! Amen" (Jude 24).

Thank You, Heavenly Father, for Jesus's teaching us to pray and how to pray. I pray for the one reading this to submit to You and experience Your love, protection, and deliverance. In the name of Your perfect Son Jesus. Amen.

New and Improved

"I, the Lord, do not change" (Mal. 3:6).

*H*ow do we express that something has been changed and
gotten better?

New, Improved, Plus, Later Generation, Ultra, Advanced Formula,
II, III, Super, Coming Soon, Under Wraps, In Development, Super-
charged, Turboboost, XL, Magna.

What is good today probably will be outdated and replaced
tomorrow. The first computer and printer I bought for our business
took up a lot of room and cost several thousand dollars. Now, computers are much smaller, much faster, and cost much less. New and
improved, right?

Anybody remember the bag phone? I had one—about the size of
that fish that got away. Most of us have replaced our cell phones, several
times—with new and improved ones, right?

Anyone remember roll-up windows in the car? Now, you could
argue that there is too much electronic stuff—and I would agree, but
cars are new and improved in many ways.

Anyone remember washing dishes in the sink and drying them by
hand? How about stoves with coal or wood for heat instead of electricity
or gas? What about before electric hair dryers when you dried your hair
with a towel or just let it drip dry?

Do you remember a time before indoor plumbing? New and
improved over trekking out to the outhouse in the frigid cold, huh?

My Grandmother, who was born in 1898, recalled a time before automobiles, before air travel, before television.

Are all these things improvements? They certainly are advancements, and can be used to help us, can't they? But, just because something is new and improved, it isn't necessarily better, is it? Better in what regard?

Our cars and trucks have many electronic options that will do different things. Many of them I don't use because I like to control these manually. Don't misunderstand me...I don't want to roll the windows up again. I also don't want to have to get up and turn the knob on the TV. Anyone remember television when there were three stations, and you had to get up to change the station? So, today we have hundreds of stations available—how many do you actually watch? How many are of any benefit to you or your family?

In our business, we talk about features versus benefits. Features describe what a particular product looks like or does. For example, several features of a particular writing pen are a removable cap, a clip for your pocket, and black ink. Those may or may not be benefits to the user. If you wanted to write in red ink, then the feature of black ink is of no benefit to you. If you wanted to use the pen with one hand only, then the feature of removable cap may not be a benefit to you. If you were not going to put it in a shirt pocket, then the clip might not be a benefit to you.

Some shoes have steel toes as a feature, but that wouldn't be a benefit to you unless your feet needed protection around machinery, for example.

One feature of the coffee urn we use is that it makes a lot of cups of coffee. That is a benefit here because we have a lot of takers. It wouldn't be a benefit at all to someone who doesn't drink coffee, would it?

Many products are sold, particularly in this country, because of new and improved features, not necessarily because of new and improved benefits.

Cell phones are a prime example. Look at the marketing campaigns—what do they focus on? Appearance, slimness, color, speed. There may be some benefit in these, but mostly it is about features, which may not be beneficial to you.

How about relationships? What about hanging out with a particular person or group of persons? A feature of hanging out with one group is that you probably are going to get into something that is no good for you or them—not beneficial.

A feature of hanging out with another group is you probably will go to church or Bible study—beneficial.

A feature of hanging out with one particular person is he or she regularly put others down—makes fun of them—not beneficial.

A feature of hanging out with someone else is he or she regularly thinks of others before himself or herself—beneficial.

Look at your life. If a biography of your life were written, what would the features be, the facts? Would there be benefits to others through your life? Are there benefits to hanging out with the Lord Jesus? "I have come that they may have life, and have it to the full," He said in John 10:10.

Is there anything that cannot be improved? I suppose an argument could be made that whatever man produces or manufactures can always be improved. No matter how good you get to be at something, there is always room for improvement, isn't there? Just when you thought you had seen the highest level of accomplishment in a particular sport, along comes one who takes it to a new level.

Just orbiting the earth was once the latest in space exploration; now we have been to the moon and way beyond. Once, the latest technology was a party-line telephone, through which folks in several different houses could receive calls over the same line—each having a unique ring. Now, people communicate from one side of the globe to the other through a miniature device with no wires connected, held in their hand.

Things are changing fast in our world. Much is being touted as better. Much is touted as making our lives better. Much is touted as making us better persons, even. Is there anything that needs no improvement?

In other words, is there anything that is perfect? We misuse the word *perfect* constantly.

Watch home improvement shows, and listen to how many times a room or some feature of the room is "perfect." There was even a computer software named Word Perfect. It wasn't.

Perfection not only needs no improvement. It *cannot* be improved. "Every good and perfect gift is from above, coming down from the Father of the heavenly lights, who does not change like shifting shadows" (James 1:17).

Perfection never changes.

Perfection never needs a facelift.

Perfection never needs development.

Perfection is never outdated.

Perfection never needs replacing.

There is no such thing as Perfection Plus.

There is no Ultra Perfection, or Advanced Perfection.

Perfection, Generation III—nope.

Perfection is the end all, be all. *Jesus* is Perfection – with no imperfection. "the Son, who has been made perfect forever." "and, once made perfect, he became the source of eternal salvation for all who obey him" (Heb. 7:28, 5:9). "Jesus Christ is the same yesterday and today and forever" (Heb. 13:8). There is no improving upon the one who is perfect.

He is perfect in love. In fact, beside the definition of love, is the picture of Jesus who is love. "God is love...perfect love drives out fear" (1 John 4:16, 18). He is perfect in truth. In fact, He is truth. He is perfect in every way.

There is one gospel—one good news, found in 1 Corinthians 15:3–4. This is it: Jesus the Christ died for our sins according to the Scriptures; He was buried; He was raised on the third day according to the Scriptures. There has never been, nor will there ever be, anyone else who is perfect; nor will die for our sins; nor will be buried to be raised again to conquer death.

There is one gospel—one Good News—it is all wrapped up in Jesus the Christ. This good news cannot be improved upon. It is timeless. It is the salvation of all who believed back then. It is the salvation of all who believe right now. It is the salvation of all who will believe at any time to come.

Don't we long for security? For that on which we count? Do you get weary of things always changing? Does it keep you off balance when people around you are changing, and not for the best?

Do you sometimes just long for stability—being able to count on some consistency, some normalcy around you? Don't we long for the important things in life to remain the same? The ones we love to always be with us? It will not be, will it?

Don't we long for security in our homes, our families, our finances, our health? We have seen so much of that security erode in recent years, haven't we? There is no new and improved product in this world that will provide security in these areas for very long. But there is Jesus, the real security provider—the eternal security provider. He is the same yesterday, today, and tomorrow. "I the Lord do not change" (Mal. 3:6).

He is the only one on whom you can depend, year in–year out; day in–day out; hour in–hour out; minute in–minute out.

Time is relative, isn't it? Have you ever had a year that just flew by; an hour that just seemed like a moment; a moment that seemed like an eternity? He holds the key to your life, your health, your past, your present, your future, your security.

When many of Jesus's followers were falling away, and Jesus asked His closest friends if they wanted to leave Him, too, here is what Simon Peter said, "Lord, to whom shall we go? You have the words of eternal life. We have come to believe and to know that you are the Holy One of God" (John 6:68–69).

The old saying goes, "Nothing is sure in this life except death and taxes." While there is an element of truth in that statement, and perhaps it looms large over us when we making funeral arrangements for a loved one, or going over tax records in April, the greater Truth is this: Jesus is sure. Jesus is surely the Lord of lords and the King of kings. Jesus is surely the Savior of each and every one who calls on His name.

He is the only one who can give you security in forgiveness for your sins—past, present, and future; security in purpose for your life in the present; security in His presence for the future.

Jesus is perfect in His love for you. He has done all He can. He was nailed to a cross for you. The death He died was meant for you and me because we are the ones who sinned, and the wages of sin is death.

If you are looking for the latest and greatest, if you are looking for the best the world has to offer, if you are looking for peace and contentment in this world, you will be disappointed, let down, and empty.

But, if you seek the perfect one, you will find Him, and in Him, you will find forgiveness, purpose, peace, and eternal life—He is Jesus. He cannot be improved upon, but you can. And He is the one to do it.

"Therefore, if anyone is in Christ, he is a new creation. The old has gone, the new has come! All this is from God, who reconciled us to himself through Christ" (2 Cor. 5:17*).

There is New and Improved...You, in Christ Jesus!

O Lord God, our perfect Father, thank You for Your perfect Son Jesus giving all for imperfect us. I pray for the one reading this to trust You to improve her or him, to give her or him new life through rebirth by the power of Your Spirit. In the name of Jesus, the New Life Giver. Amen.

New Beginnings

*H*ave you ever been betrayed? Could that have been a new beginning?

Have you ever been sold into slavery? Could that have been a new beginning?

Have you ever been seduced by one who was married to another? Have you resisted that temptation, only to be falsely accused even so? Could that have been a new beginning?

Have you ever been put in prison for something you didn't do? Could that have been a new beginning?

All the above happened to Joseph. How did Joseph respond? More importantly, what was God's response toward Joseph and through Joseph in all this?

In Genesis 37, we read about Jacob who was the father of twelve sons but loved Joseph more than all the others. He even had a richly ornamented robe made for him. Recipe for dysfunction, huh? Why did Jacob favor Joseph? Because he favored Jacob's mother over his other wife. You see, Joseph was the firstborn of Rachel, the woman for whom Jacob had worked fourteen years in order to marry, and Joseph was born to him in his old age.

We are told that Joseph's brothers hated him and could not speak a kind word to him. Joseph had dreams in which he envisioned his brothers bowing down to him, and they took it as though he intended to reign over them. Even Jacob rebuked his favorite son at the thought that he and his other sons would come and bow down on the ground before Joseph. Yet, in time, they would.

When Joseph was seventeen, Jacob sent him out to the fields to check on his brothers. They saw him coming at a distance and plotted to kill him. "Here comes that dreamer! Come now, let's kill him and throw him into one of these cisterns and say that a ferocious animal devoured him. Then we'll see what becomes of his dreams" (Gen. 37:19-20).

Now, Reuben's intention was to rescue Joseph and take him back to his father. But instead, the others stripped him of his robe—the richly ornamented one—and threw him into a cistern, which was empty. Apparently, not too disturbed by what they had done, they sat down to eat their meal. It was then that they saw a caravan of Ishmaelites approaching, who were on their way down to Egypt to trade.

Judah spoke up and questioned what they would gain if they killed him. "What will we gain if we kill our brother and cover up his blood? Come, let's sell him to the Ishmaelites and not lay our hands on him; after all, he is our brother, our own flesh and blood. His brothers agreed" (Gen. 37:26-27). How's that for some brotherly love?

So they pulled him out of the cistern and sold him for twenty shekels of silver. I wonder what that all looked like...Hey, can we interest you in this spare brother we don't need? He goes cheap.

What did they do with Joseph's robe? They slaughtered a goat, and dipped the coat in the goat's blood; took it back to their father, saying "We found this. Examine it to see whether it is your son's robe" (Gen. 37:32). They didn't say that Joseph had been killed, but they knew what Jacob would conclude. Jacob put on sackcloth and mourned many days for his son, who by now was sold in Egypt to Potiphar, the captain of the Pharaoh's guard.

So, what has happened? Joseph was betrayed by his brothers. Was God with him even so? Joseph was sold into slavery or who knows what. Was God with him even so? Was this the end of the story, or could this be a new beginning? Scripture tells us that, indeed, it was a new beginning.

"The Lord was with Joseph so that he prospered, and he lived in the house of his Egyptian master. When his master saw that the Lord was with him and that the Lord gave him success in everything he did, Joseph found favor in his eyes and became his attendant. Potiphar put him in charge of his household, and he entrusted to his care everything he owned…So Potiphar left everything he had in Joseph's care; with Joseph in charge, he did not concern himself with anything except the food he ate" (Gen. 39:2-4, 6).

All seemed to be going pretty well, but the next test was coming. "Now Joseph was well built and handsome, and after a while his master's wife took notice of Joseph and said, 'Come to bed with me!'" (Gen. 39:6-7). What did Joseph do? He refused. He stayed faithful to his heavenly Master and to his earthly master.

"But he refused. 'With me in charge,' he told her, 'my master does not concern himself with anything in the house; everything he owns he has entrusted to my care. No one is greater in this house than I am. My master has withheld nothing from me except you, because you are is wife. How then could I do such a wicked thing and sin against God?'" (Gen. 39:8-9).

Now, that should take care of that, right. Wrong! She tempted him day after day, and still he refused to go to bed with her, but that is not all—he refused to even be with her. There is a great lesson for you and me regarding temptation—get away from it. Flee from it. You and I are not strong enough to resist the temptation, but if we refuse to put ourselves in that situation, God will provide the way for our escape.

So, all good for Joseph now, right? Wrong!

Now came the accusation—she cried rape—falsely. She had grabbed his cloak as he ran out of the house and claimed that he had come on to her to make sport of her. Did the master believe her? Of course he did, and now Joseph, who did nothing wrong, who obeyed his earthly master and his heavenly Master, was thrown into prison. How would you overcome that? How do you make a new beginning of that?

The Lord was with him; He showed him kindness and granted him favor in the eyes of the prison warden. The Lord was with Joseph and gave him success in whatever he did. He was put in charge of all the prisoners and everything that was done there.

In Genesis 40, we see that the cupbearer and the baker each offended the king of Egypt, and wound up in the same prison, and each were assigned to Joseph. After they had been there for a while, each had a dream—on the same night. Joseph noticed the next morning that they were dejected, so he asked them what was wrong. They were sad because no one could tell them what their dreams meant.

You know what Joseph said: "Do not interpretations belong to God? Tell me your dreams." So the chief cupbearer told Joseph his dream, and Joseph gave him the interpretation that he would be restored to Pharaoh's service. Joseph asked the cupbearer to remember him to Pharaoh so he could get out of prison because he was, after all, innocent.

Well, the chief baker saw that Joseph had given a favorable interpretation to the cupbearer, so he wanted to learn what his dream meant. However, it was not so good for him because he would be hanged. (vv. 16–19). All came to pass, exactly as Joseph said, with the cupbearer being restored to his position and the baker being hanged. Yet, surprisingly, the chief cupbearer, who had promised to remember Joseph, did not remember Joseph, but forgot him. What about when someone promises to do you good—even to rescue you and then forgets? Had God forgotten about Joseph? How could this be a new beginning?

About two years later, Pharaoh had a dream, and no wise men of Egypt, no magicians, no one could interpret his dream. Now guess who remembered someone who could? The cupbearer told Pharaoh about a young Hebrew who did interpret dreams, and things turned out exactly as he interpreted. So Pharaoh sent for Joseph, and told him about his dream and that no one was able to interpret it, but that he had heard Joseph could.

"'I cannot do it,' Joseph replied to Pharaoh, 'but God will give Pharaoh the answer he desires'" (Gen. 41:16). Joseph heard Pharaoh tell of two dreams, which were actually one and the same.

God had revealed to Pharaoh what He was about to do. There would be seven years of abundance followed by seven years of famine—severe famine. Pharaoh should put someone in charge to store up 20 percent of the harvest during the seven good years and hold it in reserve. Pharaoh reasoned that since God had revealed all this to Joseph, and since he clearly was superior in wisdom and discernment, he was to be the one put in charge. And, so he was made second in command over all Egypt. "I am Pharaoh, but without your word no one will lift hand or foot in all Egypt" (Gen. 41:44). Joseph was thirty years old.

There were then seven years of abundance; Joseph collected food and stored it in the cities, huge quantities like the sand of the sea, so much that he stopped keeping records because it was beyond measure. During this time, two sons were born to him, Manasseh (perhaps meaning forget, as in all his troubles and all his father's household) and Ephraim. The abundance came to an end, and then the famine set in, not just in Egypt, but in all the countries, who then came to Egypt to buy food.

Now, Jacob learned that there was food in Egypt so he sent ten sons (keeping Benjamin, Joseph's younger brother, behind) to go buy food that they would not die. Unbeknownst to them, this was the first of three journeys they would make until their family would be reunited. Well, when they arrived, the one who would sell the grain to them was Joseph, the brother they would not now recognize. It had been over twenty years, and his appearance as an Egyptian man would have been greatly different than the Hebrew teenager. They bowed down to him with their faces to the ground—sound familiar? And he began to question them. He recognized them but spoke to them through an interpreter. He tested them to learn if his father and brother were still alive. He threatened to keep them all imprisoned—but one—who would go back and return with their youngest brother to verify their story. He turned away from them and began to weep. Finally, he kept Simeon and sent the others on their way loaded down with all the silver they had brought as gifts, as well as, provisions for the journey.

When they told Jacob what had happened, he lamented that now he had lost another son, Simeon, and would lose Benjamin if they took him to Egypt. He was believing that everything was against him. But, that wasn't so, was it?

So, Judah took personal responsibility for Benjamin, and Jacob finally relented. He made them take double the amount of silver this time plus the best products that their land had to offer. When they arrived back in Egypt, and Joseph saw Benjamin, he ordered them be taken to his house—not to seize them, as they thought—but to share of his bounty with them. Their meeting was interrupted by Joseph's hurrying out to look for a place to weep. After washing his face and collecting himself, he joined them.

Ultimately, Joseph made everyone leave except his brothers, and then he revealed himself to them. He wept so loudly that the Egyptians outside heard him, and word got back to Pharaoh.

His brothers were terrified. The consequence of our sin does terrify us sometimes, doesn't it?

Genesis 45:4–8 continues the story: Joseph's new beginning in the face of trial and tribulation ultimately meant new beginnings for his father, his brothers, and their families.

Even Pharaoh stepped in to provide carts and donkeys loaded down with the best Egypt had to offer for their journey. And, he promised them the best land in Goshen when they returned to settle down.

What was the news to Jacob?

"Joseph is still alive! In fact, he is ruler of all Egypt. Jacob was stunned; he did not believe them. But when they told him everything Joseph had said to them, and when he saw the carts Joseph had sent to carry him back, the spirit of their father Jacob revived. And Israel said, 'I'm convinced! My son Joseph is still alive. I will go see him before I die'" (Gen. 45:26-28).

So, after all these years, they were reunited, and they embraced and wept for a long time.

Jacob lived in Egypt for seventeen years to the ripe old age of 147. Joseph had his father embalmed in the Egyptian custom, which took forty days, and mourning lasted for seventy days. Joseph asked Pharaoh for permission to take his father back to the land where Abraham, Sarah, Isaac, Rebekah, and Leah were all buried. And so it was. Now, the brothers had no small concern that since their father was now dead, how Joseph was going to treat them (Gen. 50:18–21).

God is in control. Satan is not in control. What Satan intends to do, and actually does through our sinful nature is not the final say. Joseph was shunned, betrayed, and sold into slavery. Those were not ends, but new beginnings according to God Who is always in control. Joseph was seduced, and he resisted the temptation only to find himself in prison for something he did not do. That was not the end, but a new beginning according to God who is in control. Joseph was separated from his family never to see them again, but that was not the end. There would be a new beginning according to God who is in control.

There would be a reunion with his father and his brothers, and most importantly, there would be reconciliation, sweet reconciliation because it is God who is in control. There would be provision for his family in the new land—not hunger and need, maybe even starvation—in the old land because it is God who is in control.

How can where you are right now be a new beginning? Circumstances don't control us unless we let them. God is still in control. He can make every circumstance, every difficulty, a new beginning if we will trust Him.

Ours is to trust in the almighty God who is in control. "And we know that in all things God works for the good of those who love him, who have been called according to His purpose" (Rom. 8:28).

So be it in your life, and mine, this day, as we pray, "But thanks be to God! He gives us the victory through our Lord Jesus Christ" (1 Cor. 15:57).

Thank You, O Lord our God, for being in control, and I pray for the one reading this—that in whatever is going on in her or his life, You show them how You make new beginnings out of the worst of circumstances. In the name of Jesus, the new beginning Savior. Amen.

Now, I see

John 9:1–41

"As he went along, he saw a man blind from birth" (John 9:1).

*T*his poor man couldn't see Jesus, but Jesus could see him. We are told that he had been born blind, and we are told later in this passage that he was a beggar. That was about the only way that a blind man could support himself in that day. We are taught that this man was not blind because his eyes are been damaged through disease or accident but instead was blind from being defective when born—making it all the more "impossible" that his sight could be gained.

"His disciples asked him, 'Rabbi, who sinned, this man or his parents, that he was born blind?'" (John 9:2). Many treated this man's condition as a theological problem. You see, the rabbis had put forth that where there is suffering, there is iniquity. Some thought that the unborn could sin in the womb, or that a soul might have sinned before it even existed. Some believed that terrible suffering would be the punishment for sin that the parents had committed. Jesus corrected their misconception.

Here is what Jesus said: "'Neither this man nor his parents sinned,' said Jesus, 'but this happened so that the works of God might be displayed in him'" (John 9:3). God's power would be made known through this man.

The cause of the man's blindness isn't the focus but instead what God could do about it. We can so easily become wrapped up in the whys of something happening. Many times, we will not know the whys. But, of this, we are assured: God is constantly working to do good to us and through us. Romans 8:28 says, "And we know that in all things God works for the good of those who love him, who have been called according to His purpose."

Every aspect of our lives, including suffering, is an opportunity for God's glory to be made known. "As long as it is day, we must do the work of him who sent me. Night is coming when no one can work. While I am in the world, I am the light of the world" (John 9:4-5). The presence of Jesus on the earth made it day, time to do God's work. We are to work while we can before it is too late, and the darkness of death comes. What opportunities you and I have to do good toward others, and after the example the Lord Jesus set for us, we should do it.

Jesus used various and unorthodox methods to heal folks—methods that were misunderstood, and even despised, by those who were blinded by their faithlessness. Healing of blindness, by the way, was one of the signs of the Messiah's coming.

"After saying this, he spit on the ground, made some mud with the saliva, and put it on the man's eyes" (John 9:6). Mud made with spit? Really? The miracle of giving sight to the blind should be accompanied by lightning, thunder, or some impressive display of power, surely. Maybe some holy water bottled from the Jordan river? Or, if mud, how about from the Red Sea? Not ordinary dirt and spit. Besides, you would more likely think that mud would cause a seeing person to go blind than you would a blind person to see. But, if you were blind from birth, would you care what method Jesus used to give you sight?

The miracle is not in the mud; the miracle is not in the method—the miracle is in the Master.

'Twas battered and scarred,
And the auctioneer thought it hardly worth his while
To waste his time on the old violin,
But he held it up with a smile.

"What am I bid, good people" he cried,

172

"Who starts the bidding for me?
One dollar, one dollar, do I hear two? Two dollars, who
makes it three?
Three dollars once, three dollars twice, going for three."

But no, from the room far back a gray bearded man
Came forward and picked up the bow,
Then wiping the dust from the old violin and tightening up the strings,
He played a melody, pure and sweet as sweet as the angel sings.

The music ceased and the auctioneer
With a voice that was quiet and low,
Said, "What now am I bid for this old violin?"
As he held it aloft with its bow.

"One thousand, one thousand, Do I hear two?
Two thousand, who makes it three?
Three thousand once, three thousand twice,
Going and gone," said he.

The audience cheered, but some of them cried,
"We just don't understand.
What changed its' worth?"
Swift came the reply,

"The Touch of the Master's Hand."
From "The Old Violin, The Touch of the Master's Hand" by Myra
Brooks Welch

As Max Lucado said, "the same one who'd turned a stick into a
scepter, and a pebble into a missile, now turned saliva and mud into a
balm for the blind. Once again, the dull became divine, the humdrum
holy" (referencing Ex. 4; 1 Sam. 17).

"'Go,' he told him, 'wash in the Pool of Siloam' (this word means Sent). So the man went and washed, and came home seeing" (John 9:7).

Did Jesus involve the man in the healing process? Yes, the healing was not effected until he obeyed Jesus's command. Why do you think Jesus sent the man to wash in the pool before He healed him? Perhaps to affirm his obedience...the man obeyed and came home seeing.

What if he hadn't obeyed? Those who would be healed by Jesus must be ruled by Jesus. We receive God's power, His blessing, His healing, His guidance, when we act on faith, when we trust that God is telling the truth, and when we believe that God will do what He says He will do. Those who go to Jesus weak, come away strengthened; those who go to Jesus doubting, come away assured; those who go to Jesus blind, come away seeing.

Now, the story takes an interesting twist. This isn't just as simple as Jesus healing the blind man, nor is this the only lesson here. Everyone was rejoicing for this one now having sight for the first time in his life, right? Umm, not exactly.

"His neighbors and those who had formerly seen him begging asked, 'Isn't this the same man who used to sit and beg?' Some claimed that he was. Others said, 'No, he only looks like him.' But, he himself insisted, 'I am the man.' 'How then were your eyes opened,' they asked.

He replied, 'The man they call Jesus made some mud and put it on my eyes. He told me to go to Siloam and wash. So I went and washed, and then I could see.' 'Where is this man?' they asked him'...'I don't know,' he said'" (John 9:8-12).

Who did he say healed him? The man they call Jesus.

Is that where you are today? You believe there is a man they called Jesus. You believe that He did many wonderful works—maybe even miracles. But that is as far as you have gone. That is not enough.

"They brought to the Pharisees the man who had been blind" (John 9:13). Why? Probably not out of any sinister motive, but because something very unique had taken place, and these were the so-called experts on the workings of God. "Now the day on which Jesus had made the mud and opened the man's eyes was a Sabbath" (John 9:14). Uh-oh, did He forget? You know how those scribes and Pharisees are about the Sabbath. No work, no healing on the Sabbath. It would seem to be that Jesus was confronting them about their Sabbath understanding. Through their rules, no healing was to take place unless life-threatening—this wasn't life-threatening; no kneading was allowed—Jesus made mud; no journey of more than 2000 cubits (1000 yards)—to the pool and back was probably about 1300 yards.

By the way, this would have been a very public display, apparently intended by the Lord because there probably would have been a crowd around them when he placed the mud on the man's eyes; then, a guide would have escorted him through the city to the pool of Siloam, and more than likely spoken to many about what he doing. What does Jesus say to us about the Sabbath? "For the Son of Man is Lord of the Sabbath" (Matt. 12:8). "Therefore it is lawful to do good on the Sabbath" (Matt. 12:12). "The Sabbath was made for man, not man for the Sabbath. So the Son of Man is Lord even of the Sabbath" (Mark 2:27-28).

"Therefore, the Pharisees also asked him how he had received his sight. 'He put mud on my eyes,' the man replied, 'and I washed, and now I see'" (John 9:15). Simple statement of fact, isn't it?

"Some of the Pharisees said, 'This man is not from God, for he does not keep the Sabbath.' But others asked, 'How can a sinner do such miraculous signs?' So they were divided. Then they turned again to the blind man, 'What have you to say about him? It was your eyes he opened.' The man replied, 'He is a prophet'" (John 9:16-17).

Maybe it was said like, "I say He is a prophet," or "He certainly is a prophet." It is odd that they would even put this question to such a one as this, probably indicating their perplexity as to what to do. Remember, at first, he referred to the one who had given him sight as "the man they call Jesus." Now, he referred to him as a prophet. Wonder where he came up with that? Maybe he had seen more of His followers now.

Is that where you are today? You have heard of Jesus. You may believe He existed, and you may even suppose that He was some kind of prophet or great teacher. That is not enough.

The Pharisees not only rejected the man's opinion that Jesus is a prophet, but now they questioned whether he was ever really blind!

"They still did not believe that he had been blind and received his sight until they sent for the man's parents. 'Is this your son?' they asked. 'Is this the one you say was born blind? How is it that now he can see?'" (John 9:18). The parents state that he is their son, who was, indeed, born blind. But they refuse to speculate on how he gained his sight.

"'We know he is our son,' the parents answered, 'and we know he was born blind. But how he can see now, or who opened his eyes, we don't know. Ask him. He is of age; he will speak for himself'" (John 9:20-21). This seems to be an odd response, doesn't it? No celebratory tone about their son who was blind but now can see. No rejoicing here in this statement. In fact, what is evident is they are fearful of being excommunicated. They are not free to give thanks to God for this great thing He has done for their son. Their agony and guilt must have been great.

"His parents said this because they were afraid of the Jewish leaders, who already had decided that anyone who acknowledged that Jesus was the Messiah would be put out of the synagogue. That was why his parents said, 'He is of age; ask him'" (John 9:22-23). The Jewish leaders weren't really accomplishing much, were they? So, "A second time they summoned the man who had been blind. 'Give glory to God by telling the truth,' they said. 'We know this man is a sinner'" (John 9:24). This was not an invitation to praise God for His healing! They really didn't want the truth, they wanted him to confess his sin and then they wanted to undermine Jesus.

"He replied, 'whether he is a sinner or not, I don't know. One thing I do know. I was blind but now I see!" (John 9:25). No one can take away your testimony of what God has done for you.

"Then they asked him, 'What did he do to you? How did he open your eyes?' He answered, 'I have told you already, and you did not listen.

Why do you want to hear it again? Do you want to become his disciples, too?'" (John 9:26-27). He was giving indication that he was at least considering becoming a disciple of Jesus, wasn't he?

Is that where you are today? You have heard about Jesus. You believe that He is someone much greater than anyone else. You have seen what He has done in others' lives. You are considering becoming His follower. But that is not enough.

"Then they hurled insults at him and said, 'You are this fellow's disciple! We are disciples of Moses! We know that God spoke to Moses, but as for this fellow, we don't even know where he comes from.' The man answered, 'Now that is remarkable! You don't know where he comes from, yet he opened my eyes. We know that God does not listen to sinners. He listens to the godly man who does his will. Nobody has ever heard of opening the eyes of a man born blind. If this man were not from God, he could do nothing.' To this they replied, 'You were steeped in sin at birth; how dare you lecture us!' And they threw him out'" (John 9:28–34).

Who is blind now?

"Jesus heard that they had thrown him out, and when he found him, he said, 'Do you believe in the Son of Man?' 'Who is he, sir,' the man asked. 'Tell me so that I may believe in Him'" (John 9:35-36). Notice that it says "when He found him"—tells us that Jesus was looking for him, doesn't it?

He is looking for you, as well, so that you will put your trust in Him. "Son of Man" is the title Jesus often used for Himself, and equates to the one sent from heaven—the Messiah.

"Jesus said, 'You have now seen him; in fact, he is the one speaking with you.' Then the man said, 'Lord, I believe,' and he worshiped him. Jesus said, 'For judgment I have come into the world, so that the blind will see and those who see will become blind. Some Pharisees who were with him heard him say this and asked, 'What? Are we blind, too?' Jesus said, 'if you were blind, you would not be guilty of sin; but now that you claim you can see, your guilt remains'" (John 9:37-41).

You see, the sight they think they have (and really don't) must be taken from them if they are to receive true sight. They claim to see and therefore do not recognize their need for the only one who can give them sight.

In 1736, an eleven-year-old boy began life as a seaman on his father's ship. He eventually became captain of his own ship, which was a slave ship, traveling up and down the West African coast collecting slaves to sell to visiting traders. It was a cruel, heartless way of life. Twelve years later, he was convicted by the Holy Spirit that he was lost and needed the Savior. He was converted in a personal relationship with Jesus, the Christ. Eventually, he came to believe that what he was doing was inhumane and wrong. He became a strong and effective crusader *against* slavery. He eventually became a pastor, holding services even outside the walls of the Anglican church in any large building that was available. Shortly before his death, he said this, "My memory is nearly gone, but I remember two things: That I am a great sinner and that Christ is a great Savior." He also wrote hymns, probably the most famous of which says this:

"Amazing grace—how sweet the sound—that saved a wretch like me! I once was lost but now am found, was blind but now I see" (John Newton).

The blind man first knew Jesus by name only. That is not enough.

He then believed Jesus to be a prophet. That is not enough.

He then considered becoming a follower of Jesus. That is not enough.

Then he came to believe Jesus is Lord, and confessed Him before others with, "Lord, I believe, and he worshiped Him." That is enough.

Will you believe that Jesus is your Savior, and confess Him as your Lord?

O Lord God, thank You first of all for looking for us, and then upon finding us, giving us sight—spiritual sight—to believe in the Savior Jesus. Be it so, O Lord God for the reader of this message. In the name of Jesus, the Healer of all that ails us.

O HOLY MORN

O holy morn, the sun is brightly shining,
It is the dawn when our Savior arose.
The world now would see God's victory defining
That He is Lord o'er all heaven's foes.
He sent His Son to conquer death and sin,
The long-awaited Messiah, Holy One.
He paid the price, His life, our souls to win,
No other name but Jesus Christ has power to save, it's His alone;
Prince of peace, the great I Am, O Hallelujah, praise His name.

O blessed morn when we sing a brand new song,
No longer would our final breath be drawn in fear.
He was lifeless and alone, and lay entombed so long
That hope was gone for those ones He loved so dear;
But heaven's light began to pierce the darkness,
Father breathed new life into His Son.
Jesus is alive! Let all creation now confess
He's King of kings; He's Lord of lords; He came to save. His
work is done.
He's cleansed my soul, He makes me whole,
And I am His forevermore.

When I survey the blood-stained cross at Calvary
Where Jesus hung between heaven and earth,
How can it be that He gave Himself completely,
Filling my soul with the joy of heavenly worth?
O for a thousand tongues to sing His name,
Lamb of God Who shed His blood for me.
I fall on my knees, His righteousness I now proclaim!

He came to be The Way of Life and set us free, O Glory be,
His Kingdom come, His will be done through you and me eternally.
So, fall on your knees, His righteousness we now proclaim!
He came to be the Way of Life and set us free, O Glory be,
His Kingdom come, His will be done through you and me eternally.

Odds and Even

*H*ave you ever been at odds with someone? Are you at odds with someone right now? Things just aren't right between you. One of you offended the other; feelings are hurt. One of you betrayed the other; trust is broken. One of you rejected the other, perhaps, even without cause. One of you threw the other's kindness back in their face. One of you broke the relationship, and now, there is a gulf between you.

Being at odds with someone is a bad place to be. It is unsettling. It is worrisome.

Oh sure, you can deal with it; you've been there before. You have put it out of your mind, and you move on. It isn't the end of the world. But understand that being at odds with someone means no close relationship, in fact, no right relationship. Things are not evened out. The apple cart is upset. The books are out of balance. Things need to be made right.

Are you at odds with God? If you are, then you won't enter into His presence.

The truth is: on our own, every one of us is at odds with God. You might say, well how are we at odds with God? Well, what is God like?

God is Love

God is Good

God is Pure

God is Righteous

God is Forgiving

God is Protective

God is Compassionate

God is Merciful

God is Gracious

God is Perfect

Then, how can we be at odds with Him? What has caused this? Well, what are we like? Could it be our fault? Look at the attributes of a perfect God, and then answer that. Pretty clear, isn't it? God is not in the wrong. You and I are in the wrong.

You and I are the ones who have offended our heavenly Father.

You and I are the ones who have betrayed our heavenly Father.

You and I are the ones who have rejected our heavenly Father.

You and I are the ones who have thrown His kindness right back in His face.

You and I are the ones who have broken the relationship.

Romans 3:23 says it this way: "for all have sinned and fall short of the glory of God." Isaiah 53:6 says it this way: "We all, like sheep, have gone astray, each of us has turned to his own way, and the Lord has laid on him the iniquity of us all." Not one of us is righteous, not you, not me, not your mom.

Romans 3:10-12 says, "There is no one righteous, not even one; there is no one who understands; there is no one who seeks God. All have turned away, they have together become worthless; there is no one who does good, not even one." None of us, that is.

Even the apostle Paul confessed: "For I have the desire to do what is good, but I cannot carry it out. For I do not do the good I want to do, but the evil I do not want to do – this I keep on doing. ... What a wretched man I am! Who will rescue me from this body that is subject to death?" (Rom. 7:18-19, 24).

But there is one, and only one, righteous one—God's only Son, and He is the only one who is not at odds with the heavenly Father. In fact, not only is He not at odds with the heavenly Father, He is *even with,* in fact, *one with* the heavenly Father. He is in right relationship with the heavenly Father. He is the spirit and image of the heavenly Father.

Hebrews 1: 3: "The Son is the radiance of God's glory and the exact representation of his being."

Colossians 1:15: "The Son is the image of the invisible God."

John 10:30 records Jesus's words: "I and the Father are one."

He is even with—equal to—the heavenly Father. He is not at odds because He committed no sin. We are at odds because we did commit sin. We do commit sin. He is sinless. We are sinners.

The righteous heavenly Father cannot abide unrighteousness. He cannot abide sin. Therefore He cannot abide you and me in our unrighteousness and sinfulness. The only way that you and I can enter into God's presence is by becoming righteous. We can no more do that than we can transport ourselves to the moon by snapping our fingers. So, how could we ever be welcomed into the Father's presence? Let's look to Jesus, the sinless one.

He is the Way, and the Truth, and the Life, and not one of us comes to the Father except through Him (John 14:6). We need to be like Him, but really, *could* we ever be like Him? Maybe for a nanosecond, we could be like Him? Nah. On our own, we could not be like Jesus for any length of time or in any fashion. But, what if we committed only one or two sins? How many sins have you committed in your life? I'm well beyond one or two (in the last few minutes). The thing is—one sin—let alone multitudes of sins—means that we are not like Jesus. One sin—let alone multitudes of sins—means that we are at odds with the Father, and on our own, we would always be.

God the Father and God the Son knew this before they began all of creation. God knew that He would create you and me, and that we would disobey Him. He knew that you and I would break His commandments. He knew that you and I would be destined to an eternal hell, where all the disobedient ones would be cast. He would not have it that way. He would do something. And He did.

First Timothy 2:4-6 says it this way: "God our Savior, who wants all people to be saved and to come to a knowledge of the truth. For there is one God and one mediator between God and mankind, the man Christ

Jesus, who gave himself as a ransom for all people." Second Peter 3:9, this way: "The Lord is not slow in keeping his promise, as some understand slowness. Instead he is patient with you, not wanting anyone to perish, but everyone to come to repentance."

He had the plan already in place so that you and I could be reconciled to Him and welcomed into His presence. Reconciliation means in right relationship. The books are balanced. All is evened up. Nothing is at odds. But, in order to reconcile, the score has to be settled. The books have to be balanced. Nothing can be at odds. This is not something that you and I could ever do. We could never do enough, never have enough, or never be enough to bring reconciliation.

So, God called upon His Son to be the Mediator between Himself and man. A mediator brings resolution, reconciliation, and that is exactly what Jesus has done. It doesn't depend on us, for if it did, we would have no hope. It depended on Jesus, and He came through for you and me.

Romans 5:6, 8: "You see, at just the right time, when we were still powerless, Christ died for the ungodly...But God demonstrates his own love for us in this: While we were still sinners, Christ died for us." The godly for the ungodly. The sinless one for the sinful ones. No, you and I could never be righteous as Jesus is. But we can take upon ourselves the righteousness of Jesus. How? By placing our faith in Jesus's righteousness, the Father reckons us as righteous.

How can it be that our salvation comes through His crucifixion? How can it be that our life comes through His death? God's ways are not our ways. It was true for Abraham. It is true for you and me.

"Abraham believed God, and it was credited to him as righteousness" (Rom. 4:3). Do you believe God? What has God said that you just don't believe? He says He loves you—"For God so loved the world (you) that he gave his one and only Son, that whosoever (you) believes in him shall not perish but have eternal life" (John 3:16). Do you believe Him?

He says that He wants you to repent of your sins so you will not perish—"unless you repent, you too will all perish" (Luke 13:3). Do you believe Him?

He says that He wants you to come to a knowledge of the truth and be saved—"Then you will know the truth, and the truth will set you free...So, if the Son sets you free, you will be free indeed" (John 8:32, 36). Do you believe Him?

He says that He is preparing a place for you with Him for all eternity—"I am going to prepare a place for you. And if I go and prepare a place for you, I will come back and take you to be with me that you also may be where I am" (John 14:2–3). Do you believe Him?

He says that He created you to be in right relationship with Him, here and now, and eternally—"that God was reconciling the world to himself in Christ, not counting men's sins against them. ... Therefore, if anyone is in Christ, the new creation has come: The old has gone, the new has here! All this is from God, who reconciled us to himself through Christ" (2 Cor. 5:19, 17–18). Do you believe Him?

If so, why are you still at odds with your Creator? If you do not believe Him, then you need to understand that you make Him out to be a liar.

First John 5:10–12: "Whoever does not believe God has made him out to be a liar, because they have not believed the testimony God has given about his Son. And this is the testimony: God has given us eternal life, and this life is in His Son. Whoever has the Son has life; whoever does not have the Son of God does not have life."

The Father tells the truth, always. Satan is the liar, the father of lies (John 8:44). The one not to be trusted is the one who would destroy you, for all eternity—Satan. The one to be trusted is the one who would give His life for you, so that you can have eternal life. The one to be trusted is the one who came to earth to become like you and me in experiencing temptation, pain, rejection, loneliness, betrayal, judgment, and death, all far more than you and I ever face or experience.

The one to be trusted is the one, the only one, who can save you—Jesus, the Christ, Jesus, the Son of God. Jesus doesn't just even up the odds so we have a fighting chance. He overcomes all odds so that we don't just have a chance. We have *assurance* of forgiveness in Him, peace in Him, salvation in Him, new life in Him, everlasting life in Him. In Christ Jesus, we are no longer at odds with our Creator.

It is a beautiful place to be in the here and now, but nothing to be compared to what it will be like beyond this life—in an eternal place of no suffering, of no sin, of no sorrow, of no hatred.

That is what God offers to all who are at odds with Him—in other words, each and every one of us, apart from Jesus. But, joined together with Jesus, new life is ours—the old is gone, behold the new has come, for all who will surrender to the Lord Jesus and follow Him.

O Lord God, thank You that we don't have to be at odds with You. That is not how You want it to be, and You have done all You can to reconcile with us. I pray that this reader will no longer be at odds with You but instead be reconciled with You through Christ Jesus, the Great Reconciler. Amen.

On What Foundation Do You Stand?

*W*hat do you stand for? What are your roots? Are you firmly planted? Are you on solid ground? Or are you on shifting sand? Are you blown by the winds of opinion? Current philosophy? Are you firmly planted in God's Word? God's Truth? In Jesus?

Are you rooted in sand that shifts with the tide? Have you ever stood on the seashore and tried to plant yourself in one place? What happened as the tide rolled in? The sand gave way under your feet, and it became impossible to stay rooted there, didn't it? Ever feel like your life is like that? Just when you think you are anchored, the storms come and all of a sudden nothing seems secured.

Life is like that. This world is like that. Seems that hardly anything stays the same for very long, especially those things that we want to remain constant. I often lament about so many things changing, and changing so fast. My moaning and griping doesn't help a thing, by the way. How can we overcome this, or cope with it, because surely this world isn't going to accommodate us, isn't going to succumb to our wishes or demands. Where do find security? Solid rock security?

My wife and I had our house built many years ago, and it is built on solid rock—literally. We wanted it to have only a couple of steps up to the front door, but the builder called one day to let us know that they had dug down as far as they could—until they hit solid rock. If we wanted to go deeper, they would have to blast through the rock, which we opted not to do. So, we have a few more steps than originally planned, but we are sitting on solid rock. Now, that doesn't mean nothing can bring this house down, but it has stood strong for many years.

There is a more important truth paralleled here—the truth of a solid rock: The Solid Rock.

So, on whom can you rely? On what are you banking? Money in the walls of your house? Money in the bank? Your looks? Your strength? Your education? Your wits? Your family? Your spouse? What happens when these fail? What happens when these let you down? What happens when you are at your wit's end?

We can listen to others' opinions. It seems like everyone has one, whether sound or not.

I am reminded of a call-in show I heard one time, on which a controversial subject was being discussed. The host had invited comments from callers expressing their various viewpoints. However, he cut off one particular caller who began with what the Bible had to say about this subject. The host made clear that he only wanted to hear people's opinions and not what the Bible said.

Yet, what God has to say about anything is more important than what anyone else has to say. Sadly, no, tragically, that is the habit of the world, and of most individuals in the world, who would listen and adhere to opinions of others, that may not lead to truth and security. Some roads lead here, some roads lead there, some roads lead nowhere, but only one road—through Jesus—leads to the Truth.

Psalm 127:1 says "Unless the Lord builds the house, the builders labor in vain." What have you built, or what are you building, and is the Lord over the project? Jesus said:

"Therefore everyone who hears these words of mine and puts them into practice is like a wise man who built his house on the rock. The rain came down, the streams rose, the winds blew and beat against that house; yet it did not fall, because it had its foundation on the rock. But everyone who hears these words of mine and does not put them into practice is like a foolish man who built his house on sand. The rain came down, the stream rose, and the winds blew and beat against that house, and it fell with a great crash" (Matt. 7:24–27).

"Why do you call me Lord, Lord, and do not do what I say? As for everyone who comes to me and hears my words and puts them into practice, I will show what they are like. They are like a man building a house, who dug down deep and laid the foundation on rock. When a flood came, the torrent struck that house but could not shake it, because it was well built. But the one who hears my words and does not put them into practice is like a man who built his house on the ground without a foundation. The moment the torrent struck that house, it collapsed and its destruction was complete" (Luke 6:46–49).

If the Lord who created all that is, including you and me, isn't your anchor, your solid rock, your foundation, then you, my friend, build in vain. If your building materials are of your own making or any man's making, then, what you build will not last; what you build is only temporary. What you build is no match for Satan. It will be nothing more than a house of cards that will come crashing down when the storms blow hard enough. But you know that, don't you?

That is not what your heavenly Father desires for you. First Timothy 2:4 tells us "This is good, and pleases God our Savior, who wants all people to be saved and to come to a knowledge of the truth." Second Peter 3:9 tells us "He is patient with you, not wanting anyone to perish, but everyone to come to repentance."

He desires that you come to Him in repentance of your sinfulness—and we all have sinfulness; come to Him to be saved through His Son Jesus; come to Him and know the truth. Those who are anchored to the Lord God Almighty—the Solid Rock—will not perish.

One of the old hymns speaks it clearly: "On Christ the Solid Rock I stand. All other ground is sinking sand, all other ground is sinking sand. My hope is built on nothing less than Jesus's blood and righteousness. I dare not trust the sweetest frame, but wholly lean on Jesus name."

Did He who gave His life—suffering and dying in your place—not do enough for your consideration of Him, your belief in Him, your trust in Him, to be all you need when all else fails?

It would be best if you trusted in Him even when you have other options, and not when you are so far down that you have nowhere else to turn. But, either way, He waits with open arms to embrace you and to be the foundation for your life.

When He is your foundation—your Lord—then He is your Savior. It is then—that truly no matter what comes against you—your anchor in Him will hold. No matter what storms of life rage against you—and they will rage against you... no matter how the world tosses you about— and it will toss you about... Jesus will still be there to stand beside you, to hold you, to carry you through it all.

How do I know this? I know it because God says it to be so. That is enough. But I also know it because God has proven it in my life—that He keeps His promises. He will do the same for you. And, you see, He isn't the solid foundation just for the here and now. That would be great, but not enough, because we spend only a tiny speck of time in this life compared to the life to come. No, He is our foundation for all eternity. "For we know that if the earthly tent we live in is destroyed, we have a building from God, an eternal house in heaven, not built by human hands" (2 Cor. 5:1). "Trust in the Lord forever, for the Lord, the Lord himself, is the Rock eternal" (Is. 26:4).

What kind of house are you building? What kind of life are you building? Is your life based on, rooted in, your work? Nothing wrong with working hard; in fact, God instructs us to do just that—to observe the industry of the ant and emulate it.

Is your life based on, rooted in, your education? Nothing wrong with learning; in fact, God instructs us to study to show ourselves approved.

Is your life based on, rooted in, your family? Nothing wrong with family; in fact, God instructs us to honor, respect, and provide for our families.

But, is our salvation, our hope, and our security found in our family, our education, or our work? Isn't our salvation, our hope, our security really found in that which is not of this world? Who among us has a promise of our family's presence beyond this moment, or job security beyond this moment? Who among us will receive eternal security because of our educational level?

What we trust in ought to be more secure than shifting sand, shouldn't it?

There are many good things for us to love, work on, and delight in on this earth; however, there is only one solid Rock on which we can stand. He is Jesus. Anything else on which we stand will shift, give way, or go away...all but Jesus. He alone is our Rock, our Refuge, our Deliverer, our Fortress, and our Savior.

"I love you, O Lord, my strength. The Lord is my rock, my fortress, my deliverer; my God is my rock, in whom I take refuge. He is my shield and the horn of my salvation, my stronghold" (Ps. 18:1–2*).

Do you want false hope, or do you want real hope? Do you want to rely upon a house of cards, or on a fortress, a stronghold? Real hope is offered by Jesus—and Jesus alone. False hope is offered by all else.

Have you ever purchased a product or service only to find out it didn't live up to its billing? We all have, many times. That is the way of the world. Nothing this world offers will bring you the peace, the forgiveness, and the freedom that is offered you by Jesus Himself. And He is the only one who can offer it to you because He is the only one who has earned that right. What did it take for Him to earn that right? It was by giving all He had.

You see, He had it all. He was in the perfect place—heaven—with His Father and all the adoring heavenly hosts in His service. You see, He is "in very nature God." Yet, He gave all that up, setting aside His deity, "rather, he made himself nothing by taking the very nature of a servant, being made in human likeness. And being found in appearance as a man, he humbled himself by becoming obedient to death—even death on a cross!" (Phil. 2:6–8). Why would He do that for you? For me? Love. Love that has always been because He has always been. Love without end.

"As the Father has loved me, so have I loved you." "Greater love has no one than this: to lay down one's life for one's friends." Jesus tells us from John 15:9 and 13.

Are you His friend? You are if you claim Jesus as your Savior and follow Him as your Lord.

He doesn't ram anything down your throat. He doesn't pin you to the wall until you cry uncle. No, He allowed himself to be pinned to the wall—nailed to a tree, to die the most excruciating death imaginable, and all to save you. All so that you would ultimately have all you need and all that your heart deeply desires. We all need to be loved. We all need to be cared for. We all need to be included in a family of support and fellowship. God's family is like that.

In God's family, you are loved, cared for, supported, and secure. We are adopted by our heavenly Father into His eternal family because Jesus is the one leading the way, because He is the Way. There is no adoption into God's family apart from Jesus. He is the Way, the Truth, and the Life (John 14:6).

God's family is the solid rock family. It doesn't break up; it doesn't collapse, it doesn't fail, and it doesn't end. It is the family for all time.

It is your family if you choose Jesus. I pray that you do, and then you and I will spend eternity together with all God's family, anchored to the Solid Rock of Ages.

O Lord our God, we thank You that You await us to join your eternal family. We thank You that You are our Solid Rock in Christ Jesus, and I pray that the reader of this message will be anchored in nothing less that Jesus's blood and righteousness. In His blessed name. Amen.

Puffed Up or Praising Up

*W*hat do you do when others look up to you? Brag on your-self? Do you puff up with pride or do you praise up to the One who gives you life and being?

We have the opportunity every day to look within ourselves for whatever minute, temporal, earthly good we may find, or we have the opportunity every day to look outside ourselves and above to the eternal One, our Creator God, for great, eternal, heavenly good that He offers.

Puffed up or praising up, which is it to be? God's Word gives us clear examples of both.

Consider Pharaoh of Egypt. He was the most powerful human being of his day, with all the earthly reasons to be puffed up with pride. Yet, he had not the power to summon one iota of what he needed to stand against the power of Almighty God. But he tried.

Over and over, he was confronted by Moses and Aaron to let the Israelites go free from his slave-ownership of them. Over and over, his pride controlled his decisions. Pride leads to a hardened heart and dis-obedience. "Pharaoh's heart became hard; he would not listen to Moses and Aaron, just as the Lord had said" (Ex. 7:22).

Plague upon plague, tragedy upon tragedy, and finally Pharaoh gave in—for the moment. "During the night Pharaoh summoned Moses and Aaron and said, 'Up! Leave my people, you and the Israelites! Go, wor-ship the Lord as you have requested. Take your flocks and herds, as you have said, and go. And also bless me" (Ex.12:31–32).

But pride does not give way easily. It puffs us up in ways that lead us to believe we are in control of things that we are not. "When the king of Egypt was told that the people had fled, Pharaoh and his officials changed their minds about them and said, 'What have we done? We have let the Israelites go and have lost their services!' So he had his chariot made ready and took his army with him" (Ex.14:5–6).

The result? All Pharaoh's horses and chariots, horsemen and troops pursued the Israelites and perished in the Red Sea after the Lord had delivered His people safely across to the other side. Pharaoh shook his puny fist at the Lord Almighty, and all the glory he thought was his—all that he was puffed up about—was swallowed up that fateful day as the true glory of the Lord was revealed in delivering His people.

Now consider Joshua, who also had reason to be puffed up with pride. But his pride was not in himself nor his accomplishments, but in serving the Lord Almighty. He had survived servitude under the cruel taskmasters of this same Pharaoh in Egypt. He had crossed the Red Sea on dry ground as the Lord rescued His people from that very slavery. He then faithfully served as Moses's aide, accompanying him up the holy mountain when God gave Moses the commandment tablets. At Moses's command, he became a military leader, rounded up an army to fight the mighty Amalekites who had attacked them, and subsequently led his troops to victory.

As the representative of his tribe of Ephraim, he was one of the twelve spies sent by Moses to check out the land of Canaan, the land promised to them by the Lord. Ten of the twelve spoke fearfully of the obstacles that stood in their way, but Caleb and Joshua spoke confidently in the Lord and His will—that He would win the victories they would need to take over the land. Only those two of the twelve would eventually enter the Promised Land. Ultimately, Joshua would be chosen to take over for Moses after he died and to continue leadership of the Israelites.

Joshua demonstrated that his pride was not in himself, even though he may have had reason to be puffed up about many things. He showed that his pride was in trusting the Lord Almighty, in praising up the Lord Almighty, and in serving the Lord Almighty.

Finally, note the challenge he put to the people—same challenge for you and me today—to choose for themselves what or whom they would serve, "But as for me and my household, we will serve the Lord" (Josh. 24:15)—to the praise of the Lord Almighty!

Consider Nebuchadnezzar, king of Babylon. He was powerful, prideful, and puffed up. His armies had overrun Jerusalem and captured the best of the best among the Israelites. Now he would teach them the ways of the Babylonians. They would be his to mold and make them what he wanted them to be, just like all his other subjects. On his whim, he could summon all the magicians, the enchanters, the sorcerers, the astrologers—in other words, all the "wise men" at any time, for any reason. As he did when he had dreams which troubled him and kept him from sleep. He expected someone from among all these to interpret these for him because he could have them put to death if they didn't. Well, none were able, and so he issued an order of execution for them all.

Now consider Daniel. He had reason to be puffed up with pride. After all, he had stood firm "not to defile himself with the royal food and wine" from the king's table, and led his friends Hananiah, Mishael, and Azariah to join him so that they had only vegetables and water for the trial period. "At the end of the ten days they looked healthier and better nourished than any of the young men that ate the royal food" (Dan. 1:8, 15).

But instead of being prideful in his own wisdom and power, Daniel was praiseful of the Lord Almighty who gave him wisdom and understanding, even to interpret dreams of an evil king. So, when Daniel learned about the death sentence that had been issued for all the wise men of Babylon, "Daniel went in to the king and asked for time, so that he might interpret the dream for him" (Dan. 2:16). Then Daniel and his friends turned to the only One who could save them. They pleaded for mercy from the Lord Almighty to save them all from execution.

God delivered to Daniel the interpretation, and Daniel praised Him: "Praise be to the name of God for ever and ever; wisdom and power are his. He changes times and seasons; He deposes kings and raises up others. He gives wisdom to the wise and knowledge to the discerning. He reveals deep and hidden things; he knows what lies in darkness, and light dwells with him. I thank and praise you, God of my ancestors: You have given me wisdom and power, you have made known to me what we asked of you, you have made known to us the dream of the king" (Dan. 2:20–23).

Would Daniel take credit for the interpretation before Nebuchadnezzar? When asked by the king if he was able to interpret it, "Daniel replied, 'no wise man, enchanter, magician, or diviner can explain to the king the mystery he has asked about, but there is a God in heaven who reveals mysteries" (Dan. 2:27-28a).

A God in heaven indeed! Daniel praised up and glorified his God in heaven before a king who glorified his own self. The same king who had a monument constructed to glorify himself. How puffed up does one have to be to set up a ninety-foot-high golden image of himself for all to bow down to or be put to death? But not all would bow down and worship this idol. Hananiah, Mishael, and Azariah would not, instead praising the God of heaven and trusting that He would deliver them. When Nebuchadnezzar saw them delivered from the death furnace by the Lord Almighty, even he proclaimed that "no other God can save in this way" (Dan. 3:29).

But alas, he later reverted to his previous pride, "as the king was walking on the roof of the royal palace of Babylon, he said 'Is not this the great Babylon I have built as the royal residence, by my mighty power and for the glory of my majesty?'" (Dan. 4:30).

The next thing he knew—as had been foretold through Daniel—he became a creature whose "body was drenched with the dew of heaven until his hair grew like the feathers of an eagle and his nails like the claws of a bird" (Dan. 4:33). As he was taught humility by the Almighty's hand, Nebuchadnezzar praised the Most High, saying "And those who walk in pride he is able to humble" (Dan. 4:37). I wonder if he had the image of gold to himself destroyed.

Instead of being puffed up by his accomplishments or status in this foreign land, Daniel continued to praise up to the Almighty consistently in the face of opposition; even when he was given a death sentence in the lion's den. He trusted the Lord God who shut the mouths of the lions and delivered him. Daniel consistently and faithfully trusted, praised, and served the Lord God Almighty.

Consider Herod Agrippa I, king of Judea, from a family of ruthless rulers who valued their own desires above all else. The Herods were into power and puffed up with shameless pride. He was the grandson of Herod the Great, who sought to kill the newborn King of the Jews. He was nephew to Herod Antipas, who had John the Baptist beheaded, and who ridiculed and mocked Jesus before sending Him back to Pilate, where He would be condemned to die. And this Herod Agrippa had James, the brother of John, put to death with the sword and imprisoned Peter. The Lord Almighty delivered Peter from the prison miraculously, and when Herod could not find Peter, he had the prison guards executed. Powerful, yes. Prideful? Well, how about when he was acclaimed by the people as a god?

"On the appointed day Herod, wearing his royal robes, sat on his throne and delivered a public address to the people. They shouted, 'This is the voice of a god, not of a man.' Immediately, because Herod did not give praise to God, an angel of the Lord struck him down, and he was eaten by worms and died" (Acts 12:21–23).

Pride doesn't look up. Pride looks down as if from a superior position. Herod was deceived into believing that he was something that he wasn't. There is only one true God—the Lord Almighty, and it is He who is to be praised and served.

Now consider Paul and Barnabas. They had reason to be puffed up with pride. Throngs of people would follow them and listen to their bold teaching and instruction. They witnessed the power of the Lord Almighty as demons were being cast out and the sick were being healed. They were even held up by the people of Lystra as gods.

"In Lystra there sat a man crippled in his feet, who was lame from birth and had never walked. He listened to Paul as he was speaking. Paul looked directly at him, saw that he had faith to be healed and called out, 'Stand up on your feet!' At that, the man jumped up and began to walk. When the crowd saw what Paul had done, they shouted in the Lycaonian language, 'The gods have come down to us in human form!' Barnabas they called Zeus, and Paul they called Hermes because he was the chief speaker. The priest of Zeus, whose temple was just outside the city, brought bulls and wreaths to the city gates because he and the crowd wanted to offer sacrifices to them" (Acts 14:8–13*).

So did Paul and Barnabas become puffed up or were they praising up to their God in heaven?

"But when the apostles Barnabas and Paul heard of this, they tore their clothes and rushed out into the crowd, shouting: 'Men, why are you doing this? We too are only men, human like you. We are bringing you good news, telling you to turn from these worthless things to the living God, who made heaven and earth and sea and everything in them. In the past, he let all nations go their own way. Yet he has not left himself without testimony: He has shown kindness by giving you rain from heaven and crops in their seasons; he provides you with plenty of food and fills your hearts with joy.' Even with these words, they had difficulty keeping the crowd from sacrificing to them" (Acts 14:14–18).

The living God is the one, and the only one, to be praised, and the apostles made that clear. Puffed up—no way; praised up—amen.

Consider Lucifer, brightest of all the angels of heaven, who was so puffed up with pride that he believed he could ascend to the throne of God:

"How you have fallen from heaven, O morning star [Lucifer in the Latin], son of the dawn! You have been cast down to the earth, you who once laid low the nations! You said in your heart, 'I will ascend to heaven; I will raise my throne above the stars of God; I will sit enthroned on the mount of assembly, on the utmost heights of the sacred mountain. I will ascend above the tops of the clouds; I will make myself like the Most High.' But you are brought down to the grave, to the depths of the pit" (Is. 14:12–15*).

Jesus even stated, "I saw Satan fall like lightening from heaven" in Luke 10:18 as his disciples were recounting how Satan's demons were submitting to them in the name of Jesus.

God created this angel who became Satan, not as evil, to do evil, but as good, to do good—and to serve the Lord God Almighty. He was blameless until he gave in to wickedness (Ezek. 28:15).

Then his pride took over, "Your heart became proud on account of your beauty," as well as selfish ambition, "and you corrupted your wisdom because of your splendor" (Ezek. 28:17), which blinded him to the truth. That is the truth as to Who is really Lord of all, as to Who is above all and over all, as to Who has the final word in all things.

So, in his fallen state, he forfeited all the blessings of his Creator and was cast out of heaven, taking with him many angels—deceived by him, and prideful as he—to be his demonic minions. Satan leads all astray who believe him, "that ancient serpent called the devil, or Satan, who leads the whole world astray" (Rev. 12:9). But his day of judgment is coming, "And the devil, who deceived them, was thrown into the lake of burning sulfur, where the beast and the false prophet had been thrown. They will be tormented day and night forever and ever" (Rev. 20:10). Jesus referred to the "eternal fire prepared for the devil and his angels" (Matt. 25:41). Pride caused Satan to be puffed up and will lead him to his doom. Satan will be in charge of nothing in hell but will be in eternal torment just like all who choose their own way over God's way.

Now above all else, through all else, consider Jesus. No one ever had as much reason to be puffed up as Jesus. You see, it is He who is "in very nature God...He is the image of the invisible God...the radiance of God's glory, and the exact representation of his being" (Phil. 2:6; Col. 1:15; Heb.1:3).

In fact, Jesus is over all things and sustains all things—nanosecond by nanosecond. "For by him all things were created; things in heaven and on earth, visible and invisible, whether thrones or powers or rulers or authorities; all things were created by him and for him. He is before all things, and in him all things hold together...sustaining all things by His powerful word" (Col. 1:16–17; Heb. 1:3). In fact, He and God the Father are one (John 10:30) and all of creation their home; a creation so vast and beyond our imagination that we humans will never know, let alone see, the extent of all that is.

Reason to be puffed up with pride—who has more than the one who owns it all? Than the one who oversees it all? Than the one who gives life and takes it away? Than the one who will be glorified and praised forever and ever? Yet, it is this very One—Jesus, Son of God— who set aside His pride, His position, and His glory in heaven to be obedient to the Father's plan to save the lost, to rescue the perishing, and to deliver the condemned. His plan was that His Son Jesus would be the Savior, the Rescuer, the Deliverer...only not in the way we would expect.

In our world, such a one would ride in on a white steed, guns a-blazing, or leading a squadron of x-wing fighters. In our world, such a one would come as a larger than life, a Paul Bunyan-esque figure ready to take on all comers. In other words, such a one would come with fanfare, with hype, with headlines. All the things that cause us to stand back and be impressed.

But, what if such a one didn't come that way at all? How would he come—this Savior? As a helpless baby, born in a stable, in a remote town away from home? As one of us regular folk? As an infant to a working class couple? As one without privilege and prestige? As one who would not stand out in a crowd because of any physical attractiveness? Without hype and without fanfare?

Hype? Not really. Fanfare? Well, there was the heavenly choir, but they apparently were heard only by the lowly shepherds tending their flocks by night. Headlines? Not so much, although God the Father had made clear—over and over—throughout the ages that His Son would come, and would come in such a way. God doesn't always use headlines for His messages. But His messages are always the headlines in the big picture. Human events capture headlines day to day, but God and His will is the Headline for all eternity.

So, what about this Jesus—come to earth as one of us? How did He demonstrate praising up to his Father and not puffing up with pride for all He had? God called him to leave the perfect place with Himself—where no there is no sin and darkness—to be born into a sin-sick and dark world, and to become the sacrifice on a cross for all of mankind's depravity.

"Christ Jesus: Who, being in very nature God, did not consider equality with God something to be grasped, but made himself nothing, taking the very nature of a servant, being made in human likeness. And being found in appearance as a man, he humbled himself and became obedient to death—even death on a cross!" (Phil. 2:5–8*).

Who among us can begin to fathom this? Not one. We cannot comprehend of royalty set aside for servanthood. We cannot comprehend one so pure bearing upon himself all our filth and sinfulness—each and every one of us. We cannot comprehend a love so deep, so true, so unselfish, so sacrificing.

Jesus paid it all. Jesus set aside all, for which we ourselves would be prideful, in order to be obedient to the Father. Without His love and His obedience, we have no hope. Our sin has separated us from God, and Jesus is the bridge between us—the Mediator. "For there is one God and one mediator between God and mankind, the man Christ Jesus, who gave himself as a ransom for all people" (1 Tim. 2:5).

Repentance must replace our pride so that we agree with God that we cannot save ourselves; that we have nothing to boast about; nothing to be prideful about; that we are totally dependent on Jesus and His sacrifice for our salvation.

Jesus did all He could; it is a completed work.

But for you, it is completed only if you believe God and praise up to Him with your life surrendered.

Choose you this day whom you will believe and whom you will serve.

O Lord our God, thank You for Jesus who was an example for us in perfection and humility—two attributes that don't fit together in our world. Thank You that we can praise up to You because You alone are praiseworthy. I pray it be so in the life of this reader, to Your glory. In the name of perfect—yet humble–Jesus. Amen.

Raised to New Life

*W*hen you think of bones lying around on the ground, what comes to mind? The dead. The remains of something that once lived. Lifelessness. When you think of a valley full of bones, what comes to mind? A battlefield of the dead. Fallen heroes. Defeat. Hopelessness. What an image of despair and sadness would be a valley filled with bones. Yet, can there be a message of hope for you and me in such a valley?

Over 2600 years ago, a man was called in a vision to go out to such a valley. That man had been serving the Lord as a twenty-five-year-old Jewish priest to God's chosen people in the temple in Jerusalem, but then there was an invasion by the enemy. The Babylonians were the enemy, and they came to exert their authority over the Jews and to collect taxes. Furthermore, to weaken the Jewish people, they took captive to Babylon 10,000 of their elite—1000 miles away—near what is now Bagdad, Iraq.

These included royalty, soldiers, artisans, and priests, and we are told in 2 Kings 24:14 that only the poorest people were left in the land. Among those taken captive were Ezekiel and Daniel, as well as Hananiah, Mishael, and Azeriah, more commonly known as Shadrach, Meshach, and Abednego.

It is interesting to note that Daniel ended up finding favor with the king, and he served the Lord there in the king's court. By the way, Jeremiah was older than these but ministered during the same time period to those left behind in Jerusalem.

Ezekiel, on the other hand, now a priest without a temple, ended up among the Jewish exiles, and he served the Lord there—only now as a prophet. His message over a twenty-two-year ministry was two-fold: One message was of doom: God was going to allow the Babylonians to destroy what remained of the Jewish nation (they had already invaded in 605 BC, and now again in 597 BC), and most Jews who survived the onslaught would be exiled. Why? Because of Israel's sin. Ezekiel 5:7-9 tells us:

"Therefore this is what the Sovereign Lord says: You have been more unruly than the nations around you and have not followed my decrees or kept my laws. You have not even conformed to the standards of the nations around you. Therefore this is what the Sovereign Lord says: I myself am against you, Jerusalem, and I will inflict punishment on you in the sight of the nations. Because of all your detestable idols, I will do to you what I have never done before and will never do again."

They were to have no other gods before the one true Lord. Neither are we. We are to fear the one true Lord. We are to take Him seriously. We are to obey His teaching, and honor Him with our lives. For the one who rejects the one true Lord, hell awaits—an eternal destination of torment and suffering, a place of separation from the Lord and His home, and all that is good. For the one who believes and trusts in the one true Lord, heaven awaits—an eternal destination of love and peace...a reserved place in the presence of the Lord Jesus and His home, and all that is good.

Now, the second message from Ezekiel was one of hope: God would eventually send the Jews back home to rebuild their nation to a new level of glory. So, what happened in this vision of Ezekiel 37:1-3? "The hand of the Lord was on me, and he brought me out by the Spirit of the Lord and set me in the middle of a valley; it was full of bones. He led me back and forth among them, and I saw a great many bones on the floor of the valley, bones that were very dry." We are told that the bones were not just dry, but very dry—long dead, far beyond any hope of resuscitation.

God then asked Ezekiel an interesting question, "Son of man, can these bones live?"

What would your answer be? Honestly? I'm thinking, no, not a chance.

Ezekiel responded, "Sovereign Lord, you alone know."

What do these bones symbolize? The chosen nation, which had been defeated; run out of their own country; held captive. They were in despair. Seemingly, all that they had held dear was now lost. It seemed hopeless. Have you ever felt that way? Do you feel defeated, in despair, and hopeless today? Most, perhaps all, of us have been there. Some of us have seen the Light. I pray that in this moment we both see the Light.

What did God say next to Ezekiel? "Then he said to me, 'Prophecy to these bones and say to them , 'Dry bones, hear the word of the Lord! This is what the Sovereign Lord says to these bones: I will make breath enter you, and you will come to life. I will attach tendons to you and make flesh come upon you and cover you with skin; I will put breath in you, and you will come to life. Then you will know that I am the Lord" (Ezek. 37:4-7).

There it is—our ultimate purpose in life—to know that *He is Lord*!

Do you know that God is the Lord? Is it with your mind only, or do you know Him in your heart of hearts as Lord of your life?

Is anything too hard for the Lord? Has He raised the dead to life? How about the Lord raising the widow's dead son back to life through Elijah (1 Kin. 17)? How about the Lord raising the Shunammite woman's dead son back to life through Elisha (2 Kin. 4)? How about the Lord Jesus Himself raising Jairus's dead daughter back to life (Matt. 9)? How about the Lord Jesus Himself, in the town of Nain, raising the widow's dead son back to life (Luke 7)? How about the Lord raising Tabitha, a disciple of the Lord Jesus, who had died, back to life through Peter (Acts 9)? How about the Lord raising Eutychus, who fell to his death from a window on the third floor—by the way, having fallen asleep while Paul was teaching—raising him back to life through Paul (only fitting, right?—Acts 20)? How about the Lord Jesus Himself raising Lazarus, who had been dead for four days, back to life (John 11)?

Is anything too hard for the Lord? The Lord is working in lives right now around you and me to change them and draw them unto Himself. There have been those around you and me brought back to life, so to speak, having been given hope by the heavenly Father, having been raised up out of the pit to walk in a newness of life.

Nothing is too hard for the Lord.

What did Ezekiel do? What would you do if you were standing in a valley full of bones, and there is only one other voice speaking to you? Do what that voice tells you?

"So I prophesied as I was commanded. And, as I was prophesying, there was a noise, a rattling sound, and the bones came together, bone to bone. I looked, and the tendons and flesh appeared on them and skin covered them, but there was no breath in them" (Ezek. 37:7).

So, think about that. The bones had connected, one by one with each other. None missed its place. They stood as though they were living, but they had no breath in them.

When we surrender our lives to Jesus as Lord, His Spirit indwells us, and changes us to walk anew in His ways. But until you do that, then you are like these in this valley. Your bones are connected; you have tendons, flesh, and skin covering the bones. But you are dead in your sins, and you will be dead in your sins until you repent of your sins and trust in Jesus as Lord of your life.

God Almighty calls to you in this moment to allow His Holy Spirit to breathe His life into your dead soul. God Almighty calls you to repent of your sins. Jesus said, "But unless you repent, you too will perish" (Luke 13:3). We are told in Second Peter 3:9: "The Lord is not slow in keeping His promise, as some understand slowness. Instead he is patient with you, not wanting anyone to perish, but everyone to come to repentance."

"Then He said to me, 'Prophesy to the breath; prophesy, son of man, and say to it, This is what the Sovereign Lord says: Come breath, from the four winds and breathe into these slain, that they may live.' So I prophesied as he commanded me, and breath entered them; they came to life and stood up on their feet—a vast army" (Ezek. 37:9-10).

This is a picture of restoration—new life—for the nation of Israel, but it is also a picture of new life for you and me. We are dead in our sins, lifeless and without hope in this state. God calls you to repent and put your hope in His Son Jesus who died for you.

Listen to God speaking from Ephesians 2:4,8-9: "But because of his great love for us, God, who is rich in mercy, made us alive with Christ even when we were dead in transgressions—it is by grace you have been saved." By His grace does He breathe His Spirit into the inner being of whomever trusts in Him. "For it is by grace you have been saved, through faith—and this not from yourselves, it is the gift of God—not of works, so that no one can boast. For we are God's handiwork, created in Christ Jesus to do good works, which God prepared in advance for us to do."

So, you see, we cannot breathe new life into ourselves any more than we could raise up dry bones, put them together, and put life within them, but God can. God does. We cannot ever earn God's favor by what we do, what we have, what we are. That favor—salvation—has already been earned for you and me by the sinless one—Jesus, the Christ. It is the gift of God—the greatest gift ever offered, and it is offered to everyone.

But, only those who believe that they need it—only those who want it—will receive it.

Are you one of those? If you are, then confess to your Creator, your heavenly Father, that you are a sinner; that you cannot save yourself; that you believe that Jesus is the only hope you have and the only hope you need; that you are surrendering your life to Jesus as Lord; that you are submitting your will to His will for your life. In doing this, you are claiming Jesus as your Savior.

"If you confess with your mouth, 'Jesus as Lord,' and believe in your heart that God raised Him from the dead, you will be saved. For it is with your heart that you believe and are justified," (Justified, just as if I never sinned, making right everything with the Lord God) "and it is with your mouth that you confess and are saved. As the Scripture says, 'Anyone who trusts in him (Jesus) will never be put to shame'... For, everyone who calls on the name of the Lord will be saved" (Rom. 10:9–11, 13*).

Will you?

O Lord God, thank You for examples throughout Your Word of death to life, of hopelessness to hope, of despair to victory. I pray for the one reading this message to trust in Your power to breathe new life even into dry bones. In the name of Jesus, the Resurrection and the Resurrector. Amen.

Repentance unto Relentance

"For *all* have sinned, and fall short of the glory of God" (Rom. 3:23). "For the wages of sin is death" (Rom. 6:23). "We *all*, like sheep, have gone astray; each of us has turned to our own way" (Is. 53:6).

And there is a price to be paid for our sin – death. "Death is the destiny of every man" (Eccl. 7:2). "For as in Adam, all die" (1 Cor. 15:22). "Just as people are destined to die once, and after that to face judgement" (Heb. 9:27).

*A*ll quotes from the Bible; all make it clear that we are sinners and destined for death.

But that is not the whole story.

Some believe that we live this short time on earth, then die...and that is all there is to it. I don't. Because that is not what God says. He didn't plan for us to disobey Him, sin against Him. That is not what He wanted from us. But He knew we would, and that created the sin vs. righteousness problem. God can only abide righteousness. We can only enter His kingdom through righteousness.

We have none, so what can we do. We can repent for the forgiveness of our sins. In fact, we must repent in order to be saved. In Luke 13:3, Jesus said, "Unless you too repent, you will all perish." Second Peter 3:9 tells us, "God is patient with you, not wanting anyone to perish, but everyone to come to repentance."

God is clear about the penalty for sin. It is death. Blood must be shed for the forgiveness of sins. So, who among us has sinned? All of us.

Each one of us. God clearly told Adam that if he disobeyed, he would ultimately die. Adam did. And that is what you and I have done. We have disobeyed God. We have broken His commandments. That is not what He wanted, yet it is what we have chosen. And God is not surprised; He knew this, and He made a way for us unto salvation instead of damnation. You see, God relents in His judgment of those who repent.

Jonah was a prophet of the Lord God in the time period of around 800–750 BC. He lived in Galilee not far from Nazareth in the northern Jewish nation of Israel. Jonah apparently took great pride in the favored status of Israel as God's chosen people. And, he apparently had great disdain for Israel's enemies, namely, the Assyrians. Now, God called Jonah to go preach repentance. God called him to go preach repentance in a great city. The problem was that city was Nineveh, seat of the Assyrian empire.

You and I might have balked, too. After all, the Ninevites were known to be cruel, and they plotted evil against the Lord. Their society was rife with prostitution, witchcraft, and human exploitation of all kinds. Their habits were unspeakably cruel, unimaginable in terms of torture and sadistic nature. Just one example in the artwork, which hung on their palace walls, depicted dead Jewish soldiers impaled on poles just like fence posts. By the way, Nineveh was located in what is now Iraq, near Mosul.

God took note of the wickedness in the Ninevites, and told Jonah to go and preach to them about their wickedness.

Now, think about that, a Jew going to Nineveh with a death threat would be akin to sending a rabbi to Berlin in the early 1940s to tell Hitler he is doomed.

Why was God sending Jonah there in the first place? So they would be aware of what they were doing? So Jonah could lord it over them? So God could lord it over them? No, so they would *repent*, and God would *relent* in His judgment of them. Sounds like a plan of love and mercy.

But Jonah wasn't into that—he opted for self-preservation (or so he thought), and he headed the opposite direction. He fled to Joppa and boarded a ship that was sailing for far away Tarshish. He could go down below on that ship and hide; God would lose track of him and call somebody else, and that would be that.

Does God lose track of anyone? Does anyone fly under God's radar? Can you guess Who knew what Jonah was up to, and exactly where he was?

Well, what do you know...a great wind blew up on the sea, a violent storm so severe that it threatened to break up the ship. All the sailors were afraid, and each cried out to his own god. They threw cargo into the sea to lighten the load so the ship would ride higher on the waves. Jonah was down below in a deep sleep, but the captain found him and asked him how he could sleep. He then told him to get up, pray to his God, and maybe He would hear and not destroy them all.

The sailors wanted to get to the bottom of who was responsible for this calamity. They cast lots, and so much for flying under the radar. The truth came out—Jonah was the one causing all this trouble.

Note to self: when you disobey God, you are not the only one hurt in the process; it has consequences for others as well.

Jonah fessed up: I am a Hebrew, and I worship the Lord (funny way of showing it, huh?), the God of heaven, who made the sea and the land. Well, you see I didn't particularly care for that last assignment, so I thought I would sneak away, and maybe God would just go to plan B. Actually, they asked him what he had done, and he told them that he was running away from the Lord—Jonah is candid if nothing else.

They asked what they should do, so he told them to pick him up and throw him overboard. But first they tried rowing like crazy, yet it wasn't getting them anywhere. So, after pleading for God's mercy in advance, they pitched him overboard. The sea grew calm.

Whew, all is well...oops, what about Jonah who is likely to drown out there in the sea? The Lord provided. Provided what? A great fish that would swallow Jonah and hold him inside for three days and three nights.

Jesus would later say, "For as Jonah was three days and three nights in the belly of a huge fish, so the Son of Man will be three days and three nights in the heart of the earth" (Matt. 12:40). Do you think Jonah could have ever imagined that the coming Messiah would someday compare their two experiences?

If you were Jonah, what would you do? Be distressed and figure that your life was nearing its end? That is probably what Jonah did, and then remember that his Lord is over all, and cry out to Him for help.

"In my distress I called to the Lord and he answered me. From deep in the realm of the dead I called for help, and you listened to my cry. You hurled me into the depths, into the very heart of the seas, and the currents swirled about me; all your waves and breakers swept over me. I said, 'I have been banished from your sight; yet I will look again toward your holy temple.' The engulfing waters threatened me, the deep surrounded me; seaweed was wrapped around my head. To the roots of the mountains I sank down; the earth beneath barred me in forever. But you, Lord my God, brought my life up from the pit. When my life was ebbing away, I remembered you, Lord, and my prayer rose to you, to your holy temple" (Jon. 2:2-7).

And then this profound testimony, "Those who cling to worthless idols turn away from God's love for them" (Jon. 2:8). "Those who cling to worthless idols forfeit the grace that could be theirs" (Jon. 2:8*).

Had Jonah been clinging to the worthless idol of pride? What worthless idol are you clinging to right now? What was Jonah clinging to now? The hope that God would have mercy on him and rescue him. Jonah gave thanks, and recommitted to make good on his vows. OK, Lord, You have my attention, and this isn't where I want to finish my ministry. I vow to do what you want me to, and I am ready to go. Salvation comes from the Lord.

"But I, with shouts of grateful praise will sacrifice to you. What I have vowed I will make good. I will say, 'Salvation comes from the Lord'" (Jon. 2:9). "And the Lord commanded the fish, and it vomited Jonah onto dry land" (Jon. 2:10). Ever thought that being vomited could be a good thing?

God restated the mission (in case it had slipped Jonah's mind)— go to the great city of Nineveh and preach what I tell you to preach. Jonah obeyed.

Nineveh was a large, important city, and it took three days for Jonah to cover it, proclaiming that, in forty days from now, God would overturn their city. "Forty more days and Nineveh will be overthrown" (Jon. 3:4). The king of Nineveh believed what he heard,

"When Jonah's warning reached the king of Nineveh, he rose from his throne, took off his royal robes, covered himself with sackcloth, and sat down in the dust. This is the proclamation he issued in Nineveh: 'By the decree of the king and his nobles: Do not let people or animals, herds or flocks, taste anything; do not let them eat or drink. Let everyone call urgently on God. Let them give up their evil ways and their violence. Who knows? God may yet relent, and with compassion turn from his fierce anger so that we will not perish" (Jon. 2:6-9).

What did God do? Their repentance closed the door of God's justice and opened God's door for mercy. Their repentance led to God's "relentance."

Jonah rejoiced with them. Not. In fact, he was greatly displeased and angry.

By the way, you know what Jonah's name means? His name means dove, and even though he doesn't remind us of one, he was the bringer of peace to this great city.

But now Jonah is angry. Here is what he said, "Isn't this what I said, Lord, when I was still at home? That is what I tried to forestall by fleeing to Tarshish. I knew that you are a gracious and compassionate God, slow to anger and abounding in love, a God who relents from sending calamity. Now, Lord, take away my life, for it is better for me to die than to live" (Jon. 4:1-3).

Was it because God would be compassionate to an enemy of Israel? Was it because God should only be compassionate to the Israelites? Was it because God no longer would favor Israel as His chosen nation? If God wouldn't kill these 120,000 heathens, then Jonah wanted God to kill him. "Take away my life for it is better for me to die than to live" (Jon. 4:3).

God asks Jonah if he has any right to be angry. Jonah didn't get his way, so yeah, probably so.

Well, Jonah sat down at a place to observe what would happen next. The Lord God provided and grew a vine up over Jonah to give him shade and ease his discomfort. Jonah was happy about the vine. Doesn't that sound like you and me? We are happy when we have it good. When we are comfortable, and waited on, we like it. But then let us experience some inconvenience, some discomfort, no matter how menial sometimes, and we are put out. God provided a worm, which chewed at the vine, and it withered. Then, God provided a scorching east wind, and the sun blazed down on Jonah's head so that he grew faint. Well, that did it. Now Jonah was really angry.

God asked him if he had a right to be angry about the vine, which, by the way, he didn't put there in the first place, and Jonah said, "And I am so angry I wish I were dead" (Jon. 4:9). He rejoiced at his own comfort under the vine, but was depressed and self-absorbed about the discomfort of no vine. Was the issue really the vine, the wind, the sun? Would this really tip the scales for one who had journeyed so far, and even survived the belly of a fish for three days and three nights? Perhaps the issue was God wasn't living down to Jonah's expectations.

Don't we sometimes have expectations of God that would require Him to lower Himself to our level? God didn't do what Jonah wanted God to do. Remember, if we try to conform God to our image, we are making Him something in our minds that He is not. He does not exist to please you or me. We exist to please Him. God is slow to punish and eager to forgive. His justice is abated in the wake of repentance.

"When God saw what they did and how they turned from their evil ways, he relented and did not bring on them the destruction he had threatened" (Jon. 3:10). The Ninevites repented, and God relented. So it is with you and me. You can repent, and God will relent in His judgment of you.

You don't have to pay the wages of your sin. Jesus has already paid the wages of your sin. Jesus paid it all / all to Him we owe / sin had left a crimson stain on you and me / He makes it white as snow (Jesus Paid It All).

The choice is yours—you can choose that when God the Father looks at you, all He sees is your sinfulness. That is what will happen if you do not repent and surrender to His will. And that leads to judgment and an eternal hell, separated from your Creator and loving heavenly Father.

Or, you can choose that when God the Father looks at you, all He sees is the righteousness of His Son, Jesus. When you repent and surrender to His will, you take on the righteousness of your Savior Jesus.

"This righteousness is given through faith in Jesus Christ to all who believe" (Rom. 3:22).

O Lord our God, thank You for Your forgiveness and mercy even to us sinners. You have shown Yourself faithful to save all who repent. I pray for the one reading this to do just that and receive Your grace and everlasting life. In the name of Jesus, the Redeemer. Amen.

Stain Removal

*C*offee had been spilled on that step. Only one stain on only one step, yet, there it was. It was an ugly stain, brown, dirty-looking on the otherwise green carpet. I would go up and down those steps to my office many times daily, and on each of those trips, there was that constant reminder of the soiled carpet. It would seem to catch my eye more than any of the other steps. It even seemed that I would just have to look to confirm what I already knew—yep, it's still there.

You know what that's like, don't you? How about that scab over a wound that you continue to pick at? How about that sore in your mouth that your tongue seems to go to continually just to see if it is still there? Well, this stain wasn't going away on its own. It wouldn't just disappear. You know what it reminded me of? It reminded me of sin in my life. An ugly reminder of disobedience, of waywardness, of selfishness, of pride. Try as I might to focus elsewhere, it is still there. That stain on my heart.

Now, it is interesting to note that it seemed easier to ignore the stain when I was going down the steps. I generally go down quicker than I go up, and the faster pace allowed me less time to pay attention to it. As I went up the steps more slowly, my eye was more easily drawn to the stain. That also reminded me of my life. The fuller the schedule, the faster the pace, the more easily distracted I am. I was distracted from things that need attention. How about you?

Does busyness seem to distract you from what is important? You know what seems to get derailed in the faster pace—when I am distracted? My spiritual life. My marriage. My family.

Now, my faster pace could be related to generally good things that could even be family, could be work, could be recreation or entertainment. But it could just be nonproductive personal habits—wasting time, wasting talent, wasting resources. Or worse, it could be destructive personal habits. I have been guilty of all these and more.

Any of these things could lead me, or you, to overlook, even though temporarily, that stain on my heart, or your heart, that needs to be cleansed. We can push it out of our minds for a while—ignore it—but it still cries out for attention. Just because we don't look at it or pay attention to it doesn't mean that it has gone away.

Our loving heavenly Father has placed within each of us the need to love Him and trust Him. Our loving heavenly Father has placed within each of us the desire to be in right relationship with Him and with others. Someone once said that there is a void in each of us in the shape of the Lord Jesus. We can try to fill that void with other relationships, with work, with recreation, with booze, with drugs, with sex, but the bottom line is that none of these fill that void. Only Jesus fills that void.

What does that require? Repentance of our sins, belief in Jesus as Savior, and trust in Jesus as Lord.

You see, we all have stains on our heart from sin that can only be cleansed by blood—and only the blood that the Savior Jesus shed on Calvary's cross. He gave Himself as a ransom for you and me, "For there is one God and one mediator between God and mankind, the man Christ Jesus, who gave himself as a ransom for all mankind" (1 Tim. 2:5). You see, only the righteous will stand before God and be recognized as His children, His heirs alongside Jesus, the only begotten Son. Who among us is righteous? Do we have any righteousness on our own? Some think so.

Jesus tells us in Luke 18:9–14: "To some who were confident of their own righteousness and looked down on everyone else, Jesus told this parable: 'Two men went up to the temple to pray, one a Pharisee, and the other a tax collector.'"

The Pharisees were religious leaders of the Jews who, for the most part, believed that God's grace extended only to those who kept the law. Their behavior showed that tradition was often more important than scripture, and their behavior showed a belief that they would be justified, or made right before God, by their works. Many religions today teach that salvation will be "earned" by your works, Yet, God makes clear that we are saved by grace, not of our works, but for the purpose to do good works after we are saved. Salvation unto good works...not good works unto salvation.

Tax collectors, also referred to as publicans in scripture, were outcasts, generally hated and considered as traitors because they collected taxes for the Roman government.

Now, back to Jesus's parable:

"Two men went up to the temple to pray, one a Pharisee, and the other a tax collector. The Pharisee stood by himself and prayed: 'God, I thank you that I am not like other people—robbers, evildoers, adulterers—or even like this tax collector. I fast twice a week and give a tenth of all I get.' But the tax collector stood at a distance. He would not even look up to heaven, but beat his breast and said, 'God, have mercy on me, a sinner.' I tell you that this man, rather than the other, went home justified (made right) before God. For all those who exalt themselves will be humbled, and those who humble themselves will be exalted'" (Luke 18:10-14).

As it is written, "there is no one righteous, not even one" . . . "Therefore no one will be declared righteous in God's sight by the works of the law" (Rom. 3:10, 20).

The Pharisee prayed about himself, believing God would accept him for his own righteousness, but it won't happen that way. The tax collector pleaded with God for mercy because he recognized that he had no righteousness of his own. You see, we all, like sheep, have gone astray, and turned each one of us to our own way; we each have sinned and fallen short of God's glory, as we are told in Isaiah 53:6 and Romans 3:23. If you try to earn your salvation, your own entry into heaven, you know what will happen? You will fail. Because you cannot. You and I have broken God's laws, and there is the stain of sin on our hearts.

Go back with me to the step with that stain, that ever-present stain. That damnable stain.

I spoke about the faster pace going down. Well, going up the steps is a different matter. The pace is usually slower, and especially later in the day. Fatigue is setting in, and when it does, the stain begins to be more noticeable. Just like in life, we pay more attention to it as we move more slowly. The reminders of our sin are particularly noticeable as we struggle with life's daily challenges.

Satan uses the worries and cares of the day to try and lead us to despair and depression, and then worse behavior. He lays the guilt trip on us to weigh us down, weaken us, and then destroy us. But, while he is trying to break us down, our loving heavenly Father is there to lift us up. He wants us to slow down—be still and know that He is God—to slow down and take note of what we need the most. The loving Father wants our guilt to lead to freedom, not destruction. He wants us to recognize that our dependence is on Him for everything, including cleansing of sin.

Cleansing of sin leads to restoration, peace, and contentment. Just like that carpet that needed to be deep cleaned, my heart and soul need to be deep cleaned. Your heart and soul need to be deep cleaned.

In fact, only the blood of the Lamb of God can be the cleansing agent we need.

You are being called from an empty way of life, to be, in fact, *redeemed* from an empty way of life—not because of any great thing you can do, not because of anything you can bribe God with, not because of who your family is, but *only* because of the precious blood of Christ. First Peter 1:18-21, 23 says:

"For you know that it was not with perishable things such as silver or gold that you were redeemed from the empty way of life handed down to you from your ancestors, but with the precious blood of Christ, a lamb without blemish or defect. He was chosen before the creation of the world, but was revealed in these last times for your sake. Through him you believe in God, who raised him from the dead and glorified him, so your faith and hope are in God...For you have been born again, not of perishable seed, but of imperishable, through the living and enduring word of God."

This is so if you are putting your trust in the one Lord and Savior Jesus.

How has God loved you? By giving His one and only Son Jesus to die in your place. By sending His one and only Son Jesus to be one of us, to endure all that we face and so much, so much more. Without His mercy, you and I are condemned. But in His mercy, Jesus shed his blood so that you and I can be forgiven and cleansed. But in His grace, Jesus offers the full and meaningful life in the power of His Spirit this day and the next and the next.

It begins with agreeing with our heavenly Father that we need to repent. Without repentance, there is no forgiveness, but where there is repentance and trust in the heavenly Father, there is mercy and grace abounding. He wants me to be cleansed so I can be free to live in right relationship with Him. He wants you to be cleansed so you can be free to live in right relationship with Him.

You see, when you are convicted of sin, and you hear messages of condemnation, of how God doesn't love you, of how you are hopeless, of how that stain from what you have done will never be washed away, please know who is sending this message. That is Satan, the liar. He is the father of lies. In fact, it is his native language. That is Satan, the thief. He is the one who would take away every good thing in your life. That is Satan, the murderer. He is the one of whom God says, "He comes to steal and kill and destroy" (John 10:10). He wants your sin, my sin, to lead us *downward* to where he is.

Now, compare that to your Creator. He wants the conviction of your sin to lead to repentance, and *upward* to where He is. Why? Because without repentance, there is no salvation. Jesus said, "But unless you repent, you too will all perish" (Luke 13:3).

Does God want anyone to perish? Listen to this: we are told in 2 Peter 3:9 that the Lord is patient with you, not wanting anyone to perish, but everyone to come to repentance. You see, if our guilt leads us to repentance, then it will lead us upward to the Father, not downward to Satan. When Jesus was set free from the nails of the cross in death, He went down to grave first, but then, in new life, He went upward to be with the Father.

So it is with you and me; whoever repents of sin and believes in Jesus as the Lord of all, then that individual will experience death to the old and life to the new. He not only cleanses my heart, your heart, but He restores our hearts to just like new. "Therefore, if anyone is in Christ, he is a new creation; the old has gone, the new has come!" (2 Cor. 5:17*).

The psalmist prayed "Create in me a pure heart, O God" (Ps. 51:10). The loving Father does exactly that—purifies our hearts by faith in Him (Acts 15:9). Now, I ask you, what stain is ever before you? What stain will not go away?

We need to continually look into our hearts—ask the Father to show us our hearts—to see what stains need to be removed. He takes our sins and makes them white as snow, as we confess them to Him. It is a continual process, this keeping of my heart pure and clean before the Father, this keeping of your heart pure and clean before the Father. But He is up to the task. He is ever faithful to forgive as we confess our sins to Him (1 John 1:9).

What stains are ever before you, not carpet stains, but heart stains. Would you look at your heart, and ask God to look into your heart? Let Him take the stains—the sins—there, and remove them by the blood of His perfect Son, Jesus, the Christ. Forgiveness and cleansing are realized only through the Savior because of His death for you and me.

Would you like your heart to be pure, restored to the innocence of childhood? Jesus said, "unless you change and become like little children, you will never enter the kingdom of heaven" (Matt. 18:3).

So His call is to humble yourselves, recognizing your heart is not pure, and that God is the only one who can purify it through the shed blood of His perfect Son Jesus.

You know, I did finally deep clean that stain out of the carpet on that step. You can't tell it was ever there, or can you? When that carpet is removed one day, what will be revealed beneath? The carpet pad underneath will still show that stain, won't it?

In the same way, our efforts can make the outside look good, but our efforts to really remove the stain are futile. The Pharisees were like that— putting on a great outward appearance, but Jesus said that they were like white-washed tombs (Matthew 23:13)—empty of life on the inside.

So, it is with sin. Only God can deep clean; only God can truly cleanse through and through.

And He is faithful to do just that, as you repent and trust in Him.

O Lord our God, thank You that You are able to cleanse through and through, and thank You that You are willing and able to do just that in the life of the one reading this. Be it so, Lord God, according to Your will in Christ Jesus, the one without stain or blemish. Amen.

Tax Collectors, Samaritans, and Centurions

*H*ave you ever been shunned? Have you ever been looked down upon? Have you ever been considered an outcast? Has it been because of your appearance? The color of your skin? The way you talk? Where you're from? The kind of work you do?

God offers you good news.

Because, you see, God is no respecter of persons because of any of these things. God doesn't love someone because they are white any more than He loves them because they are black. God doesn't love someone because they speak fluently any more than He loves them because they stutter. Job refers to God as the one who shows no partiality to princes and does not favor the rich over the poor, for we are all the work of His hands (Job 34:19).

Each one of us has been created in His image. Each one of us has been created in love, to be loved by God Almighty. And each one of us has been created to love God Almighty. In James, Acts, and Romans, we are told that God does not show partiality or favoritism. He has no teacher's pets. He loves each one of us, and He calls each one of us to love one another as ourselves (James 2:1, 8; Acts 10:34; Romans 2:11).

What comes to mind when you hear the words, tax collectors, Samaritans, and centurions? These groups of folks were not thought of very highly in Jesus's day. They were, for the most part, looked at with scorn and distrust. They were outcasts in many respects, not to be trusted, and not to be associated with.

So what was Jesus doing in their presence? Why didn't He look at them the same way that the Jewish leaders did? Does He look at some of the folks around you—whom you look down upon—the same way as you do? We are told in Matthew 9:9–12, Mark 2:13–17, and Luke 5:27–31 that Jesus actually called a tax collector to be His disciple—a tax collector becoming an apostle of the Lord? This tax collector had the given name Levi, son of Alphaeus, but became known as Matthew—his name as Jesus's disciple. Matthew means "gift of the Lord."

Tax collectors were also known as publicans—not a favorable label. They worked for Rome and had a bad reputation for being traitors because many demanded more than what was owed so they could pocket the difference. Why would Jesus call a tax collector to follow Him? You see, it isn't what we are when Jesus calls us that is important. What is important is what we *become* when Jesus calls us to follow Him.

Jesus said to Levi, "Follow me," "and Matthew got up and followed him" (Matt. 9:9). Later, they were having dinner at Matthew's house—a great banquet, in fact—with a large crowd of whom? Tax collectors! Jesus was asked why he ate and drank with tax collectors and sinners. What did Jesus say? "It is not the healthy who need a doctor, but the sick...For I have not come to call the righteous, but sinners" (Matt. 9:12).

There was another tax collector whose home Jesus visited. In Luke 19, when Jesus entered Jericho, a man ran ahead and climbed a sycamore tree just so he could see Jesus when He came that way. But Zacchaeus didn't just see Jesus, Jesus saw Zacchaeus, and "looked up and said to him, 'Zacchaeus, come down immediately. I must stay at your house today'" (Luke 19:5).

The people muttered that Jesus had gone to be the guest of a sinner. What happened to this sinner in the presence of Jesus? He stood up and said to Jesus, "Look, Lord! Here and now I give half of my possessions to the poor, and if I have cheated anybody out of anything, I will pay back four times the amount." Jesus then said the most important words any of us can hear: "Today salvation has come to this house" (Luke 19:8, 9). "For the Son of Man came to seek and to save the lost" (Luke 19:10).

To seek and to save what was lost – the mission of the Savior. It doesn't matter that the lost man was a tax collector. What matters is Jesus saving the man who was a tax collector.

Another tax collector who humbled himself before the Lord was spoken about in Luke 18:9–14; he wouldn't even look up to heaven. He beat his breast. He said, "God, have mercy on me, a sinner" What did Jesus say about this tax collector? He went home justified before God because he didn't seek to exalt himself, but instead humbled himself, and was saved.

Matthew, Zacchaeus, this one at the temple—all tax collectors, outcasts, looked down upon by the religious leaders of that day—yet, each one changed by the Lord Jesus, who came to call sinners, and who came to seek and save that which was lost.

What about Samaritans? Half-breeds, foreigners, despised and shunned by the Jews at large. Would Jesus associate Himself with such people as the Samaritans? Would He even hold one up as an example in the parable found in Luke 10:25–37? There was a man going up from Jerusalem to Jericho, when he was attacked by robbers. They stripped him. They beat him. They robbed him. They left him half dead.

Would anyone stop, get involved, and help him? A priest—religious leader—didn't; he passed by on the other side. A Levite—a lay leader in the synagogue—didn't; he passed by on the other side.

But there was one who took pity on the poor man. He knelt down and bandaged his wounds. He put the poor man on his own donkey and led him into town. He took him to an inn, paid for a room for him, and promised to cover any other expenses that the man would have there. This kind man was a Samaritan. And Jesus said, "Go and do likewise" as this Samaritan had done in showing mercy and compassion; in sacrificing for someone else. Who emulated Jesus? Not the priest, not the Levite, only the Samaritan.

Is it important what ethnic background this man had? Jesus's blood covers the sins of all folks who put their trust in Him. It doesn't matter your skin color or nationality or ethnicity or background or upbringing or station in life. Jesus came to seek and to save that which was lost, and to show mercy to each who will receive.

Jesus cited another Samaritan for his faith in Luke 17:11–19. This Samaritan was even a leper—another stigma in that day. Folks were to stay away from him because he was a Samaritan and because he was a leper. What is Jesus doing around one such as he? He is loving him.

There actually were ten lepers who called out to Jesus to have pity on them. Jesus did exactly that, and sent them to show themselves to the priests because they would be cleansed. They would all come back, praising God, for being healed, right? Wrong. How many came back? Only one, who threw himself at Jesus's feet, praising Him, thanking Him in a loud voice. This one was a Samaritan. Jesus asked where were the other nine who received healing as well. Was no one found to return and give praise to God except this foreigner? Jesus told him to rise and go—his faith had made him well.

A Samaritan, whose faith was in the Lord Jesus. What is this world coming to? We had better be coming to Jesus.

Do you remember Jesus speaking to the woman at the well in John 4? Jesus revealed truth to her, and because she gave testimony about Jesus to the other Samaritans from that town, many believed in Jesus. A female Samaritan missionary – whoever heard of such a thing? God has. The people urged Jesus to stay with them. He stayed two more days, and you know what happened? Many more Samaritans became believers in the Lord Jesus. They testified, "We know that this man really is the Savior of the world" (John 4:42).

Savior of the world, Indeed!

Tax collectors. Samaritans. And now, what about centurions? Would Jesus hold up a military officer—a centurion—as an example for the people?

In Matthew 8:5, we are told that when Jesus entered Capernaum, a centurion came to Him, asking for help. It was probably not very common to see a Roman soldier asking a Jewish rabbi for help. But here he was, asking for help for his servant, who lay paralyzed and suffering terribly at home. Jesus said He would go, but the centurion said that he would not even deserve for Jesus to come under his roof. Remember what Jesus said about humbling oneself? The centurion not only was humble but gave testimony about recognizing Jesus's power and authority. He believed that all Jesus had to do was say the word, and his servant would be healed. Jesus didn't have to go there in order for His power and authority to bring healing. All He had to do was speak it.

Think of this: "When Jesus heard this, he was amazed and said to those following him, 'Truly I tell you, I have not found anyone in Israel with such great faith'" (Matt. 8:10). Jesus amazed, and at a centurion? He held up the centurion for his faith, and told him to go and it would be done just as he had believed. His servant was healed that very hour. A Roman soldier believed in the Lord Jesus.

We are told of another centurion in Luke 23:47—this one the Roman military official in charge of Jesus's crucifixion. When Jesus completed His mission on the cross at Calvary, and breathed His last, this centurion "seeing what had happened, praised God and said, 'Surely, this was a righteous man.'" Now, we don't know for sure what was in this man's heart, but it would seem to be that he recognized that through all the torture, the scorn, the ridicule, the shame, the cruel death on this cross—which he likely would have seen many times before—that through it all, he saw that this was no ordinary man, no man like he had ever seen before, no mere mortal, but instead the righteous one, the Son of God.

What is this world coming to when tax collectors, Samaritans, and centurions put their trust in the Lord Jesus? What would our world come to today if the outcasts, the downtrodden, and the despised put their trust in the Lord Jesus? You see, it doesn't matter where you come from, who your people were or are, what your ethnicity is; it doesn't matter whose blood flows through your veins, it only matters that His blood covers you and cleanses you of your sins.

He told us in Mark 10:45 that He did not come to be served, but to serve and to give his life as a ransom for many. Are you one of these? He shed His blood for you. He gave His life for you.

You see, we make the mistake over and over again of looking at the outside, judging a book by its cover, so to speak. We make up our minds way too quickly by what we see on the surface. If we look at Jesus by the pictures we see, the paintings we see, we probably are not impressed. Very likely, He looked nothing like most of these images anyway. But, that isn't the point. Isaiah 53:2-3 says, "He had no beauty or majesty to attract us to him, nothing in his appearance that we should desire him. He was despised and rejected by mankind, a man of suffering, and familiar with pain. Like one from whom people hide their faces, he was despised, and we held him in low esteem." Despised and rejected; experiencing suffering and pain; held in low esteem. Does Jesus understand fully one who is looked down upon, shunned, cast out? Does Jesus understand you? Yes and Yes.

Can you face the fact that it doesn't matter to God what you look like, how you talk, where you live, that God is no respecter of persons because of any of this? What matters is your heart. What matters is whether you are covered by the blood of the Lamb. Continuing in Isaiah 53:4-5, "Surely he took up our pain and bore our suffering, yet we considered him punished by God, stricken by him, and afflicted. But he was pierced for our transgressions, he was crushed for our iniquities; the punishment that brought us peace was on him." He took your punishment, my punishment, not under duress, but willingly! He bore all your sins, and mine, on that cross, so you and I could be free.

God gives us this testimony in 1 John 5:11–12: "And this is the testimony; God has given us eternal life, and this life is in his Son. Whoever has the Son has life; whoever does not have the Son of God does not have life."

God calls you to put your trust in His Son Jesus, the Messiah, the Christ, the Savior of the world.

Jesus is the *only hope* we have. Jesus is the *only hope* we need.

He stands ready with open arms to save you (Rev. 3:20).

O Lord our God, thank You that You call us to come to You no matter our stature or station, no matter our appearance or accomplishment. May the one reading this believe You and come to You in faith and submission. In the name of the one punished, pierced, and crushed for our sin, Jesus. Amen.

The Advocate

So many words are written and spoken today about our rights. So many folks are looking for someone to stand up for them, *needing* someone to stand up for them.

To look out for their interests.

To be an advocate for them.

We have more methods to communicate with one another today perhaps than ever before... but just because we have so many, that doesn't mean it is working well for us.

It doesn't really mean that we connect.

It doesn't mean that we are being heard.

It doesn't mean that we have a sense of belonging.

It doesn't mean that we aren't left out, disenfranchised.

It hurts when we don't belong.

It hurts when we are left out.

It hurts when we don't have a voice.

Can we always find someone to take up our cause?

Can we *ever* find someone to take up our cause?

Is there always a sympathetic ear when we need one?

Do you have a sympathetic ear when you need one?

You can probably reflect on times when you had no one to listen to your case.

You probably have had moments in the dark hours of the night when you felt all alone.

You probably have memories of being left out.

You probably have had experiences where you didn't belong.

You probably have felt that no one understands what you are going through.

It is not uncommon. But that doesn't do you much good, does it?

So, is there anything, *anyone* who can help you?

Who can help you any hour of the day or night?

Who can help you every minute, every hour, every day?

Who can even help you with pain of the past?

Who will assure you that you can belong, in fact who will adopt you as His own?

Who will give you a life that is meaningful beyond that which you have ever known?

Who will strengthen you when you are weak?

Who will give you peace in the midst of chaos?

Who will fill your heart with hope when you are barely hanging on?

Who will bring contentment to your soul that nothing else will?

Perhaps you can't imagine that there is someone who can or will do this for you. Perfectly understandable, because most folks in this world have not experienced this. But you can.

Meet Jesus.

Because when you meet Jesus—truly meet Jesus—you will meet God, your Heavenly Father who loves you beyond your wildest imaginations, and you will meet the Holy Spirit, your Counselor, your Intercessor, your Advocate. You may have heard about Jesus, maybe even know quite a lot about Him. You likely have seen many images of Jesus. You probably have heard His name invoked in various ways. You may have read numerous opinions about Him.

But this isn't about the images you have seen. I have no doubt that many artists were well intentioned in their portrayal of events in His life; however, I also have no doubt that His physical appearance was unlike most of these images. Also, this isn't about the various ways you have heard His name invoked. It may be that His name has been more misused in your presence, or even by you, than called upon in the right way. And, this isn't about your opinions, my opinions, or anyone else's opinions about Him because all those added up don't amount to a hill of beans.

This is the call to meet the *real* Jesus. The Jesus revealed to us by His Father, our Creator. The one we truly see only through the eyes of faith.

In our world that is so focused on the outside—how we look, how we talk, how we carry ourselves—God said this about His Son, "He had no beauty or majesty to attract us to him, nothing in his appearance that we should desire him" (Is. 53:2). Don't look to the cover of GQ magazine to find Jesus. You won't find Him idolized in *People* magazine. He likely did not look like most of us have Him pictured in our minds or as depicted in our artwork. That's the point; He did not take on the human form to be the best-looking among us. He did not become one of us to be *unlike* most of us. He did not dwell among us to lord it over us. He came to identify with us. Most of us don't have perfect outward appearances, don't walk down runways as models to be photographed for our physical beauty, and don't appear on magazine covers for our sex appeal. Good news! Jesus identifies with you and me.

Even though we may try to lord it over someone else, most of us have no authority to do so. We certainly have no God-given right to do so. Jesus came as a servant. "rather, he made himself nothing by taking the very nature of a servant, being made in human likeness" (Phil. 2:7). He came to serve others, including you and me. "For even the Son of Man did not come to be served, but to serve, and to give his life as a ransom for many" (Mark 10:45).

The King of heaven came down here to be an earthly servant. He set aside kingly robes for swaddling clothes, and His birth was highlighted by the facts that he was born in a remote village; that his parents had sought anyplace they could find to stay for the night where their child could be born in safety; that he was laid in a feeding trough for common livestock; and that the news of his birth was proclaimed first to the humblest of folks—the shepherds out on the hillside. He came to identify with you and me. Would you look beyond any image that you may have of Jesus and see his humility? It isn't what he looked like that is important, what is important is *what* He is and *who* He is.

His name: Jesus's name has been misused and abused more than any other throughout history. Why? Satan would have it no other way. If he can lead anyone to see Jesus and Jesus's name for something other than the truth, then he wins in his lying and deceiving influence.

This is what God the Father did: He "gave him the name that is above every name, that at the name of Jesus every knee should bow, in heaven and on earth and under the earth, and every tongue acknowledge that Jesus Christ is Lord, to the glory of God the Father" (Phil. 2:9–11). Please understand that Jesus means "the Lord saves," and his earthly parents were "to give him the name Jesus, because he will save his people from their sins" (Matt. 1:21).

In the name of Jesus there is power to save, "Salvation is found in no one else, for there is no other name under heaven given to mankind by which we must be saved" (Acts 4:12). God the Father wants you to know this. Satan does not.

When we use the name of Jesus, it must be to praise His name above all others, to thank Him for what He has done to save us, to be our Deliverer, to call upon Him to help us, and to help others. "Everyone who calls on the name of the Lord will be saved" (Rom. 10:11).

You may have heard many opinions about Jesus. You may have had several opinions yourself. But opinions are not the answer. God's truth—His testimony—about His Son are the answer:

"Whoever believes in the Son of God accepts this testimony. Whoever does not believe God has made him out to be a liar, because they have not believed the testimony God has given about his Son. And this is the testimony: God has given us eternal life, and this life is in his Son. Whoever has the Son has life; whoever does not have the Son of God does not have life" (1 John 5:10–12).

Whoever knows Jesus–truly knows Jesus–knows the Father, the heavenly Father. "I and the Father are one...anyone who has seen me has seen the Father...The Son is the radiance of God's glory and the exact representation of his being" (John 10:30; 14:9; Heb. 1:3).

This is a call to receive Jesus, to know Jesus. Why? Because without Jesus, you will never have contentment. Without Jesus, you will never have peace. Without Jesus, you will never have salvation. Without Jesus, you will never have the Advocate.

You see, Jesus has already been your Advocate. He has already stood up for you. He has stood in for you. He has, in fact, already taken the punishment that was due you. Punishment for what, you may ask. Punishment due each and every one of us, "For all have sinned and fall short of the glory of God...There is no one righteous, not even one... For the wages of sin is death...All we like sheep have gone astray, we have turned each one of us to our own way" (Rom. 3:23; 3:10; 6:23; Is. 53:6).

We deserved death for our sinfulness. Jesus did not. He was without sin. Yet it was Jesus who stood up for us when the penalty was to be paid. It was Jesus who went to the cross in your place and mine. It was Jesus who atoned for you and me. What greater advocate could there be than one who would lay down his life for you?

That is not just so you can live in the here and now, but so you can live forever beyond this life in a place of unspeakable goodness and joy. Jesus came to give us life everlasting, not because we deserve it, but in spite of the fact that we don't.

God's laws require a sacrifice to cover sin, and Jesus stepped forward to be that sacrifice. Can you fathom it? Probably not. Can you believe it? Yes, you can, and for your eternal good, you must.

Yes, for sure "the wages of is death, but the gift of God is eternal life in Christ Jesus our Lord," and, for sure "we have turned each one to our own way, and the Lord has laid on him the iniquity of us all" (Rom. 6:23; Is.53:6). Where there is sin, there must be atonement for that sin in order for there to be forgiveness.

We all want forgiveness, don't we? Forgiveness is what is missing in all religions that teach salvation by works. Because we can never do enough good deeds, never be "devout" enough, to earn God's forgiveness.

But forgiveness can be ours according to our loving heavenly Father's plan through Christ Jesus, His Son. Yet it cannot be unless we confess our sin and repent of it.

When we repent, we avail ourselves to the grace and mercy that God our Father offers in His Son Jesus. Jesus who completed the work of atoning sacrifice at Calvary. He could do no more for you and me, yet His love for you and me would let Him do no less. Hallelujah to the Savior—your Savior and mine.

As for the here and now, Jesus left us His Spirit to be our Counselor, our Advocate before the Father, to take up our cause, to teach us, to comfort us, to correct us, to keep us pointed in the right direction—toward Jesus. "But the Advocate, the Holy Spirit, whom the Father will send in my name, will teach you all things and will remind you of everything I have said to you." (John 14:26) "the Spirit helps us in our weakness. We do not know what we ought to pray for, but the Spirit himself intercedes for us with groans that words cannot express" (Rom. 8:26*).

You see, you really do have someone—Someone—who hears your heartbeat, who feels your heartache; who stands up for you against the enemy; who steers you away from temptation; who is available all hours of the night and day; and Someone on whom you can count to guide you and teach you in the way that is best.

Job spoke of this one long ago in the midst of unspeakable tragedy and loss. As he lamented, "My spirit is broken, my days are cut short, the grave awaits me," yet still he looked up and proclaimed "even now my witness is in heaven; my advocate is on high. My intercessor is my friend as my eyes pour out tears to God; on behalf of a man he pleads with God as one pleads for his friend" (Job 17:1; 16:19–21).

Job knew that in the midst of his suffering, his loneliness, his confusion, and his misery that still he had one who knew him and spoke for him and pleaded his case before the heavenly Father.

And so do you and I.

If you will believe God, your Heavenly Father, if you will agree with Him that you, indeed, have failed—as we all have—and that you want

Him to change you, forgive you, save you, He will. Jesus has made all this possible by being the Lord and Savior you need. When He bore your sins on the cross, He made things right for you with the Father, unless of course you choose another way. But all other ways lead to damnation—eternal damnation.

No one comes to the Father except through Jesus, "I am the way and the truth and the life. No one comes to the Father except through me" (John 14:6). And in receiving Jesus, you will also receive the Advocate—His Spirit. Jesus also said, "and I will ask the Father and he will give you another advocate to help you and be with you forever—the Spirit of truth"..."he will guide you into all truth" (John 14:16; 16:13).

Just as Jesus is perfect, and an exact representation of His Father, so is the Holy Spirit perfect, and He will guide you and me to do what is right; He will teach you and me the truth; He will encourage you and me; He will hear our prayers, even help us in our praying; He will comfort us in our sorrow; He will shine a light—the Light of Jesus—on our paths continuously.

So you see, you do have Someone with whom you can connect, Someone who understands, Someone who cares, Someone who saves.

He is Jesus.

Will you put your trust in Him and live a life—full and everlasting?

That is the hope and plan of the one who created you, the one who died for you, the one who would indwell you—both now and forevermore.

O Lord our God, thank You that You have come to save us through Christ Jesus Your Son, and that You have come to be our Guide, our Advocate as Your Holy Spirit indwells us daily. I pray it is so for the one reading this in the name of Jesus who made it all possible. Amen.

The Lord Is My Shepherd

To whom do you belong? The answer to that question determines where you will spend eternity.

Do you belong to the Prince of Peace? Or, do you belong to the prince of darkness?

Do you belong to the Good Shepherd, Jesus? Or, do you belong to the cruel taskmaster, Satan?

Do you belong to the Lover of your soul? Or, do you belong to the one who would destroy your soul?

If you don't belong to the Good Shepherd, then you are owned by Satan. But it doesn't have to be that way—it will only be that way if you choose it to be. The Twenty-third Psalm is beautiful poetry. It is often quoted, often recited, many times at funerals. But there is much more to that Psalm than we often realize.

David knew what it was like to own sheep, to tend his sheep, to lead his sheep. He knew the 24/7 responsibility of taking care of his sheep. He knew all the planning that went into every day so that he could lead his sheep out to where they would have exactly what they needed in food and clean water. He knew what he had to do to protect them and keep them safe. He knew what was required for their security and calmness.

Did you know that we have a lot in common with sheep? Sheep do not do well on their own. Neither do we do well on our own. Sheep need someone—a shepherd—to watch over them, provide for them, protect them, love them. We need someone—a shepherd—to watch over us, provide for us, protect us, love us. Now, the lot in life for sheep depends on the type of shepherd who owns them, whether that shepherd is gentle, kind, brave, selfless, or whether that shepherd is cruel, selfish, uncaring, insensitive. Sheep cannot choose in whose care they are. You and I can.

"The Lord is my shepherd, I shall not want" (Ps. 23:1**). "The Lord is my shepherd, I lack nothing" (Ps. 23:1).

The Psalmist, David, proclaims proudly that it is the Lord who is his shepherd. It is with admiration, appreciation, and devotion that David speaks of his Lord. The good shepherd makes ample provision for his sheep. He prepares the field, the path that his sheep will travel that day, to make sure that they will have enough to sustain them. Now, it isn't always a field lush with knee-deep alfalfa as we may have pictured it. In fact, much of the area around which David and other shepherds would have led their sheep is desert-like. The path might actually have only a tuft of grass here, and a sprig of grass there, but the good shepherd knows that where he leads his sheep, there will be enough. Will there be enough for two or three days? Probably not, but they don't need enough for two or three days; they only need enough for today.

God doesn't promise us a storehouse full, but He does promise to meet our needs. "And my God will meet all your needs according to the riches of his glory in Christ Jesus" (Phil. 4:19). With the Lord as my Shepherd, I shall not lack for what I need, and neither will you, if the Lord is your Shepherd. In Jesus, we can be, and should be, utterly satisfied and content. Jesus said in John 10:10–11: "I have come that they may have life, and have it to the full. I am the good shepherd. The good shepherd lays down his life for the sheep."

Sheep are identified with their shepherd by a distinctive earmark. So, the sheep of the Good Shepherd Jesus are identified with Him by distinctive traits. Those belonging to Jesus want to follow Him, to be like Him, and do the things that Jesus does. Are you His; do you belong to Jesus; and are you under His direction?

"He makes me lie down in green pastures" (Ps. 23:2a).

The shepherd starts his sheep out early in the morning, walking them steadily and grazing them along the way. After being on the move for a while, there comes a time when they need rest. They are hot, tired, and thirsty. But they will not rest unless they are free of fear, hunger, and pests. So, the good shepherd finds a cool, safe, quiet spot for them to lie down and rest. And, they are comforted because he is nearby.

Likewise, we need to take time to rest, to "Be still and know that I am God" (Ps. 46:10). Jesus took time to be quiet and pray; so should we. Elijah spoke of God's still, small voice, which we hear more easily when we stop and rest and listen. A flock that is restless, discontented, and agitated never does well. Sounds like us, doesn't it? But, as the good shepherd continually provides for them what they need, they sense that he has things under control, and they find rest. Some sheep, however, are just prone to be restless, discontented, also, like many of us.

Phillip Keller wrote in *A Shepherd looks at the 23rd Psalm* of one ewe who was like this. She was one of the most attractive sheep he ever owned. She was beautifully proportioned with an excellent coat of wool. Her head was clean, and she had bright eyes. She bore sturdy, healthy lambs. But she was always looking for something beyond the best grazing field. She would look for any place that she could get out, and you know where she often ended up—feeding on a bare, brown, inferior pasture. She repeatedly had to settle for so much less than what she had. She began to lead other sheep astray, and finally Keller writes that he had no choice but to put her down. Her eyes were on something other than the good shepherd and what he provided.

How often have you settled for so much less than what the Good Shepherd offers you? When our eyes are on the Good Shepherd, Jesus, we will find rest, contentment, and peace. Jesus said in John 6:35, "I am the bread of life. Whoever comes to me will never go hungry, and whoever believes in me will never be thirsty."

"He leads me beside still waters" (Ps. 23:2b).

Still waters; quiet waters. Water is essential for the well-being of the sheep—about 70 percent of their body is composed of water. Why still waters? Because sheep are poor swimmers. If they were to step out into a swift current, their coat of wool would soak up the water, and they would likely drown were it not for the good shepherd to rescue them. But what if there is no still water to be found?

Just like the green pastures don't just happen on their own, neither do pools of clean, fresh water. The good shepherd will often have to provide such waters, sometimes forming a dam across the stream so there will be a pool from which his sheep can drink. If the good shepherd doesn't provide and lead them to the good water supply, where will they drink? Oftentimes, they would drink from polluted potholes where they would pick up parasites and germs. Have you done that? Have you settled for polluted places where you will be infected and harmed?

Jesus tells us: "Whoever believes in me will never be thirsty" (John 6:35b). Believing in Jesus is to trust Him, take Him in, spend time with Him. Learning that He will provide that which you need. "Taste and see that the Lord is good" (Ps. 34:8).

Sheep often graze early in the morning on dew-drenched vegetation. This is a clean and pure source of water. What a picture for you and me, finding nourishment early in the morning from time with the Lord Himself—feeding on God's Word. "Satisfy us in the morning with your unfailing love, that we may sing for joy and be glad all our days" (Ps. 90:14).

"He restores my soul" (Ps. 23:3a**). "He refreshes my soul" (Ps. 23:3a).

Each sheep receives one-on-one attention from the good shepherd. He touches them, rubs their noses and ears, reassures and encourages them. That requires face-to-face contact.

You remember how David faced and defeated Goliath in the power of the Lord? But, what happened to David after that? He strayed away from God's power; he sinned against God and man; he was overcome with guilt; he repented; he came face to face with the Lord; and the Lord restored his soul.

Forgiveness comes when we repent, when we come clean before the Lord face to face. We are then restored—revived—refreshed.

David knew what it was like to be downcast or cast down. This is an old English shepherd's term for a sheep who is turned over on its back without the ability to get up by itself. It is a downcast or cast down sheep. Without help, such a sheep will die. It points up how important for the good shepherd to know his sheep, count his sheep, and be aware of where they are. And when he finds one in this state, he rolls it over, lifts it up, stands it on its legs, straddles it to rub its limbs to restore circulation, all the while speaking words of encouragement.

Now, a sheep could end up in the downcast state for several reasons, but one of the main ones is too much wool. We can be so encumbered, so weighted down by the things of this world, that we too become downcast. It is then that we should turn to the Good Shepherd Jesus to be lifted up, encouraged, loved, and restored.

"He leads me in paths of righteousness for His name's sake" (Ps. 23:3b**). "He guides me along the right paths for his name's sake" (Ps. 23:3b).

We need guidance. We need someone to show us the way. Sheep have no sense of direction. Dogs, cats, and horses can often find their way back after being lost, but not sheep. For one thing, they have poor eyesight. The paths in that day were often bordered on one side by a steep drop-off, and so, danger was ever present. But, with the good shepherd leading the way, the sheep would be at peace knowing he would lead them safely. Likewise, the Good Shepherd doesn't point out to us a place where he wants us to go where He Himself has never been. No, He leads us on the right path, the path that brings us good, and leads us home.

It takes planning and careful attention to detail for the good shepherd. Likewise, the Good Shepherd, Jesus, has the perfect plan, and He knows every detail about where He wants to lead us. The Lord does not drive us or force us to go where we cannot safely go. Instead, He leads us on the right path, the path of righteousness so that we will identify with our Master, so we will do the things that He does—for our good and for His glory. Proverbs 3:6 instructs us to "In all your ways submit to him, and he will make your path straight." It lies in His will, doing what He asks us to do.

"Yea, though I walk through the valley of the shadow of death, I will fear no evil, for You are with me" (Ps. 23:4a**). "Even though I walk through the darkest valley, I will fear no evil, for you are with me" (Ps. 23:4a).

Facing death can lead us to feel helpless and alone. Jesus knows what that is like. He faced death. He died. And He arose. He promised never to leave us or forsake us (Heb. 13:5). I think of His presence in the fiery furnace with Hananiah, Mishael, and Azeriah (Dan. 3); of His presence with Daniel in the den of lions (Dan. 6); of His presence with Stephen as he was stoned to death (Acts 7); they were not alone in their valley of the shadow of death. These valleys are places to trust, places to lean on the everlasting arms. He is there with us. Remember, shadows cannot hurt us. And, besides, Jesus drives even the shadows away.

"your rod and your staff, they comfort me" (Ps.23:4b).

We long for protection and safety, don't we? Sheep are pretty help-less creatures, easy prey for the enemy. The good shepherd uses the rod—which is a hard, heavy club—as a weapon against the predator. It is also used to discipline his sheep for their own good. And he uses it to examine his sheep, parting the wool to expose sores or areas that need attention. His staff—which is about eight feet long with a crook on the end—is often used to lift the sheep out of thorny patches, ledges, and other dangerous places. It is a symbol of the shepherd's strength and power. He uses the staff to guide his sheep along, to touch them for that reassuring and comforting contact.

"You prepare a table before me in the presence of my enemies" (Ps. 23:5a).

Some of the enemies of the sheep are poisonous plants, which can be fatal; and thorny bushes, which can lead to sores and infections; not to mention the predators lurking about. The good shepherd digs these plants up and roots them out, preparing the field–the table–for his sheep so that they have a safe place to graze. Just like a farmer can't simply plant his crop and forget about it... he has to go in and chop down or dig up weeds again and again, so the good shepherd has to continually prepare the table for his sheep. He is always on the lookout for predators and where they may hide.

The Good Shepherd Jesus is out ahead of His own, preparing the heavenly table around which all of us who belong to Him will one day sit in His presence. He longs to see you at that table, so much so that He went to the cross for you.

"You anoint my head with oil; my cup overflows" (Ps. 23:5b).

We get hurt in life, don't we? Bruised and banged up. So it is with sheep. The good shepherd examines each one individually to remove the briars and thorns; to pour oil on the sores. He provides refreshing water as he is caring for them and loving on them. Like the child who wants his mom to kiss the sore place, so the sheep look to the good shepherd to be treated and comforted.

Likewise, the Good Shepherd Jesus examines each one of us and knows what hurts we have, not just on the outside, but on the inside, and He will treat and comfort each one of His own. He calls His sheep by name, they hear His voice, and know His voice (John 10). The Good Shepherd Jesus anoints us with His Holy Spirit so that we are set apart to do His work. There is no higher calling than to say yes to the Father today. It is then that we truly know what the full and meaningful life is all about. It is then that we are filled to the measure of all the fullness of God.

"Surely your goodness and love will follow me all the days of my life, and I will dwell in the house of the Lord forever." (Ps. 23:6)

When I was younger, I didn't understand how "Shirley" fit in here. (I think it is clearer now). The Good Shepherd Jesus is all about goodness, love, and mercy. The Good Shepherd treats His sheep so. He longs to show His love to you, and He longs for you to show your love to Him. For those who put their trust in Him, there awaits the house of the Lord—the presence of the Lord, the glory of the Lord, all around, for all time. No more of all the things that bind us, hurt us, cause us to suffer, bring us heartache, bring us pain, bring us down—no more of these. Only what Jesus is, and only what Jesus does, will be present—love, joy, peace, gentleness, righteousness, faithfulness, in this everlasting house of the Lord.

Charles L. Allen tells the story in *God's Psychiatry* of two men on a platform, both called to be a part of special program before a vast audience of people. Each of them would recite the Twenty-third Psalm from memory. The younger man, trained in speech and drama technique, presented first. The crowd cheered his eloquence and clapped for an encore that they might hear his wonderful voice again. Then, the older gentleman, leaning on his cane, stepped forward, and in feeble, shaking voice, recited the same words from the beloved Psalm. When he finished, there came no sound from the listeners as before. Folks seemed instead to be praying. After some silence, the young man stood to make this statement, "Friends, I wish to make an explanation. You asked me to come back and repeat the Psalm, but you remained silent when my friend here was seated. The difference? I shall tell you. I know the Psalm, but he knows the Shepherd!"

Please know the Shepherd, my friend, and entrust yourself into His care.

O Lord God, thank You for being our Good Shepherd in Christ Jesus, for being the one who watches over us, provides for us, and delivers us. I pray it is so for the one reading this in the name of the Good Shepherd who laid down His life for this one, and for me. Amen

Unless...I Will Not Believe

*W*hat is your "unless" that keeps you from believing in Jesus? For Thomas, one of the disciples, it was seeing and touching the actual wounds in Jesus's body.

Jesus had been crucified to death, had been buried, and had been raised from the dead. He had appeared to many in the days after His resurrection, including the other disciples, but Thomas, not being with them, had not yet seen the risen Lord.

John 20:24–25 explains, "Now Thomas (called Didymus), one of the Twelve, was not with the disciples when Jesus came. So the other disciples told him, 'We have seen the Lord!' But he said to them, 'Unless I see the nail marks in his hands and put my finger where the nails were, and put my hand into his side, I will not believe.'"

What is your unless... that keeps you from believing in Jesus as the one who is risen from the dead? What keeps you from "tasting and seeing that the Lord is good" (Ps. 34:8)? What keeps you from trusting in the Lord with all your heart—not leaning on your own understanding—and acknowledging Him in all your ways so that He will make your path straight (Prov. 3:5–6)?

What keeps you from believing that Jesus has overcome death, over-coming the world so that you have hope and peace? Jesus said this, "I have told you these things, so that in me you may have peace. In this world you will have trouble. But take heart! I have overcome the world" (John 16:33). What keeps you from believing that you need Jesus? He said "I told you that you would die in your sins; if you do not believe that I am the one I claim to be, you will indeed die in your sins" (John 8:24*).

Do you want to die in your sins? Would you choose eternal separation from the one who loves you beyond your wildest imagination? Would you choose everlasting damnation? Do you want the worst you have ever experienced multiplied a million times over, and not just for a moment, but for all moments for all time? Could you possibly want a place of torment and anguish to be your fate?

That is without a doubt not what your Creator wants for you. That is not His plan for you.

God says that He has loved you so very much that He gave His one and only Son to die on a cross for you, so that you would believe in Him and not perish but have everlasting life. You see, God did not send His Son into the world to bring you condemnation, but to bring you salvation (John 3:16–18). Jesus said that He came to seek and to save the lost (Luke 19:9).

Unless you believe that you are lost apart from Jesus the Christ, you are deceived. Know this, God does not deceive. He tells the truth. Jesus is the Truth. He proclaimed that He is the Way, and the Truth, and the Life, and that no one will come to the Father unless they come through Jesus (John 14:6).

The deceiver is Satan. He comes to you in order to steal from you, to kill you, and to destroy you. Jesus comes to you to bring you life, and life to the max (John 10:10).

Satan is a murderer and a liar, in fact, the father of lies. "He was a murderer from the beginning, not holding to the truth, for there is no truth in him. When he lies, he speaks his native language, for he is a liar and the father of lies" (John 8:44).

So believe this. You and I have sinned. We have broken the commandments, probably every one of them, probably every one of them more than once. But, it isn't about the tally of the ones we have broken or the number of times we have broken them. It is the fact that we have broken them. We are sinners. Sinners need saving. "for all have sinned and fall short of the glory of God" (Rom. 3:23).

You know what the glory of God is—Jesus. Do you think you have fallen short of Jesus?

Let's see, Jesus gave up paradise to come into this sin-sick world where He would be subjected to the worst of all humankind. He would put others' needs above His own—not just for a moment, but for all His time here on earth. He would meet the needs of those around Him, both physically and spiritually. He fed them. He healed them of every kind of infirmity and sickness. He delivered them from demons. He raised them from the dead.

But more importantly than all these, He gave them hope. He forgave them of their sins. He freed them from the bonds of Satan. He brought to them everlasting life. He is the Light of the world. He is the Bread of life. He is the living Water.

Yet, He was mocked. He was ridiculed. He was rejected. He was falsely accused. He was betrayed. He was abandoned. He was stripped. He was beaten. He was starved. He was slapped. He was spit upon. He was condemned. He was not the one chosen to be released by the very ones He came to save. He was nailed to a cross. He was crucified as a criminal. How do you compare to that? Have you fallen short of Jesus? What is your unless?

If you could only see Him, or touch Him, then you would believe. But that isn't the problem. There were likely many who saw Him in the flesh, perhaps even touched Him, perhaps even followed Him for a while, who still did not believe in Him. The problem is not evidence, the problem is disobedience. We are warned in Hebrews 3:12 to see to it that we do not have a sinful, unbelieving heart that turns away from the living God. Disobedience is in our hearts.

And, it doesn't matter what color our skin is; it doesn't matter what kind of upbringing we had; it doesn't matter what level of education we have; it doesn't matter what amount of money we have earned in our lives or how we earned it; it doesn't matter what awards we have attained; it doesn't matter how many times we haven't been chosen for the team; and it doesn't matter how many friends we have or don't have—disobedience is in our hearts, and we need Jesus.

Jesus is the only hope we have. Jesus is the only hope we need. We don't need more evidence or more proof of anything. If we don't desire to be reborn into a new nature with a new heart, then no amount of evidence or proof will matter. No matter how many of your unlesses are met, without becoming new in Christ Jesus, it won't matter.

God draws you to Him by the power of His Spirit. If you resist His Holy Spirit, then you are giving in to the disobedience of your heart. If you yield to His Holy Spirit, then you will be led to repentance of your sin, to faith in the Lord Jesus, and to a new life in Him. There will be no peace in your heart, in your life, apart from Jesus because you will never receive forgiveness for your sins apart from Him.

Thomas spoke out of his resistance to believe—to trust—in what the Lord Jesus had told them... that He would, indeed, be crucified but would arise from the grave on the third day. We don't know for sure if Thomas—having stated his unless to the others—even reached forth his hand to touch the wounds of the Savior, but, you see, he didn't have to. Whatever happened in that moment, of this we can be sure. God's Spirit moved upon Thomas to draw him to Jesus, and lead him to confess "My Lord and my God!" (John 20:28).

Where are you in this moment? Is there an unless this or unless that, that keeps you from crossing the bridge of faith? Are you doubtful about Jesus? Jesus does not rebuke us for doubt, but He does rebuke us for unbelief.

Doubt is often an intellectual problem—unanswered questions and problems. Our world is full of those.

Unbelief is a moral problem—rooted in our hearts.

If you or I had to have the answers to every question, solve every problem, allay every doubt before believing in the Lord Jesus, then you and I would never have any hope of forgiveness, peace, and everlasting life.

We must choose to step out on faith, try the Lord, and see that He is faithful. He is true. Everything He says He will do, He does. He says He will save you. He will.

What is going to take for you? What are the conditions God must meet before you will believe?

Maybe if you really saw someone raised from the dead, that would do it. Probably not. Thomas had seen that. He was there when Jesus raised Lazarus—in the grave four days—from the dead.

Did you know that Thomas had shown great courage earlier? You see, it was in Judea, where Mary, Martha, and Lazarus lived that Jesus had been threatened. The Jews there had intended to stone him (John 10:31). So, the threat of death hung over Him as He returned there to raise Lazarus. It was Thomas who spoke up to the others "Let us also go, that we may die with him" (John 11:16).

A person can be courageous and yet be unbelieving. It is a choice to be unbelieving. If you are without Christ, you are without hope. You have no lasting peace. You exist in unforgiveness of your sins. You are destined for an eternal hell.

Thomas spent a week—apart from the other disciples—and therefore had missed opportunities to be with the Lord. So, the others had already seen the resurrected Jesus, had been encouraged by Him, had heard His words of peace, and had their fears removed.

I imagine that was a pretty miserable and lonely week for Thomas. But he did return to the fold, and when he did, Jesus appeared again among them, and Thomas chose to believe. His conditions didn't have to be met. He just needed to believe.

Unless this or unless that will happen for you, then you will not believe.

Unless this person will come through for you, then you will not believe.

If only that one thing changes to make your life better, then you will believe.

If only that for which you have waited so long materializes, then you will believe.

What if this or that doesn't happen? Will you throw away eternity? If only circumstances change, then you will believe. What if circumstance don't change? Will you call God a liar?

"Whoever does not believe God had made him out to be a liar, because they have not believed the testimony God has given about his Son. And this is the testimony: God has given us eternal life, and this life is in his Son. Whoever who has the Son has life; whoever does not have the Son of God does not have life" (1 John 5:10–12).

If only...

Unless...

These are conditions that puny man cannot put upon our Creator God and expect that He will meet them. Because, you see, He has met all the conditions He needs to meet to save you.

You are a sinner. You will die in your sins. You need a Savior. There is one. He is Jesus. He took your sins on the cross. He paid your ransom. He conquered death. He rose again. So can you believe in Him?

Now is the time to believe. Now is the time to confess Jesus, your Lord and your God.

"That if you confess with your mouth, 'Jesus as Lord', and believe in your heart that God raised him from the dead, you will be saved...For everyone who calls on the name of the Lord will be saved" (Rom. 10: 9–10, 13).

What if Thomas had not seen Jesus anymore before Jesus ascended into heaven? Would he have believed in Him? I don't know, but it doesn't matter. Jesus made sure that Thomas would see Him again in the flesh. He even said to him, "Put your finger here; see my hands. Reach out your hand and put it into my side. Stop doubting and believe."

Again, we don't know whether Thomas put his finger there or reached out his hand to touch Jesus's side, but we do know that he believed. He exclaimed, "My Lord and my God!" (John 20:27-28).

"Then Jesus told him, 'Because you have seen me you have believed; blessed are those who have not seen and yet have believed'" (John 20:29). Jesus spoke of you and me. We have not seen Him in the flesh. But we can see Him through eyes of faith.

He stands with open arms to receive you. He is making sure to encounter you, to appear before you, face to face, to stand at your door and knock so you will open and invite Him in and so that you have every opportunity to be saved. He is pursuing you by the power of His Holy Spirit. He did all He needed to do in the flesh. Now, His Spirit is continually at work, doing all He can, to draw you to Him through faith, in order that you spend eternity with Him.

Will you proclaim Jesus as your Lord and your God?

O Lord our God, thank You for removing any need we have for unlesses. Thank You for being truthful to the one reading this and to me so that we can count on what You say. We have no right to put any conditions on You who have loved us without conditions. I pray that Your Spirit speaks and draws this one to You now in the name of our Savior Jesus. Amen.

Unrequited Love

*H*ave you ever loved with no return? Have you ever given yourself to someone who gave you nothing back? Have you ever done what you could, maybe all you could, to show someone how important they are to you, only to see that you were not so important to them? Have you ever been considerate of someone else, only for them to be inconsiderate toward you? Have you ever been compassionate toward someone, but you were met with indifference from them? Have you ever shown mercy toward someone and received only scorn back from them? Have you ever proven trustworthy to someone, and yet they still wouldn't trust you? Have you ever been unselfish and giving to someone, and yet, in return, they were ungrateful to you?

As you can see, I am not just talking about romantic relationships but all relationships. It could be with your spouse, a friend, a family member, a co-worker, or a neighbor. In any case, doesn't it hurt when you are doing right by them, and they are not doing right by you? You are laying it all out there for them, yet they have shut themselves off from you. It hurts badly when they are uncaring toward you, doesn't it?

When they are unappreciative toward you.

When they are indifferent toward you.

When they are scornful toward you.

When they are hateful toward you.

When they reject you.

How are you treating Jesus? Are you trusting Him? Are you trusting in Him? Why should you? Only because He has done all the above and countless more for you.

In the Gospel accounts, there is record upon record upon record of Jesus reaching out to the hurting, the suffering, the lonely, the forgotten, the helpless, the rejected, the scorned, the ugly, and the lost. Listen to what John wrote at the end of his Gospel writings: "Jesus did many other things as well. If every one of them were written down, I suppose that even the whole world would not have room for the books that would be written" (John 21:25).

In all that He has done, and is still doing, Jesus has given you every reason to love Him. Why would you settle for less than Jesus? Why does He do what He does? *Love.* Because He loves you and me. Oh, how He loves you, Oh, how He loves me, Oh, how He loves you and me.

He began loving you before you came to be. He saw everything that you would ever be, and He loved you. He sees who you are today and who you were yesterday, and who you will be tomorrow, and He loves you—still.

He knows your every sinful thought, your every sinful act, and He loves you—still. He knows your act, and mine. He knows your pretense, and mine. He knows your prideful motivation, and mine. How can Jesus know so much about you? He created you.

"He (Jesus) is the image of the invisible God, the firstborn over all creation. For by him all things were created; things in heaven and on earth, visible and invisible, whether thrones or powers or rulers or authorities; all things were created by him and for him. He is before all things, and in him all things hold together" (Col. 1:15–17*).

You exist, you live, you breathe because He holds you together. He knows everything about you, and He loves you—still. He has walked where you walk. Jesus stepped out of perfect heaven into our imperfect world to live as one of us.

"In the beginning was the Word, and the Word was with God, and the Word was God. He was with God in the beginning. Through him all things were made; without him nothing was made that has been made" (John 1:1–3). "The Word became flesh, and made his dwelling among us" (John 1:14). Why? He came to identify with us.

He knows what you are going through—the hurt, the rejection, the despair, the temptation, the trial. He has been there, He has earned your trust... so trust Him to help you through it. "For we do not have a high priest who is unable to sympathize with our weaknesses, but we have one who has been tempted in every way just as we are- yet he did not sin" (Heb. 4:15).

He is not like authority figures that you and I have faced who tell you to do something that they themselves have never done nor would ever do. They can't show you because they don't know how. It is hard to lead someone where you yourself have never been. Jesus leads you through dark places where He has been. Jesus leads you through tough places where He has been.

But, it isn't just that He has been there, done that. We say that like we know all about it. Been there, done that. But with Jesus, it is different. There is nothing that you face this day that He hasn't already faced, and already faced it down. There is nothing that you will face tomorrow that He hasn't already faced, and already faced it down.

You see, you and I need someone to understand what we are feeling, what we are facing, but, more than that, we need someone who will *help us* where we are. He is that Someone. He understands. He meets our needs. He helps us where we are. He came to seek out and save the lost. "For the Son of Man came to seek and to save the lost" (Luke 19:10).

In Luke 15:4–6, Jesus speaks of one sheep out of a hundred that was lost, and how the owner searched and found it, then wanted all around him to join in rejoicing because he had found his lost sheep. How about something even more insignificant than one sheep? How about a lost coin (Luke 15:8–9)? The woman found her lost coin and called her friends and neighbors together to join her in rejoicing. What is Jesus teaching us here—that in the same way, there is rejoicing in heaven, in the presence of the angels of God over one sinner who repents.

In Luke 19:1-9, Zacchaeus had acquired great wealth as a tax collector, apparently not all of it honestly. He was wealthy and prominent in his community. He had gained considerable worldly goods, but he, himself, was lost. Jesus came to him and called him to a new life, a life not of selfishness but a life of surrender. Zacchaeus submitted to the Lordship of Jesus, and he was changed. He was saved to a new life, and life everlasting. As the new man in Christ, he surrendered half of his possessions to the poor.

And more than that, all that he had cheated, he repaid—not just what he owed them (which would have been noteworthy)—not twice what he owed them—not three time what he owed them—no, he repaid them what he owed them times four. You see, he was rich, but he was lost—without Jesus. He surrendered to Jesus as Lord of his life, and he was saved, not only unto an eternal heaven, but saved to finally live a life of purpose and fulfillment here on earth.

Jesus came to seek and save the lost. Each of us is lost without Jesus. We are like a ship without a sail, misguided, without purpose, and headed in the wrong direction. You see, if you are not headed in Jesus's direction, you are headed the wrong way. "We all, like sheep, have gone astray, each of us has turned to his own way" (Is. 53:6a).

And who suffered because of this? Certainly, we have, but Jesus suffered most of all, "and the Lord laid on him the iniquity of us all" (Is. 53:6b).

He was led like a lamb to the slaughter.

He had done no violence, yet violence befell Him.

He had no deceit in Him, yet He died for the deceitful.

He did not oppress anyone, yet He was oppressed.

He did not afflict anyone, yet He was afflicted.

He cursed no one, yet He was cursed.

He brought healing to the multitudes, yet He suffered at the hands of the multitude.

He brought joy to the people, yet endured agony.

He brought life to those He created, yet He was crucified unto death.

Unrequited love? No one knows like Jesus. He paid it all.

I asked questions earlier about what have you received in return for good things you have done. What has Jesus received in return? The majority of all He created will reject Him, according to Matthew 7:14: "But small is the gate and narrow the road that leads to life, and only a few find it." But the good news is that you can be one of those few. Sin has left a crimson stain on your soul and my soul. But Jesus makes it white as snow.

Does Jesus want you to be saved? Does Jesus want you to repent? Second Peter 3:9 tells us God is not slow in keeping His promise as some understand slowness. He is patient with you, Why? He does not want you to perish because He wants all to come to repentance. First Timothy 2:4 shows us that God, our Savior, desires that all men be saved and come to a knowledge of the Truth; do you hear that? God wants you to be saved and to come to a knowledge of the Truth. What is Truth? Jesus is Truth. God calls us to come to Jesus.

"For there is one God, and one mediator between God and men, the man Christ Jesus, who gave himself as a ransom for all men" (1 Tim. 2:5*). Jesus had told His disciples that He was going to lay down His life, and He would be going away to a place that He would prepare for His followers to come. He told them that they knew the way to the place where He was going. But Thomas said to Him, "Lord, we don't know where you are going, so how can we know the way" (John 14:5). Jesus answered, "I am the way and the truth and the life. No one comes to the Father except through me" (John 14:6).

So, what is the Truth? Jesus.

What is the Way? Jesus.

What is the Life? Jesus.

But, to everyone who calls on the name of the Lord Jesus, to everyone who believes in his or her heart that God raised Him from the dead, to everyone who confesses Jesus as Lord before others, salvation comes. Forgiveness comes. Peace comes. It is not because of anything you or I have done, or anything that you are or I am, it is only because of what Jesus is and what He has done.

We come to Him in repentance of our sins. We come to Him, surrendering our lives. He becomes Lord of all of you. You see, He is Lord of all, no matter what you do. Jesus is Lord. You will bow before Him and acknowledge that He is Lord. You will do it either by invitation while you have breath here on this earth, or you will do it in judgment beyond the grave.

"Therefore God exalted Him to the highest place and gave him the name that is above every name, that at the name of Jesus every knee should bow, in heaven and on earth and under the earth, and every tongue confess that Jesus Christ is Lord, to the glory of God the Father" (Phil. 2:9–11*).

The Father's desire is that you bow before Him now, and agree that He is Lord of your life—submit to Him as Lord of your life. He then becomes Savior of your soul for all eternity.

His love for you then is not unrequited.

His love for you then is rewarded in you with Him for eternity.

O Lord our God, thank You for love so amazing, so divine, so everlasting to be unlike any other. Thank You for Your patience to wait for us in our disobedience. I pray for the one reading this message to respond to Your love in surrender and trust. In the name of the ultimate lover of all, Jesus. Amen.

What Is Truth?

*W*hat is truth in our world today? Is truth different today than it was last year? Last century? Last millennium? Does truth change? "What is truth?" is a question that was posed by Pilate, the Roman governor, to Jesus, as the Son of God stood before him as a man condemned to die. Pilate had already questioned the charges brought against Jesus by the Jewish leaders. He even commanded them to take him themselves and deal with him according to their laws. They objected on the grounds that they had no rights by which to execute him. So, here is what happened next:

"Pilate then went back inside the palace, summoned Jesus and asked him, 'Are you the king of the Jews?' 'Is that your own idea,' Jesus asked, 'or did others talk to you about me?' 'Am I a Jew?' Pilate replied. 'Your own people and chief priests handed you over to me. What is it you have done?' Jesus said, 'My kingdom is not of this world. If it were, my servants would fight to prevent my arrest by the Jewish leaders. But now my kingdom is from another place.' 'You are a king, then!' said Pilate. Jesus answered, 'You say that I am a king. In fact, the reason I was born and came into the world is to testify to the truth. Everyone on the side of truth listens to me.'

'What is truth?' retorted Pilate. With this he went out..." (John 18:33–38).

Was Pilate really interested in the answer to that question? My belief is probably not because if he was, there likely would be more exchange between Jesus and Pilate recorded before he left Jesus's presence.

Many times folks will ask that question rhetorically as if to say, "What is truth anyway?" not convinced that anyone can really know.

This perhaps is born out of our world today in which we often hear conflicting reports about what is true, particularly in the realm of politics, in the realm of conflicts between nations and cultures, and in the realm of religion.

Can truth be known? If so, how?

Who do we believe?

We have heard stories told that have been handed down generation through generation by folks who weren't actually there when the events happened. Typically, the stories become a little more dramatic, juicier, or fantastic through the different tellings.

Wouldn't it be great if we could hear it right from the one who was there? That person would have been an actual eyewitness. They could speak of it firsthand. Surely they would know the truth, right? I reckon so, if their memory was accurate, or if they weren't trying to downplay some aspect of it, or glorify some other aspect of it. Oftentimes, our own agenda clouds our vision of the truth or reality,

Wouldn't the police and the courts have a much easier task if they could count on reliable eyewitnesses who saw it all and related it accurately in detail? But we know that is not the case oftentimes. Instead, different eye-witnesses give different accounts, making it difficult to determine the truth.

What if there was one who was trustworthy in every way, could be believed on every point, who always tells the truth, who wrote the book?

What if this one was there in the very beginning of it all, has seen everything that has ever taken place in all of creation, is still living today, is still communicating with us today, and who understands the whys and wherefores like no one else?

What if this one actually wants *you* to know the truth in every way, in fact, wants every one of us to know the truth in every way so that we can be free from the pitfalls and destruction that lies and deception cause.

What if this one proved himself trustworthy to you and me in ways that no one in all history has ever done?

What if this one literally has done everything he could so that you would believe him, trust him, and in so doing, experience a life far beyond your imagination?

Friend, to understand truth, we do, in fact, need to go back to the very beginning. For it is there where it all began for you and me; there is where the foundation for all that is was laid. That is where *our* foundation was laid; there is where we find the one who gave us life and purpose. Wouldn't He be the one who knows the truth?

Many speculate about how we got here, why we are here, and what will become of us. But who among us mortals knows for sure? I will look to the Immortal One, our Creator, for those answers, what about you?

Will you look to the created or the Creator? The Creator has not left us alone to figure it all out. He does not want us to be confused, unsure, without hope. He does not see you as the number six billion, eight hundred twenty-four millionth human being that he has created, although He would know the actual count.

No, instead He sees you as one that He lovingly gave breath, and as one He lovingly wants to spend time with, not only in the here and now, but for all eternity. Truly, He does see you as one who, like every one of us, does not naturally want the same things He wants. But just as truly, He sees you as one who needs exactly what He offers. So, back to the beginning, the genesis:

"In the beginning, God created the heavens and the earth...In the beginning was the Word, and the Word was with God, and the Word was God. He was with God in the beginning. Through him all things were made; without him nothing was made that has been made...The Son is the image of the invisible God, the firstborn over all creation. For in him all things were created; things in heaven and on earth, visible and invisible, whether thrones or powers or rulers or authorities; all things have been created through him and for him. He is before all things, and in him all things hold together" (Gen. 1:1; John 1:1–3; Col. 1:15–17).

Who better to know about this life than the one who gives it?

Who better to know about heaven and earth than the one who created them?

Who better to know about all things than the one who holds them all together?

How easy it is for us to wander and to be led away from the truth. Try walking a straight line to a designated spot with a blindfold on. Likely as not, you will begin to stray off the line, and the further you go, the more off the line you will get. Even though you ever so slightly veered off at the beginning, eventually you will miss the mark by a lot.

A hardened criminal, who had committed brutal murders, was asked where it all began. He responded that it began early in his teens when he stole a pack of cigarettes and wasn't caught. He strayed off the mark slightly at the beginning, but years later he had wandered way off the mark. He had been deceived by the deceiver who lies to us and wants us to follow anything but the truth. Satan uses lies, but he also uses half-truths and anything that plants seeds of doubt to lead us astray.

The story was told about a sea captain, whose first mate regularly drank too much, which kept him from carrying out his duties. The captain was recording these episodes in the ship's logs in order to deal appropriately with this misbehavior when they reached land. Concerned that the captain might be doing just that, the first mate snuck in and read the damaging entries. So he made an entry of his own, "Captain sober today." Those were true words since the captain didn't even drink, yet deceitful as a half-truth.

Remember Satan's tactics in the Garden of Eden? Recorded in Genesis 3, he didn't call God a liar to Eve's face; no, he planted seeds of doubt about God's motives when he asked, "Did God really say, 'You must not eat from any tree in the garden?'" Of course, that isn't what God said. He actually said, "You are free to eat from any tree in the garden; but you must not eat from the tree of the knowledge of good and evil, for when you eat from it you will surely die."

Now Eve, in response to Satan's question, ever so slightly misquoted what God had told her. She said, "We may eat from the trees in the garden, but God did say, 'You must not eat fruit from the tree that is in the middle of the garden, and you must not touch it, or you will die.'"

Once she veered from what God had told her—even though just a bit—she was now led further away by Satan when he said this, "You will not certainly die,' the serpent said to the woman. "For God knows that when you eat from it your eyes will be opened, and you will be like God, knowing good and evil." Eve was now hooked by the enticing barb of the "father of lies," and what started out as an inch off track was growing into a mile. Eve saw that the fruit "was good for food, and pleasing to the eye, and also desirable for gaining wisdom", so she took some and ate it. Adam joined right in the disobedience, as they each put their trust in the cre-ated—former angel, now devil—rather than their Creator. Truth was what God spoke, not what Satan spoke. Truth is always what God speaks, so believe Him.

Truth is the standard that leads us on the right path.

God's truth lights our way so we are not groping in darkness, "Your word is a lamp for my feet and a light on my path" (Ps. 119:105). If we don't have a true standard to go by, then anything goes. And when anything goes, there is no security, no peace, and no assurance of anything except chaos. This is not how our Creator wants it to be. In fact, He states clearly that He "wants all to come to a knowledge of the truth." Why? Because "God our Savior wants all men to be saved" (2 Tim. 2:4).

What did Jesus say to Pilate, that He came "to testify to the truth" and that "everyone on the side of truth listens to Him." In fact, Jesus stated that He is "the truth." If you want to see the truth, then see Jesus. If you are on the side of truth, then listen to Jesus.

We often hear the phrase "the truth will set you free" in our world today, and sadly it is often misapplied. If the truth being cited is anything other than Jesus and His teachings, then the meaning is lost. Jesus teaches us "If you hold to my teaching, you are really my disciples. Then you will know the truth, and the truth will set you free" (John 8:31–32). We aren't set free unless we first know Jesus and hold to His teachings. It is in His life and His teachings that we know the truth. "So if the Son sets you free, you will be free indeed" (John 8:36).

Jesus, as God's only Son, and the exact representation of the Father, is the only one who can lead us in truth and bring you and me into His family. He became like one of us so we can become like Him by adoption. God the Father offers you and me adoption into His eternal family through Jesus and His sacrifice.

All who would come to the Father will come to Him only through Jesus, the Son of God. Jesus said, "I am the way and the truth and the life. No one comes to the Father except through me" (John 14:6). That sounds clear to me, how about you?

Many look for other ways, and Satan tempts us to believe that Jesus isn't the only way. I will believe Jesus who always tells the truth.

Satan would have us believe that we can make it on our own, that we can summon all we need from within, and that we are the masters of our own fate, all of which play right into his deadly plan.

The truth is that we are all lawbreakers of God's laws. "We all, like sheep, have gone astray, each of us has turned to his own way...All have sinned and fall short of the glory of God" (Is. 53:6; Rom. 3:23).

"See to it that no one takes you captive through hollow and deceptive philosophy, which depends on human tradition and the basic principles of this world rather than on Christ" (Col. 2:8*).

The truth is that we are condemned to die because of our sin. "For the wages of sin is death...They perish because they refused to love the truth and so be saved" (Rom. 6:23; 2 Thess. 2:10).

The truth is that nothing we can do, nothing we can say, nothing we can be, could ever be enough to save us. "There is no one righteous, not even one; there is no one who understands, no one who seeks God. All have turned away, they have together become worthless; there is no one who does good, not even one...Therefore no one will be declared righteous in God's sight by the works of the law" (Rom. 3:10–12, 20).

The truth is that we need a Savior. Christ Jesus came into the world to save sinners...Our eternal citizenship is in heaven. And we eagerly await a

Savior from there, the Lord Jesus Christ...Jesus, Who rescues us from the coming wrath (Luke 19:10; 1 Tim. 1:15; Phil. 3:20; 1 Thess. 1:10).

The truth is that the one to save us must be without any sin—the perfect sacrifice. "For you know that it was not with perishable things such as silver and gold that you were redeemed from the empty way of life handed down to you from your ancestors, but with the precious blood of Christ, a lamb without blemish or defect . . . For we do not have a high priest who is unable to empathize with our weaknesses, but we have one who has been tempted in every way, just as we are—yet he did not sin" (1 Pet. 1:19; Heb. 4:15).

The truth is there is only One, He is Jesus, the Christ. "For there is one God and one mediator between God and mankind, the man Christ Jesus, who gave himself as a ransom for all people...I am the way and the truth and the life. No one comes to the Father except through me...Just as people are destined to die once, and after that to face judgment, so Christ was sacrificed once to take away the sins of many; and he will appear a second time, not to bear sin, but to bring salvation to those who are waiting for him...Salvation is found in no one else, for there is no other name under heaven given to mankind by which we must be saved" (1 Tim. 2:5; John 14:6; Heb. 9:26–28; Acts 4:12).

The truth is that He went before the executioners and was crucified in my place, in your place. "But we do see Jesus"..."he suffered death, so that by the grace of God he might taste death for everyone."..."We are going up to Jerusalem, and the Son of Man will be delivered over to the chief priests and the teachers of the law. They will condemn him to death and will hand him over to the Gentiles to be mocked and flogged and crucified"..."When they came to the place called the Skull [Calvary], they crucified him there" (Heb. 2:9; Matt. 20:19; Luke 23:33).

The truth is that He died and was buried. "When he had received the drink, Jesus said, 'It is finished.' With that, he bowed his head and gave up his spirit...and since the tomb was nearby, they laid Jesus there" (John 19:30, 42).

The truth is that He was raised from the dead and is alive today. "Why do you look for the living among the dead? He is not here; He has risen! Remember how He told you, while He was still with you in Galilee: 'The Son of Man must be delivered into the hands of sinners, be crucified and on the third day be raised again'...Christ Jesus, who died—more than that, who was raised to life—is at the right hand of God and is also interceding for us. Who shall separate us from the love of Christ?" (Luke 24:5–6; Rom.8:34).

The truth is that he conquered death and the grave, and all who follow him will do the same. "Jesus said to her, 'I am the resurrection and the life. The one who believes in me will live, even though they die; and whoever lives by believing in me will never die'" (John 11:25–26).

The truth is that we must repent of our sin in order to follow Him and to call upon His name. Repentance causes us to empty ourselves out of that which separates us from God, and causes us to make room for The Spirit of Christ within us.

"But unless you repent, you too will all perish...I have declared to both Jews and Greeks that they must turn to God in repentance and have faith in our Lord Jesus...Those controlled by the sinful nature cannot please God...And if anyone does not have the Spirit of Christ, he does not belong to Christ...those who are led by the Spirit of God are sons of God" (Luke 13:3, 5; Acts 20:21; Rom. 8:8, 9, 14*).

The truth is that we must die to self to be alive in Him. "He himself bore our sins in his body on the cross, so that we might die to sins and live for righteousness; by his wounds you have been healed...I have been crucified with Christ and I no longer live, but Christ lives in me....And he died for all, that those who live should no longer live for themselves but for him who died for them and was raised again" (1 Pet. 2:24; Gal. 2:20; 2 Cor. 5:15).

The truth is that if we have Jesus, then we have life. "God has given us eternal life, and this life is in his Son. Whoever has the Son has life" (1 John 5:12).

The truth is that if we don't have Jesus, then we don't have life. "Whoever does not have the Son of God does not have life" (1 John 5:12).

The truth is that the old nature—the one with which we are born—will never satisfy, never fulfill, never save. We must be born again from above. "Jesus replied, 'Very truly I tell you, no one can see the kingdom of God unless they are born again...Therefore, if anyone is in Christ, he is a new creation; the old has gone, the new has come! All this is from God, who reconciled us to himself through Christ" (John 3:3; 2 Cor. 5:17–18).

The truth is that we can amass all the world has to offer, and yet have nothing. Only in Christ Jesus do we have the full and meaningful life. "For whoever wants to save his life will lose it, but whoever loses his life for me will find it. What good will it be for a man if he gains the whole world, yet forfeits his soul? Or what can a man give in exchange for his soul?...I have come that they may have life, and have it to the full" (Matt. 16:25–26; John 10:10).

The truth is that everyone who lives, who has ever lived, or will ever live will come to acknowledge that Jesus is Lord of all, either by willing submission before the grave unto salvation, or without choice after the grave unto judgment. "Therefore God exalted him to the highest place and gave him the name that is above every name, that at the name of Jesus every knee should bow, in heaven and on earth and under the earth, and every tongue acknowledge that Jesus Christ is Lord to the glory of God the Father" (Phil. 2:9–11).

The truth is that Jesus is King of kings and Lord of lords (Revelation 19:16).

The truth is that Jesus is the *only hope* we have.

The truth is that Jesus is the *only hope* we need.

O Lord our God, thank You for revealing Truth to us through Jesus – The Truth, and through Your written Word, and through Your Spirit. You have made Your purpose clear for each of us, including the reader of this message, that we believe You unto salvation and the meaningful life. In Jesus, our Hope. Amen.

Wheaties Box

*W*heaties, the Breakfast of Champions—Champions, what champions have appeared on the Wheaties box? Michael Jordan has appeared the most; Tiger Woods second. Athletes featured have been female and male; many different ethnicities; covering a wide range of sports including baseball, football, basketball, tennis, golf, swimming, boxing, wrestling, track & field, hockey, gymnastics, skating, soccer, cycling, volleyball, auto racing, motocross, and even aviation.

Who is on your Wheaties box? Who is your champion? What if you could put anyone on your Wheaties box? Would your champion be an athlete? A singer? A political leader? A man or woman in uniform? Actor or actress? Parent? Grandparent? Aunt or uncle? Pastor, priest, or other religious leader? Policeman? Fireman? Teacher? Why would you choose that particular person?

When I was a boy, my choice would have been Mickey Mantle. Why? He was muscular, athletic, magnetic. He ran fast, hit home runs, threw hard. He had an infectious smile. He had a way about him that drew others to him. Not far behind would have been Johnny Unitas, Arnold Palmer, and Rod Laver. As you can see, I looked up to those who rose to the top in their sport.

Of course, my Dad was right there with them because I looked up to him in every way. Dad was strong and athletic. I never could seem to get enough of our time together. Would your champion be someone whom you have observed on TV or from afar, but probably who will never know who you are? Would your champion be your choice because he or she is famous? Attractive? Wealthy? Powerful? Influential? Successful? Sacrificial? That last one doesn't really fit with the others, does it?

But, think about it, who has made sacrifices for you? Perhaps you can name a parent or parents, (my parents made many sacrifices for me, and I am forever grateful to them), grandparent or grandparents, or other guardian? We can all be grateful to those in our armed forces who have fought and are still fighting to protect our freedom and to keep it assured.

Maybe no one comes to mind. But, there is one who has made the ultimate sacrifice for you, one who deserves your honor and respect. He is greater in stature, greater in courage, greater in power, greater in strength, even greater in influence, but most importantly—greater in love—than anyone—*anyone*!

Now, what about his attractiveness? In Isaiah 53, we are told that he possessed no comeliness, no beauty, no attractiveness that we would be drawn to him or desire him for *that* reason. Apparently, he would not have been a candidate for sexiest man alive, or a contender for the GQ magazine cover. How many of you can identify with that? Just about all of us can, can't we? But, as far as sacrificing for you, loving you, *no one* ever gave up more for you so that you would have more than you ever dreamed possible. He is the champion of all champions.

Here is what we are told in Colossians 1:15–17**: "He is the image of the invisible God, the firstborn over all creation. For by Him all things were created that are in heaven and that are on earth, visible and invisible, whether thrones or dominions or principalities or powers. All things were created through Him and for Him. And He is before all things, and in Him all things consist." Now, that is some kind of influence, some kind of power, isn't it? Nothing can face him down. He will not be stopped—in fact, He cannot be stopped—by all the evil forces ever assembled.

We have heard the hypothetical question.. what happens when the unstoppable force meets the immovable object. Jesus is more than either of them. He is King of kings. He is Lord of lords. He is the Alpha (the beginning) and the Omega (the end). He is *Jesus*, the Christ.

Look with me on the Garden of Gethsemane. It was the day before Jesus would be nailed to a cross.

I reckon that Satan celebrated as Jesus fell on his face and wept in the garden. He was asking the Father for another way as sweat drops of blood fell from his forehead. He would experience all the physical pain of the hideous, cruel crucifixion, but moreover, he would experience the ultimate shame of all the filthy sinfulness of all mankind—even yours and mine. Yet, he was to be obedient to the Father's plan.

I reckon that Satan celebrated as Jesus cried out to His Father, while his followers—his close friends—fell asleep.

I reckon that Satan celebrated when Jesus was betrayed by one of his twelve disciples—even the keeper of the money.

I reckon that Satan celebrated when Jesus was grilled by the rulers of the synagogue, while nearby, one of his closest friends was denying that he even knew him.

I reckon that Satan celebrated when Jesus was interrogated by the rulers of the land.

I reckon that Satan celebrated when Pilate gave in to the screaming crowd to release a murderer instead of Jesus, the Son of God.

I reckon that Satan celebrated when Jesus was stripped.

I reckon that Satan celebrated when Jesus was flogged.

I reckon that Satan celebrated when Jesus was mocked.

I reckon that Satan celebrated when Jesus was spat upon.

I reckon that Satan celebrated when Jesus fell to the ground under the weight of the cross.

I reckon that Satan celebrated as the nails went through Jesus's hands and his feet.

I reckon that Satan celebrated when the soldiers raised that cross upright, slamming all the weight of Jesus's body on those nails.

I reckon that Satan celebrated that most of Jesus's disciples were now nowhere to be found.

I reckon that Satan celebrated even more when Jesus cried out to his Father, asking why he had been forsaken.

Then, I reckon that Satan celebrated to the max when Jesus said, "It is finished," as he breathed his last. But, when Jesus said it is finished, it didn't mean what Satan believed it meant. When Jesus said it is finished, he proclaimed to all creation that he had faithfully completed his mission—his mission to die for you and me. What does that mean for you and me?

It means atonement. Jesus's atoning work means that God's wrath was turned aside from you and me and that your sin and my sin were taken away. It means redemption. Jesus's redemptive work means that your release and my release were obtained through payment of a ransom. Jesus's life was the ransom paid for our release. His atonement, His redemption is for all. But, it only is realized in those who would believe in Him and what He has done.

There is no redemption, no salvation for the one who rejects who Jesus is and what He has done. No man can save himself. No man can open the door to heaven except He who has the key, He who owns it all, He who is God's only Son. No man can write his own name into the book of life, no matter how good he is, no matter how whatever he is.

Only Jesus can do that, and He has done that for each one who trusts in Him. Because he paid the price, there is no more sacrifice for sin required. But Jesus's mission didn't end on the cross. It didn't end as his lifeless body lay in that cold tomb, even though I reckon that Satan and all his minions were drunk in celebration. But Satan's celebration would give way to an Easter hangover when the tomb was discovered to be empty. This Jesus who had died was dead no longer.

He was alive! He is alive!

Yes, He faced all that Satan could throw at him. Hebrews 4 says he was tempted in every way like as we are, yet was without sin. He endured all the hatred and violence, and yet responded in love. He faced it all down. He is my hero. He is my champion. Is He your hero? Is He your champion?

I mentioned Mickey Mantle earlier. He was the star of the powerful New York Yankees. He could do it all—hit with power, hit for average, run with speed, and field with efficiency. But, I learned many years later that someone else on that Yankees' team was worthier of being my hero than the Mick. Was he built like Mantle, good-looking as Mantle, fast or powerful as Mantle? No. Now, he was a great ballplayer, for sure—eight time All-Star, five time Gold Glove Award winner, World Series MVP, one of the best second basemen ever...but that isn't what speaks for him in my mind now. He was a follower of the Lord Jesus. He led Bible studies for his teammates—yes, only a few attended, but all were invited—even Mickey.

He was a family man, in fact, leaving his career in the Majors at 31 when he was still on top, so he could spend more time with his wife and daughters. He took a job as a college coach, at a fraction of what he made in the majors, to nurture his family. This is the kind of man we ought to look up to instead of so many others. His name is Bobby Richardson. He didn't seek to be our hero. And, he shouldn't be our hero. But, an example of a believer in, and follower of, the one who should be our hero, our Champion—Jesus.

Many had fallen away from following Jesus, and so He asked His closest friends, His disciples, if they, too, were going to leave Him. Here is what Simon Peter said in John 6:68, "Lord, to whom shall we go? You have the words of eternal life. We have come to believe and to know that you are the Holy One of God." The Holy One of God—now, there is a hero. There is the Hero.

He is my hero. But, more than that, He is my Savior. He is my Lord. Is He your Savior, your Lord? Has anyone ever accomplished more on your behalf? Could anyone ever accomplish more on your behalf than die for your sinfulness and offer you peace and salvation?

What title could ever compare to King of kings and Lord of lords? National champion; Olympic champion; world champion; Mr. or Miss Universe?

What trophy could ever compare to the old rugged cross? Oscar? MVP? Nobel?; Pulitzer?

Who could ever endure the challenge that Jesus faced, and come out victorious?

What victory against all odds could ever be greater than conquering death?

What opponent could ever be more formidable than the prince of darkness and death itself?

Who has done as much to earn your attention, your respect, your consideration, your devotion, your worship, your love than Jesus?

If anyone else would be on your Wheaties box, why? But, more importantly, if anyone else, if anything else but Jesus is on the throne of your life, why? He is Lord. He is Lord of all.

You see, there will be a day when every knee will bow, and every tongue will confess Jesus as Lord. You can repent and follow Him now, and you will become His for all eternity. You will receive salvation, peace, and purpose. But, if you refuse to receive Him and follow Him in this life, you will still bow before Him, but then it will be in judgment, not in grace. Please receive Him now and become a believer in and follower of the one true Hero of all time—Jesus, the Christ.

On Fathers' day, we stop to thank and honor our earthly fathers, but it is the one heavenly Father who should be recognized and honored most of all. Why? because of what we are told in John 3:16, For God, our heavenly Father, has shown His divine love for you and me in that He gave His only Son so that if you and I will believe in Him, we will have what? Not everlasting death and torment, but instead everlasting life and peace! His love is the perfect love. He is the perfect Father, doing everything He can to make you His own.

O Lord God, our Champion in victorious Jesus, thank You for the victory that is ours in trusting and obeying You as Lord. Thank You for being the Champion of the one reading this, and I pray for Your power upon and within this one in the name of Jesus, Victor over death and Champion for all sinners. Amen.

Where Are the Giants Now?

*W*hat obstacles get in your way? What difficulties are before you? What is keeping you from being who your Heavenly Father calls you to be? Maybe there are things that seem overwhelming to you. Likely, some of these things are more than you can handle on your own. They are, perhaps, like giants. So, what giants do you face?

The question really is: How do you face giants who can overpower you and who can keep you down? How do you face giants who are stronger than you, more powerful than you, and meaner than you?

Let's look for guidance in God's word (1 Samuel 17). We look first at the youngest son of a shepherd named Jesse. David was the least important among his siblings; not nearly the tallest nor largest among his brothers. He was a songwriter and musician, and he played the harp, for crying out loud. How would one such as he do against giants? Probably get stomped, wouldn't he?

Verse 4 says, "A champion named Goliath, who was from Gath, came out of the Philistine camp. His height was six cubits and a span (about 9 feet 9 inches). He had a bronze helmet on his head and wore a coat of scale armor of bronze weighing five thousand shekels (about 125 lbs.); on his legs he wore bronze greaves, and a bronze javelin was slung on his back. His spear shaft was like a weaver's rod, and its iron point weighed six hundred shekels (about 15 lbs.). His shield bearer went ahead of him." Seemingly an unstoppable force with impenetrable protection. His armor and weaponry probably weighed as much or more than the shepherd boy David.

So, what was the deal with Goliath? Well, he stood and shouted across the valley to King Saul and the Israelite army, challenging them to battle. He called for them to choose one man to come down and face him. Winner takes all. The army of the loser would become servants of the other. He defied them to send such a man to do battle.

What was the reaction of Saul and the Israelites to such a challenge? They were dismayed and terrified. This went on for forty days, Goliath coming out, issuing the call to fight, and no one answering. Now, one day David showed up to bring grain, bread, and cheese to his brothers (so, now you can add errand boy to David's resume).

So, David, for the first time, heard Goliath's defiance of the Israelite army and its king. And he saw them all run from Goliath in great fear. David started asking some questions, such as, "What will be done for the man who kills this Philistine and removes this disgrace from Israel? Who is this uncircumcised Philistine that he should defy the armies of the living God?" (1 Sam. 17:26). David was met with anger, scorn, and misunderstanding, even by his oldest brother.

So David said that he would go out against this Philistine and fight him. "David said to Saul, 'Let no one lose heart on account of this Philistine; your servant will go and fight him.' Saul replied, 'You are not able to go out against this Philistine and fight him; you are only a young man, and he has been a warrior from his youth'" (1 Sam. 17:32-33).

Remember, Goliath was a champion, one experienced in battle, and one victorious again and again in battle. Saul was right if you only look at David's physical appearance and background versus that of Goliath. But, what had David learned in his short life besides tending sheep, writing and playing music, and running errands? He had learned to trust the Lord. Because, you see, the Lord had delivered him—given him the strength and power to overcome even bears and lions.

We see that David's eyes were on something different than those around him. Their eyes were on the nine-foot giant of a man. David's eyes were on the one who had created this giant of a man, the one who created everything that is, the one who is all powerful: The Lord of all.

It is interesting to note that as Saul decided to allow David to go out, he wanted to put his armor on him. With all that on, I suspect that David looked something like the small child who is so bundled up to go out in the cold that he can hardly move, much less play in the snow. No, David took all that off, and picked up five smooth stones from the stream, put them in his shepherd's pouch, and with sling in hand, he approached the Philistine.

Can you picture it? Goliath thought it was a joke, a mockery. He was going to squash this boy who would come at him with sticks, and he was going to feed him to the birds of the air and beasts of the field.

"He looked David over and saw that he was little more than a boy, glowing with health and handsome, and he despised him. He said to David, 'Am I a dog, that you come at me with sticks?' And the Philistine cursed David by his gods. 'Come here,' he said, 'and I'll give your flesh to the birds and the wild animals'" (1 Sam. 17:42-44).

What was Goliath seeing? A sure victory.

What was David seeing? A sure victory.

What odds do you think Vegas would have given David? Probably wouldn't even give odds—no contest, it would be quick and ugly. Goliath saw victory because of the overwhelming odds he held over his opponent. David saw victory because of the overwhelming odds the Lord held over his opponent.

"David said to the Philistine, 'You come against me with sword and spear and javelin, but I come against you in the name of the Lord Almighty, the God of the armies of Israel, whom you have defied. This day the Lord will deliver you into my hands, and I'll strike you down and cut off your head. This very day I will give the carcasses of the Philistine army to the birds of the air and the wild animals, and the whole world will know that there is a God in Israel. All those gathered here will know that it is not by sword and spear that the Lord saves; for the battle is the Lord's, and he will give all of you into our hands'" (1 Sam. 17:45-47).

Goliath moved closer to attack as David ran quickly toward Goliath. He put in the stone, and slung it, striking Goliath on the forehead. He fell face down on the ground. Without a sword or spear, but with the power of the Lord Almighty, David struck down the Philistine and killed him.

David faced the giant before whom all the others cowered. How did he do it? Trusting in the Lord. "Some trust in chariots and some in horses (and some in sword, spear, javelin, and armor), but we trust in the name of the Lord our God" (Psalm 20:7).

Where was the giant Goliath now? He was face down on the ground. The tongue that defied the living God was now silenced. That same tongue that cursed the living God would one day speak again, this time confessing the living God as Lord—tragically, however, not unto his salvation, but unto his condemnation. "that at the name of Jesus every knee should bow, in heaven and on earth and under the earth, and every tongue acknowledge that Jesus Christ is Lord, to the glory of God the Father" (Phil. 2:10-11).

How do you face your giants today? Will you face them on your own, with your own weapons, with your own smarts, with your own limitations? Or, will you face them in the power of the Lord Almighty?

Let's look at another young man, the son of a blue-collar kind of man, a carpenter.

What kind of giants did Jesus face? For starters, He faced temptation by Satan himself for forty days and forty nights, and all while he was in a state of fasting. Did Jesus overcome Satan with weaponry? Yes, but not conventional sword or spear. He answered Satan with unconventional, supernatural weaponry, with the Sword of Truth—God's Word. Every time that Satan enticed Him, Jesus's responses—His defense—were the powerful words of His heavenly Father.

We are conquerors also through these same words.

Romans 8:37–39 says, "in all these things we are more than conquerors through him who loved us. For I am convinced that neither death nor life, neither angels nor demons, neither the present nor the future, nor any powers, neither height nor depth, nor anything else in all creation, will be able to separate us from the love of God that is in Christ Jesus our Lord."

What about when Jesus faced his final days on earth? What more daunting giants could a person face than what Jesus faced?

What if you were betrayed by one in whom you had placed your trust, such as Jesus was?

What if you were abandoned by your closest friends, such as Jesus was?

What if you were falsely accused, such as Jesus was?

What if you were wrongly and illegally tried, such as Jesus was?

What if you were ridiculed, such as Jesus was?

What if you were scorned, such as Jesus was?

What if you were flogged, such as Jesus was?

What if you were spat upon, such as Jesus was?

What if you were condemned to die even though guilty of no crime, nor even one sin, such as Jesus was?

What if you faced being nailed to a cross and crucified, such as Jesus was?

We sometimes wonder if it is better to know when bad things are coming or not to know.

Jesus knew exactly what was coming. This was His mission. He was born and became one of us so He could ultimately take our place on the cross. He even told his followers in order to prepare them.

Then, Jesus told his disciples that they were going up to Jerusalem.

Luke 9:51 tells us, "Jesus resolutely set out for Jerusalem." Knowing what faced He there, Jesus set his face to Jerusalem. The word resolutely means with firm determination; bold; resolved. You see, regardless of all that He faced, Jesus would do what He was called to do. It was as simple as that.

What were Jesus's words in the Garden of Gethsemane? "My soul is overwhelmed with sorrow to the point of death...Abba, Father, every-thing is possible for you. Take this cup from me. Yet not what I will, but what you will" (Mark 14:34, 36).

He prayed that this cup could pass from him. Then He prayed that, nevertheless, the Father's will be done. It wasn't just the cruelest of all manners of death that prayed on Jesus, but all the sins of all mankind that would be laid on Him who had committed no sin. Think of the worst sins you have committed, and then picture those nailing Jesus to the cross. Yes, He gave His life for you and me on that giant of a cross. And, the biggest giant of all—death—seemed to have won.

Jesus was finally dead.

Except that death had not really won because the Father raised His Son from the grave. The giant of death was slain when Jesus rose to new life. And, because he rose to new life, you and I can, too. Where is the giant of death now? "Death has been swallowed up in victory. Where, O death, is your victory? Where, O death, is your sting?" (1 Cor. 15:54-55). "But thanks be to God! He gives us the victory through our Lord Jesus Christ" (1 Cor. 15:57). "No, in all these things we are more than conquerors through Him who loved us" (Rom. 8:37).

What giants are you facing today? How will you face them? On your own power, or in the power of the one who is greater than all? It is a matter of trust.

Trust in the Lord of All.

Trust in the King of kings.

Trust in the Lord of lords.

What giant is keeping you from believing the Lord, trusting the Lord? Giant of doubt? Giant of fear? Giant of illness? Giant of temptation? Giant of a past that continues to keep you down?

Remember that no giant is as great or as powerful as that Giant who took on all that Satan could muster against Him, even death on a cross.

Jesus is the Giant that faces all other giants down.

He is the *only hope* you have. He is the *only hope* you need.

Will you believe in Him? Will you trust in Him?

O Lord our God, thank You that there is no giant, real or imagined that You cannot handle for us. I pray for the one reading this to recognize this truth and lay before You any and every giant that would hinder his or her growth in relationship with You. In the name of the true Giant, Jesus. Amen.

Worry or Trust

*D*o you ever worry? Are you ever anxious? Can you will your-self not to worry or be anxious? Do you sometimes set it aside for a period and then take it back up again?

Philippians 4:6 says, "Do not be anxious about anything."

Worrying—being anxious—about some things really doesn't make sense, such as the future, things over which you have no control. How about things that you worry about that never come to be? Mark Twain said, "I am an old man and I have known a great many troubles, but most them have never happened."

The question is often asked, "How is that working for you?" So, how is that worrying working for you? Probably not too well. Maybe you could get someone else to do your worrying for you?

The story is told of one fellow who did just that. Apparently, he wor-ried a lot, so he hired a man to be his worrier and agreed on a $200,000 yearly salary. After the man accepted the job, his first question to his boss was, "Where are you going to get $200,000 per year to pay me?" The man replied, "That's your worry."

So is God telling us—Don't worry, be happy? Hakunnah matata?

Of course not. He continues in verse 6, "but in every situation, by prayer and petition, with thanksgiving, present your requests to God." We have to confront worry and anxiety with power from the Lord—power that we don't adequately possess on our own. You see, worry and anxiety are not only not helpful, but they are counterproductive. They cause us to be troubled with cares; to be focused on our self-interests. It is destructive to our well-being and distracting to our being productive.

Corrie Ten Boom said it well: "Worry does not empty tomorrow of its sorrow; it empties today of its strength." She knew what she was talking about. This was a woman whose father, brother, sister, and nephew all perished in the World War II Nazi murder camp. Why? Because they were rescuing others, providing an escape route for Jews hunted down by the German Gestapo. But instead of worry, what? The opposing force to worry: Prayer. Worry and prayer cannot stand together.

In everything, by prayer and petition, offering up, presenting our desires to our heavenly Father. Our focus, our direction, is changed from the worry, the anxiety, to looking for help from the one who can help us, the one who wants to help us, the one who will help us. It is our telling the heavenly Father that we believe Him, that we trust Him.

God is neither too big to pay any attention to little ole you and me, nor is He too small to hear each and every one of us—even all at the same time. He is just right. He is perfect, you see.

"I lift up my eyes to the mountains—where does my help come from? My help comes from the Lord, the Maker of heaven and earth. He will not let your foot slip—he who watches over you will not slumber; indeed, he who watches over Israel will neither slumber nor sleep" (Ps. 121:1-4).

A vital part of prayer is worship and love of the Father, recognizing who He is: Creator of all that is; Lover of our souls; Lifter of our heads; our Provider; our Protector. Worshipping the Lord, adoring the Lord, is bragging on Him. It is appreciating Him for what He has done for you.

Does He need that? No.

But, you and I need to do that. We need to recognize our place before the Father, which is not to stand before Him as though we have rights, or as though we can make demands of Him. It is to kneel before Him, knowing that it is only by His mercy that we can be forgiven and escape hell for all eternity; and that it is only by His grace that we can receive His power and strength for this day and every day onward, to spend eternity in heaven.

Mercy—staying the hand of execution—you and I don't get what we deserve, which is punishment and eternal damnation.

Grace—opening up of heaven's storehouse of blessings—receiving what we don't deserve: forgiveness, peace, everlasting life.

You see, He bought you and me with a price—the ultimate price—the life of His one and only Son, Jesus. So, we should ever be grateful and thankful to be the recipients of His divine love. These lead us to "with thanksgiving." It is easy to overlook this, but we mustn't. It is vital also. Do you have any trouble being thankful for each of the men and women who have given their lives in service to our country so we can have the freedom we do? Do you have any trouble being thankful for someone who helped you out when you were in desperate need? Do you have any trouble being thankful for someone who tended to you when you were sick?

Now, should you and I have any trouble, or hesitancy, in being thankful to our heavenly Father who loves us so? We should be ever thanking God for His goodness and His kindness to us. Thankful, in fact, in all things—thankful that God reaches beyond our sin to draw us back to Him—to be reconciled to Him—if we will let Him; thankful that God will work good through you and me in all things if we will let Him, regardless of the circumstances (2 Cor. 5:17; Rom. 8:28).

Paul and Silas prayed and sang praises to God as they were shackled in the prison cell... after they had been stripped, and beaten, and flogged. What law had they broken to be imprisoned? None. But, because they cast a demon out of a girl (rescued her), her owners wouldn't get rich off her. Unjustly tortured and imprisoned, yes, but they praised God anyway, and as a result, the jailer and his family were saved, for all eternity (Acts 16).

"Do not be anxious for anything, but in everything, by prayer and petition, with thanksgiving, make your requests known to God." Does God know what you and I need before we ask? Yes.

So, why ask? It should be enough that God tells us to ask. In fact, He says in many ways to bring our requests before Him. It isn't to inform Him, but it is to acknowledge our dependence on Him. It is to recognize that it is He who is in control, not us. It is to agree with Him that

He is Lord over all. It is to ever change you and me into followers of the Lord Jesus.

And if you are not willing to bring your requests, your petitions before Almighty God, what does that mean? Does it mean that you are too proud to admit that you need Him? But you do need Him. Does it mean that you don't believe He wants to help you? But He does want to help you. Does it mean that you don't want to submit to His will for your life? But you do need to submit to His will for your life, we each need to do so.

When we approach God with a submissive spirit, we can approach with confidence—Hebrews 4:16, "Let us then approach God's throne of grace with confidence, so that we may receive mercy and find grace to help us in our time of need." How is it that we can do this? Because we have a High Priest who can sympathize with our weaknesses, one who has been tempted in every way just as we are... yet, He did not sin (Heb. 4:15).

So, we bring our worries and anxieties to our heavenly Father, wrap them in prayer, give thanks to Him for loving us in spite of all our sin, praise Him that He never gives up on us, and what happens— we have peace within. "And the peace of God, which transcends all understanding, will guard your hearts and your minds in Christ Jesus" (Phil. 4:7).

Peace says to anxiety—get out of the way; I am moving in. You have put your trust in the heavenly Father, and He rewards you with peace within, even when there is chaos without, even when there is uncertainty without. How is that? It is beyond our ability to understand, beyond our reasoning power.

Isaiah 26:3-4 says it like this: "You (O Lord) will keep in perfect peace those whose minds are steadfast, because they trust in You. Trust in the Lord forever, for the Lord, the Lord himself, is the Rock eternal."

I can testify to that being the case in my life, whether we faced cancer surgery; whether we faced financial ruin; whether we faced unresolved family issues, my heavenly Father has given to me His peace and kept me in His peace.

The Psalms are full of the writings of folks who were at "their wit's end" (Psalm 107), yet when they called out in their deepest need, to the Lord Almighty for help, He responded to rescue them, to deliver them, to give them peace.

Horatio Spafford gave testimony to this over 140 years ago, and it lives on in the words of the beloved hymn, "It Is Well With My Soul:"

> When peace, like a river, attendeth my way,
> When sorrows like sea billows roll–
> Whatever my lot, Thou hast taught me to say,
> It is well, it is well with my soul.

> Tho Satan should buffet, tho trials should come,
> Let this blest assurance control,
> That Christ hath regarded my helpless estate,
> And hath shed His own blood for my soul.

> My sin—O the bliss of this glorious tho't–
> My sin, not in part, but the whole,
> Is nailed to the cross, and I bear it no more;
> Praise the Lord, Praise the Lord, O my soul.

> And, Lord haste the day when my faith shall be sight,
> The clouds be rolled back as a scroll;
> The trump shall resound and the Lord shall descend,
> Even so—it is well with my soul.

You see, even in the throes of tragically losing his four daughters to drowning in the Atlantic ocean—when their ship was struck by another and sank, Horatio Spafford found God's peace to dwell on Jesus's redemption and second coming, rather than on his own sorrow.

So His peace will guard our hearts and minds in and through Christ Jesus. It is when we are seeing Jesus that the troubles around us don't loom as large. It is when we take our eyes off Jesus that our troubles, our worries, our anxieties overtake us. His peace will keep us from sinning under troubles, and from sinking under the pressures.

"Finally, brothers and sisters, whatever is true, whatever is noble, whatever is right, whatever is pure, whatever is lovely, whatever is admirable—if anything is excellent or praiseworthy—think about such things" (Phil. 4:8).

When we commit to follow Jesus, we commit to the path of righteousness, which will move us to do good works, to do the things that Jesus did. We will be becoming people of integrity, honesty, good reputation. These things aren't our goal—our goal is to follow Jesus, but these things will become who we are in Christ.

True in words—loving the truth; speaking the truth.

Noble—of good character—honorable.

Right—practicing trust in the heavenly Father, and being just toward others—doing right by them.

Pure—not giving in to sinful desires—especially when no one is watching.

Lovely—loving, pleasing toward others—putting the interest of others before your own.

Admirable—establishing a good reputation—doing things for the betterment of those all around you.

Excellent—striving to do your best in all you do, morally, physically, and spiritually, as unto the Lord Jesus.

Praiseworthy—living to be rewarded with God's praise when we leave this earth, and behaving in such a way to deserve men's praise even though that is not the goal.

Put these into practice!

What do you spend time thinking about? Your relationship with Jesus? Think about Jesus. In Jesus, all the above came to life. All the above were exampled for you and me.

Jesus is the Only Hope we have. Jesus is the Only Hope we need. Are you ready to submit your life to the Lord Jesus? He is worthy.

O Lord our God, thank You that You take away our worry, our anxiety, our fear, and replace them with peace, assurance, and faith that only come from You. Truly, You are worthy of our trust and submission, and I pray that it is so for the one reading this message. In the name of the one who brings us peace, Jesus. Amen.

Your Invitation

*Y*ou are about to be given a most important invitation. But what are you being invited to?

What if your invitation came from the mayor to attend a banquet of important locals? Would you want to go?

What if your invitation came from the governor to attend a gala held in the governor's mansion for VIPs across your state? Would you want to go?

What if your invitation came from the president of the United States to a private dinner with his family at the White House? Would you want to go?

What if your invitation came from the queen of England to attend a dinner with her family and British royalty at Buckingham Palace? Would you want to go?

Have you ever received one of these invitations? No? Well, I am so sorry for you. I had a great time with the queen last year. Not.

Or, think of some other influential, famous, or admired person from whom you would like to receive an invitation to attend a dinner for honored guests.

Or, how about being invited to some great event, such as the Super Bowl, Olympics, or World Championship of Hot Dog eating. Would you want to go?

So, you pick your fantasy invitation, and pretend you have anticipated for months, you have prepared yourself, and now you have arrived. What is likely to happen?

Your name will be checked against a ledger, a list, of some kind to verify that you, indeed, have been invited and are authorized to attend.

But what if there was a mix-up, and someone forgot to put your name on the list?

Or, what if someone misspelled your name, and so it isn't found on the list?

Or, what if they got you confused with someone else of the same name, and it really wasn't you they intended to invite in the first place?

Or, what if you found out, when you arrived, that it had been over-booked, and it turns out that there was not a place for you? You were turned away.

Major disappointment, huh?

OK, now let's pretend that you arrived, and your name was found, and you were allowed in. You have looked so forward to meeting this person you have looked up to, and being able to not only meet them, but to spend time with them, ask them questions, have fellowship with them, and maybe even learn from them.

But then, you find out that you aren't even seated at the same table with the one for whom you came, as you had thought. Worse than that, you aren't even seated in the same room with them. You aren't even served the same first-class food; in fact, it is nothing more than finger sandwiches and water.

Major disappointment, huh?

Or, you chose instead an invitation to attend a great event, and your credentials allow you in, only to find you are seated in the nose-bleed section, behind a column, next to a leather-lungs who drowns out even the marching band.

Major disappointment, huh?

Now, back to the real invitation that you actually are to receive, one that far outclasses any of these or any other invitation you can imagine.

Fantasy invitations might be to spend time with a world leader who exerts great political influence; or to spend time with a superstar athlete who makes *Sports Illustrated* covers; or to spend time with one is recognized for the millions given to charity; or to spend time with a great scientific mind, and so on.

But this invitation is offered to you to spend time with the very one around whom all creation revolves.

Your invitation is offered by the one who created all things and for whom all things were created.

The one who holds all things together.

The one who gives us life.

The one who gives us every breath.

The one who gives us hope.

If you choose to accept this invitation, then your name will be written in blood and cannot be blotted out. It cannot be overlooked. And, you will be seated—at this banquet—with the Guest of Honor.

You will enjoy the finest royal feast ever served, not only fit for a king, fit for the King of kings, fit for the Lord of lords.

Jesus tells a story of a king who sent out invitations to the wedding banquet for his son.

"Jesus spoke to them again in parables, saying: 'The kingdom of heaven is like a king who prepared a wedding banquet for his son. He sent his servants to those who had been invited to the banquet to tell them to come, but they refused to come. Then he sent some more servants and said, 'Tell those who have been invited that I have prepared my dinner. My oxen and fattened cattle have been butchered, and everything is ready. Come to the wedding banquet.' But they paid no attention and went off—one to his field, another to his business. The rest seized his servants, mistreated them and killed them. The king was enraged. He sent his army and destroyed those murderers and burned their city. Then he said to his servants, 'The wedding banquet is ready, but those I invited did not deserve to come. So go to the street corners and invite to the banquet anyone you find. So the servants went out into the streets and gathered all the people they could find, the bad as well as the good, and the wedding hall was filled with guests. But when the king came in to see the guests, he noticed a man there who was not wearing wedding clothes. He asked, 'How did you get in here without wedding clothes, friend?' The man was speechless. Then the king told the attendants, 'Tie him hand and foot, and throw him outside, into the darkness, where there will be weeping and gnashing of teeth.' For many are invited, but few are chosen" (Matt. 22:1-14).

So here is a lavish, royal feast that has been prepared, and invitations have gone out. It is an honor to be invited. It is a disgrace to the king for anyone to refuse to come. Yet, this once in a lifetime invitation was met with indifference, disinterest, even hatred.

The first group of invitees represented in this parable are the Jews, God's chosen people. He called them to be set apart out of all nations in the world. He sent His prophets throughout the Old Testament to call them to repentance of their sins and to trust in Himself as Lord of all. Yet, over and over again, they turned their backs on Him. God sent John the Baptist and the apostles to tell them that the Messiah had come, and to call them to repentance and to trust in His Son Jesus,. To try and persuade them to accept His offer.

Yet, over and over again, God's invitations were met with indifference, defiance, rejection, same as in this parable. The reasons sinners do not come to Christ and salvation through Him is not because they cannot...but because they will not. Making light of Christ and the salvation He offers is the great damning sin of the world. Maybe some rejected the offer because they were just careless. It is one thing to be careless with possessions, but a whole other thing to be careless with one's soul.

The faithful ministers of the Lord were persecuted, even killed, same as in this parable. So, the king then invited whom? Anyone else who would come: wayfaring strangers, folks out on the street, and Gentiles. God sent His followers, His ministers to take the Gospel to the Gentiles. Aren't you glad of that, Gentiles? I am. The Gospel for all, good news for all. How about you?

The feast is to gather souls who want to be a part of the wedding feast for the King's son, the same as the gospel is presented to gather souls who want to be with the Christ for all eternity. But, only those with wedding clothes can be part of this banquet.

Wedding clothes are representative of the righteousness of Christ. Only those clothed in the righteousness of Christ will be in attendance. The one not in wedding clothes represents one who believed he could attend on his own righteousness. So, what about your righteousness and my righteousness? *We don't have any.* Only Jesus is righteous, and we can only be reckoned as righteous—same as was said about Abraham—through faith in the Lord Jesus.

It is not only careless and presumptuous for anyone to believe that somehow God will favor them with salvation and eternal life apart from a relationship with the Lord Jesus, it is damning. This is evidenced by the religious leaders of Jesus's day who believed that by looking the part on the outside, and doing enough deeds in the name of religion, they would be saved. Yet, Jesus said they were like white-washed tombs, looking good on the outside, yet dead on the inside. Such a one does not wear the wedding clothes nor attend the wedding banquet.

Open your invitation.

"Blessed are those who are invited to the wedding supper of the Lamb!" (Rev. 19:9).

For I have loved you so much that I gave My One and Only Son so that if you will believe in Him and receive Him as your Lord and Savior, you will not perish but have everlasting life. You are redeemed only by His shed blood, and your name will only be written in His book of life by following Him on the path of righteousness (John 3:16; 1 Peter 3:18–19; Rev. 21:27).

You are invited to partake of the wedding supper with the Lamb of God! An event that pales all others in comparison. The invitations, events, that I mentioned earlier cannot compare. Nothing that happens on this earth can hold a candle to this gathering, this feast in the presence of the Lord of lords, the King of kings—Jesus.

Jesus is the Bridegroom—the perfect Son of God, the Messiah, the Christ, the Bread of Life, the Way, the Truth, and the Life, the one who gave all that He had for you and me, and we, who are His church, are the bride. Could it ever get any better than that? Who is His church? Not denominationalists. Only those individuals covered by the blood of the Lamb (Rev. 3:5).

When, in repentance, we kneel at the feet of Jesus at the cross and surrender to Him as Lord, what pours over us? His blood—the same blood that cleanses us of all sin, all guilt, all unrighteousness, so that we are set free to walk in newness of life in His love and in His ways. This includes the so-called good and the so-called bad in our society. All are changed in Christ; no one is good on his own, and no one is bad enough to be beyond God's saving grace.

These are the ones whose names are written in the Lamb's book of life—as if they were written in His blood (Rev. 21:27). There won't be any misspelling, no oversight, no nosebleed section, no second-rate provision, no overbooking—there is always room for the repentant sinner.

Jesus spent His time on earth with sinners. He was criticized and shunned because He did. But he came to serve, not to be served, He came to save, and only those who believe that they need to be saved—will be.

But the way to Jesus, and the way of Jesus is narrow. Jesus told us in Matthew 7:13–14: "Enter through the narrow gate. For wide is the gate and broad is the road that leads to destruction, and many enter through it. But small is the gate and narrow the road that leads to life, and only a few find it."

Jesus never said that His way is the easy way. He never said that His way is the fun way. He never said that His way is the popular way. Jesus never spent time on this earth looking for ease, for fun, or to be popular. He spent His time sacrificing for others, delivering from demons, giving sight to the blind, making the lame to walk, rescuing sinners, delivering hope, saving souls. Why? Because He loves you and me so.

Because He wants to spend eternity with you and me, to be the Bridegroom to you and me, His church, His bride. With blessings beyond our comprehension, grace beyond measure, privilege accorded only to joint heirs with the Only Begotten Son of the Father.

The invitation has been extended to you, not because of anything you have, or anything that you have done, but because what has been spoken to you by our heavenly Father in His Word, through His Son Jesus, and through the power of the Holy Spirit straight into your heart.

Will you accept His invitation to choose Jesus?

If so, then I will see you at the great heavenly banquet.

O Lord our God, thank You that You want us to be with You forever, that You want the one reading this to be with You forever. And that You are preparing a great banquet in our heavenly home where Jesus will be honored, and all of us who trust in Him will be honored in His name and in His righteousness. Amen.

About the Author

*L*arry and his wife, Rhonda, have been married since 1972, and live in Louisville, Kentucky. They are blessed with a loving, close-knit family... Zach, Missy, and Wyatt (Son, Daughter-in-law, Grandson); Rachel, Alan, Roman, and Jordan (Daughter, Son-in-law, Grandsons).

Can hope rise above the ash heap or the pandemic?
Can peace rise above the chaos and confusion?
Can forgiveness rise above your sinfulness?

As an ordinary man trusting in an extraordinary God, Larry relates messages from the Bible through the lives of ordinary folks—from all walks of life—that will encourage you, give you hope, and point you to the only Hope you have, and the only Hope you need.

Because...

Jesus does offer you hope, no matter what.
Jesus does offer you peace, no matter what.
Jesus does offer you forgiveness, no matter what.

CPSIA information can be obtained
at www.ICGtesting.com
Printed in the USA
LVHW020110160620
658145LV00012B/1010

9 781631 292354